LIBERAL LEARNING
AND THE
ARTS AND SCIENCES MAJOR
Volume 2

REPORTS FROM THE FIELDS

PROJECT ON LIBERAL LEARNING,
STUDY-IN-DEPTH,
AND THE ARTS AND SCIENCES MAJOR

ASSOCIATION OF AMERICAN COLLEGES, 1991

THIS WORK WAS SUPPORTED BY
THE FUND FOR THE IMPROVEMENT
OF POSTSECONDARY EDUCATION,
U. S. DEPARTMENT OF EDUCATION
AND
THE FORD FOUNDATION

Published by
Association of American Colleges
1818 R Street, NW
Washington, D.C. 20009

Copyright 1990

ISBN 0-911696-50-4

CONTENTS

FOREWORD

This two-volume report, Liberal Learning and the Arts and Sciences Major, presents the results of a three-year review of liberal arts and sciences majors within the context of liberal education. Initiated by the Association of American Colleges, the review has been planned and implemented in cooperation with twelve learned societies, each of which considered its own major in relation to concerns and questions addressed across the entire project.

The work of this project has been guided by a National Advisory Committee formed by AAC in consultation with the participating learned societies. Volume One of this report, *The Challenge of Connecting Learning*, was prepared by members of the National Advisory Committee. It proposes a set of organizing principles important for any arts and sciences concentration.

Volume Two contains abridged versions of twelve field reports on specific majors by task forces appointed by the participating learned societies. These reports provide presidents, academic administrators, and faculty members with a summary of important issues and recommended changes in each reviewed field. The twelve learned societies separately are publishing unabridged versions of their own reports; they are designed to stimulate dialogue and self-examination in departments and program committees.

The participating learned societies and their respective task forces are listed on page xi. Information on obtaining any or all of the twelve separate reports is on page 225.

Toward a wider dialogue

We want to emphasize that this work is preliminary. While these volumes contain specific precepts and recommendations, their primary recommendation is a call for serious faculty dialogue about central issues addressed in these pages:

☐ What is the arts and sciences major supposed to contribute within the context of a liberal education?

☐ Are there common touchstones for any liberal arts and sciences major? Should differing or competing assumptions about the purposes of a major across departments and domains be directly addressed?

☐ Have departments specified their expectations for students' liberal learning? Can faculty members explain how particular requirements and intellectual practices serve common goals for students' learning? Can students?

☐ Do faculty members review student work over time in relation to departmental goals? Are the results of such discussions used to review and revise program goals?

☐ Do program requirements and practices support students in bringing together different parts of their learning, within the major and in related fields?

☐ What can departments do to encourage fuller participation by students of all backgrounds?

☐ What are the appropriate relationships between major programs and other parts of the undergraduate curriculum? Should some part of general education be structured to provide critical and integrative contexts for study in particular majors?

These fundamental questions about majors in the context of liberal education require and deserve campuswide faculty discussion.

Integrity and the arts and sciences major

The stimulus and point of departure for this review of arts and sciences majors was the discussion of the baccalaureate degree in AAC's landmark 1985 report, *Integrity in the College Curriculum: A Report to the Academic Community*. That report challenged colleges and universities to consider what kinds of learning a student ought to achieve in any liberal arts and sciences field, whatever the student's area of concentration. These reports address concentrations themselves, asking what liberal arts and sciences majors should contribute to students' liberal learning and what kinds of curricular structures and practices are needed to support important learning.

The authors of *Integrity* minced no words on the shortcomings of the undergraduate major. "The undergraduate major...everywhere dominates, but the nature and degree of that concentration varies widely and irrationally from college to college. Indeed, the major in most colleges is little more than a gathering of courses taken in one department, lacking structure and depth."

Reports from two other AAC projects undertaken subsequent to the publication of *Integrity* echo this stringent judgment. In the 1989 *Structure and Coherence: Measuring the Undergraduate Curriculum*, a study of seniors' transcripts from liberal arts and sciences majors in thirty-five institutions, Robert Zemsky of the University of Pennsylvania raises pointed questions about the "real curriculum" that American undergraduates experience. Too many students, he reports, are taking "advanced courses" in subjects in which they have had little or no prior curricular experience. In such a context, what becomes of "depth" as a goal for advanced study?

Faculty members in another AAC project (1986–1989) on using external examiners to assess student learning in arts and sciences majors also raised questions about the effectiveness of learning in college majors. In that project, faculty members prepared comprehensive written and oral examinations in their fields for graduating seniors on their own and similar campuses. They then served as external readers and oral interviewers for seniors who took the examinations. Many examiners reported that seniors are less skilled than their instructors had expected in integrating learning across courses.

All these findings challenged AAC to ask whether recent campus reform has focused disproportionately on general education. Discussions in 1987–88 with learned societies indicated that many of them would welcome participation in a collaborative review looking simultaneously at general and field-specific goals for arts and sciences majors. In 1988–89, AAC secured funding from the U.S. Department of Education's Fund for the Improvement of Postsecondary Education (FIPSE) and the Ford Foundation to support such a review.

The review of arts and sciences majors

The project, titled "Liberal Learning, Study-in-depth, and the Arts and Sciences Major," has been coordinated by AAC and guided by a National Advisory Committee. It was structured to generate a broad dialogue about college majors that would include students as well as faculty members and administrators, campuses and specific programs as well as national organizations.

The project's National Advisory Committee first framed a set of organizing questions, the Charge to the Task Forces, which appears on page 1. The charge was the subject of an all-project conference in March 1989.

For their responses to the charge, the learned society task forces used a variety of sources, including catalogues, formal and informal campus surveys, analyses of previously available data, and discussions with students. Preliminary drafts of the reports were circulated for comment by each task force and were further discussed at the societies' annual meetings and other gatherings.

At the same time, project staff members reviewed specific major programs in disciplinary and interdisciplinary arts and sciences fields. Institutions and project participants were invited to nominate campus programs that exhibit unusual integrity and vitality in their conception and implementation of the major. More than 150 programs were nominated; a sampling is included in the "Promising Practices" section of Volume One.

AAC also surveyed students' perceptions of their learning in the major. Distributed informally by faculty members participating in the task forces and analyzed under the direction of Theodore Wagenaar, professor of sociology at Miami University of Ohio, the survey provided suggestive information on students' experience of intellectual coherence and connected learning across ten of the fields in the project.

Both the preliminary task force reports and distinctive campus practices were discussed at AAC's 1990 Annual Meeting, "Undergraduate Majors and the Claims of Liberal Learning," and the project benefitted from many who took part in that meeting. A subsequent all-project conference in February 1990 provided a further opportunity for more dialogue and reflection across participating fields. Final drafts of the reports in Volumes One and Two were completed in late 1990.

Acknowledgments

AAC and the participating learned societies are grateful to FIPSE and the Ford Foundation for their willingness to support a uniquely collaborative dialogue on the major. We thank in particular Peter Stanley, director of education and culture at the Ford Foundation, who first articulated some of the most significant issues with which the project grappled, and Charles Karelis, executive director of FIPSE, whose probing questions and continuing commitment exemplify the best traditions of liberal inquiry.

On behalf of AAC's Board of Directors and members, we also extend our thanks to the leaders of the twelve learned societies for their many contributions to this effort. We acknowledge especially the seventy-one teacher/scholars who served on the task forces. Individually and collectively, they brought a remarkably high standard of intelligence, openness, critical perspective, and simple stamina to a demanding set of activities.

With particular appreciation, we thank the scholars who served as task force scribes and took their committees' respective field reports from early drafts through numerous iterations to the final editions. Well chosen by their respective societies, the scribes served as both guides and servants to the larger communities. AAC and all of higher education stand much in their debt.

Thanks also are due to the thirteen members of the National Advisory Committee, who ably provided leadership and integration to a complex range of activities. They set a high standard for the kind of collegial engagement recommended in these two volumes.

The project is especially grateful to Jonathan Z. Smith, scribe for the National Advisory Committee. In that role, he took exemplary care that each part of the Project Charge and the Volume One report from the National Advisory Committee represent the considered views of the entire committee.

Finally, many members of the AAC staff contributed in important ways to the project and to the reports that have come from it. John Chandler, AAC president from 1985–90, was a member of the National Advisory Committee and provided his full support to the project. Associate Director of Programs Thomas Jeavons offered invaluable assistance at all stages of the project. Audrey Jones, project secretary, faithfully kept track of thirteen different arenas of activity, nearly one hundred different travel schedules, and dozens of meetings and papers; Suzanne Lightman ably coordinated two AAC annual meetings and many smaller gatherings on the topic of the major.

Rhoda Selvin, assistant vice provost at the State University of New York–Stony Brook, who was an AAC fellow in 1989, oversaw the review of promising practices in the major and organized a series of sessions on those programs at AAC's 1990 Annual Meeting. R. Lynn Kelley, dean of the college at Wilson College and a 1990 AAC fellow, has undertaken a similar task for the 1991 Annual Meeting.

Director of Public Information and Publications Sherry Levy-Reiner steered the production—in record time—of both volumes. Assistant Director of Publications David Stearman managed the production process, and Editorial Associates Kristen Lippert-Martin and Lisa Magnino carefully scrutinized the various manuscripts and proofs. Neil Manson, a graduate student in philosophy at Syracuse University, spent the summer of 1989 gathering and organizing the twelve reports. We are grateful to them all.

Majors stand at the heart of the American higher educational enterprise. The Association of American Colleges is proud to have played a leading role in bringing together disciplinary and interdisciplinary groups to engage in an extended and extending conversation about these essential topics.

–PAULA P. BROWNLEE
President
Association of American Colleges

–CAROL G. SCHNEIDER
Executive Vice President
Association of American Colleges

January 1991

PROJECT PARTICIPANTS

National Advisory Committee
JOHN W. CHANDLER
President Emeritus
Association of American Colleges

BLYTHE CLINCHY
Professor of Psychology
Wellesley College

GERALD GRAFF
Professor of English
Northwestern University

WILLIAM SCOTT GREEN
Professor of Religion
University of Rochester

PATRICK J. HILL
Professor of Interdisciplinary Studies
Evergreen State College

JANE BUTLER KAHLE
Professor of Science Education
Miami University (Ohio)

PRISCILLA LAWS
Professor of Physics
Dickinson College

PAULA McCLAIN
Professor of Public Affairs
Arizona State University

YOLANDA T. MOSES
Vice President for Academic Affairs
California State University–
Dominguez Hills

HANS PALMER
Professor of Economics
Pomona College

ROBERT SHOENBERG
Senior Fellow
Association of American Colleges

JONATHAN Z. SMITH
Robert O. Anderson Distinguished
Professor in the Humanities
University of Chicago

JOHN A. THORPE
Vice Provost for Undergraduate
Education
State University of New York–
Buffalo

Participating Learned Societies
American Academy of Religion
STEPHEN CRITES, Wesleyan
University
FREDERICK DENNY, University of
Colorado
CAROLE A. MYSCOFSKI, University
of Missouri
JUNE E. O'CONNOR, University of
California–Riverside
ALBERT RABIL, JR., State University
of New York–College at Old
Westbury
JAMES B. WIGGINS, Syracuse
University

American Association of Physics Teachers
NEAL B. ABRAHAM, Bryn Mawr College
JAMES B. GERHART, University of Washington
RUSSELL K. HOBBIE, University of Minnesota–Twin Cities
LILLIAN C. McDERMOTT, University of Washington
ROBERT H. ROMER, Amherst College
BRUCE R. THOMAS, Carleton College

American Economics Association
ROBIN BARTLETT, Denison University
W. LEE HANSEN, University of Wisconsin
ALLEN C. KELLEY, Duke University
DONALD McCLOSKEY, University of Iowa
JOHN J. SIEGFRIED, Vanderbilt University
THOMAS TIETENBERG, Colby College

American Historical Association
EDWARD A. GOSSELIN, California State University–Long Beach
MYRON MARTY, Drake University
COLIN A. PALMER, University of North Carolina
LYNDA N. SHAFFER, Tufts University
JOANNA ZANGRANDO, Skidmore College

American Institute of Biological Sciences
JACK L. CARTER, Colorado College

CHARLES CHAMBERS, American Institute of Biological Sciences
FRANK HEPPNER, University of Rhode Island
ROY H. SAIGO, Southeast Louisiana State University
GERALDINE TWITTY, Howard University
DAN B. WALKER, California State University–San Jose

American Philosophical Association
ROBERT AUDI, University of Nebraska–Lincoln
GARY ISEMINGER, Carleton College
ANITA SILVERS, San Francisco State University
LAURENCE THOMAS, Syracuse University
MEROLD WESTPHAL, Fordham University

American Political Science Association
TWILEY W. BARKER, University of Illinois
LAWRENCE W. BEER, Lafayette College
MARY ELLEN FISCHER, Skidmore College
RONALD KAHN, Oberlin College
KATHLEEN McGINNIS, Trinity College
MARIAN L. PALLEY, University of Delaware
RANDALL B. RIPLEY, Ohio State University
JOHN W. WAHLKE, University of Arizona

American Psychological Association
LAUREL FURUMOTO, Wellesley
College
DIANE HALPERN, California State
University–San Bernardino
GREGORY KIMBLE, Duke University
THOMAS V. McGOVERN, Arizona
State University–West
WILBERT J. McKEACHIE, University of
Michigan

American Sociological Association
CATHERINE BERHEIDE, Skidmore
College
KATHLEEN CRITTENDEN, University
of Illinois–Chicago
ROBERT DAVIS, North Carolina
A&T State University
PAUL EBERTS, Cornell University
ZELDA GAMSON, University of
Massachusetts–Boston
CARLA HOWERY, American
Sociological Association
THEODORE WAGENAAR, Miami
University (Ohio)

Mathematical Association of America
JEROME A. GOLDSTEIN, Tulane
University
ELEANOR JONES, Norfolk State
University
DAVID LUTZER, College of William
and Mary

LYNN ARTHUR STEEN, St. Olaf
College
URI TREISMAN, University of
California–Berkeley
ALAN C. TUCKER, State University
of New York–Stony Brook

National Women's Studies Association
JOHNNELLA BUTLER, University of
Washington
SANDRA COYNER, Kansas State
University
MARGARET HOMANS, Yale
University
MARLENE LONGENECKER, Ohio
State University
CARYN McTIGHE MUSIL, National
Women's Studies Association

Society for Values in Higher Education
(reviewing interdisciplinary majors)
ALICE F. CARSE, State University of
New York–College at Old Westbury
WILLIAM DOTY, University of
Alabama
JULIE THOMPSON KLEIN, Wayne
State University
EDWARD ORDMAN, Memphis State
University
CONSTANCE D. RAMIREZ, Duquesne
University

THE CHARGE TO THE TASK FORCES

In recent years, a number of reports and studies have assessed the impact of new challenges to traditional understandings of liberal learning, challenges reflected in such terms as the "diversification of the student body," the "knowledge explosion," "global awareness," and "blurred disciplinary boundaries." In many of these reports there has been a significant shift from a conception of education as fields, courses, and contents to one that emphasizes students' development of abilities and capacities regardless of their specific choice of curricula and courses.

Although the principal focus of most of the reviews to date has been general education, both these challenges and the recommendations they have elicited hold equally significant implications for the undergraduate major, which serves as a prime mode of self-identification for college faculty and students alike and which consumes the bulk of their energies.

It is time, we believe, for a searching appraisal of the role of the undergraduate liberal arts major and other forms of study-in-depth in baccalaureate liberal learning. As members of the National Advisory Committee convened by the Association of American Colleges to guide a review of arts and sciences concentrations, we welcome the involvement of the learned societies' task forces in this review and look forward to working with them.

The advisory committee hopes that the disciplinary and interdisciplinary task forces will begin their deliberations by considering the major in the light of broad educational goals. One way of thinking about overarching goals for the undergraduate major has been suggested by the Association of American Colleges' 1985 *Integrity in the College Curriculum: A Report to the Academic Community*, and especially by its discussion of "study-in-depth" as an integral element in undergraduate liberal education.

Integrity in the Curriculum describes study-in-depth in terms of the capacity to master complexity, the abilities required to undertake independent work, and the achievement of critical sophistication through sequential learning experiences. The report argues that the common tendency to identify the major with "coverage" of particular content results in shallow learning unless students also grasp the assumptions, arguments, approaches, and controversies that have shaped particular claims and findings. The report stresses the importance of students learning to use inquiry and argumentation strategies pertinent to particular fields of study and of their becoming conscious of developing power in mastering these strategies. The report also urges the importance of students' perceiving and working with increasingly complex interrelationships among data and concepts in their fields. "Depth," the report insists, "cannot be reached merely by cumulative exposure to more and more...subject matter." It requires that students

grapple with connections across subject matters. It implies that students develop the capacity to discern patterns, coherence, and significance in their individual learning.

The advisory committee believes that there are additional important facets of study-in-depth, including the ability to apply the approaches of a particular field across a broad spectrum of problems and issues and the development of critical perspective *on* the approaches and limitations of one's chosen field.

Taken together, these considerations suggest a twin agenda for the task forces' inquiry into the effectiveness of various forms of concentrated study as an experience of "study-in- depth": on the one hand, concern for the intellectual purpose and coherence of the major program as designed by faculty; on the other, concern for individual students' growing competence in making connections through their particular course of study.

The advisory committee would like each task force to review current campus practice in its field in light of these twin considerations and

☐ formulate a rationale for concentrated study in its field that describes the specific contributions that advanced study should make to the overall purposes of undergraduate liberal learning

☐ frame a set of recommendations

on ways to strengthen studies-in-depth in its field

☐ identify exemplary campus programs whose practices suggest promising and significant ways that study-in-depth in its field can contribute to liberal learning.

THE RATIONALE
FOR CONCENTRATED STUDY
IN SPECIFIC FIELDS

In their formulation of a rationale for concentrated study in particular fields, the advisory committee would like the task forces to consider the purposes of undergraduate liberal learning in the lives of students and the ways in which particular forms of study-in-depth ought to contribute to fulfillment of these purposes. Since the point of departure for this project has been the discussion of study-in-depth in *Integrity in the Curriculum*, we hope that the task forces will give special consideration to the arguments of that report and to our emendations of it.

As they review the purposes of study-in-depth in their particular areas, we would like the task forces to consider how majoring in a liberal arts field helps prepare students for significant aspects of their lives beyond the academy. How should particular forms of study-in-depth respond to the increasing diversity and interconnectedness of the world

confronting today's students? What curricular requirements and expectations both represent the intellectual contours of a field and foster outcomes important for liberal learning? Are there structural principles or considerations that should shape programs of study-in-depth in the liberal arts? If so, are these comparable across a representative range of arts and sciences fields? Or do they vary from field to field?

RECOMMENDATIONS
FOR STRENGTHENING
STUDY-IN-DEPTH

In requesting recommendations about ways to strengthen study-in-depth in particular fields, we anticipate that the task forces will address lively questions about content in their particular areas. But the advisory committee brings to this endeavor a conviction—to be tested in the reviews of practice—that the question, "What contents should students study in a particular major and in what order?" is only part of the discussion that should be fostered through this national review of study-in-depth. We invite recommendations that direct fresh attention both to the quality of students' engagement in their collegiate concentrations and to the kinds of engagement with content that will serve different sorts of students over the long term.

In this context, we would like the task forces to consider how students can learn—across a set of learning experiences—to test, shape, reflect on, add to, challenge, and use knowledge. How can students integrate learning gained in different courses to construct increasingly sophisticated structures of knowledge? How can students develop some sense of the intersection of disciplinary approaches and of the possibilities and problems of translating and negotiating among them? How can they gain a sense of the strengths and the limitations of the lenses through which they are learning to view issues and problems? How can they be encouraged to connect their learning with significant questions in the world beyond the classroom?

To accomplish these goals, the advisory committee proposes a series of topics designed to stimulate and focus discussion within the task forces. In proposing these topics, we do not expect that the task forces' recommendations for strengthening study-in-depth will address systematically every question raised within each topic. We do hope that the topics themselves, and the issues implied by the particular questions within each topic, will receive serious attention as the task forces frame their reviews of campus practices and formulate their recommendations.

We ask that the task forces, as they discuss these topics, envision several very different students from a broad range of cultural and academic backgrounds, most of whom will not pursue advanced study in the field of their collegiate major. For example, the sociologists might envision one student who enters community service, another who goes to law school and on to a career in corporate finance, a third who combines sociological studies with preparation for public school teaching, a fourth who returns to college at age thirty-five and hopes to continue her studies through a night school MBA, a fifth who will work in another part of the world, a sixth who will raise a family, along with those students who follow the career pattern of an academic sociologist.

In focusing on the rich diversity of today's students, we hope the task forces will suggest ways that collegiate concentrations can better support students' varied learning goals and needs while addressing common goals for all students.

The topics organize themselves into four categories:
☐ setting and reviewing goals for study-in-depth
☐ sequential learning and intellectual development
☐ students' experiences of connected knowing

☐ connections with other fields.
The task forces may wish to add a
fifth category:

☐ special considerations.

Setting and reviewing goals
for study-in-depth

What are the present practices by
which academic programs are reviewed and approved? Are present
campus practices for setting and reviewing goals adequate? If not, how
can they be improved?

Who should review and approve
goals for the major: The faculty as a
whole? A faculty committee? An external review? What considerations
should guide this judgment?

How frequently should reviews
occur?

Should criteria for reviews typically include attention to the changing character and needs of the
student body? To relations between
the discipline and other fields? To relations between the discipline and
general education? To the field's contribution to the larger society?

Much of the articulated rationale
that guides, explicitly or implicitly,
the design and implementation of
arts and sciences majors is focused
on preparation for advanced study.

To what extent is this conception
of depth appropriate for the large
number of students who are not preparing for, and do not pursue, graduate work? Are there exemplary

programs that successfully accomplish valuable educational objectives
but do not seek primarily to prepare
students for advanced studies?

Sequential learning
and intellectual development

☐ *General issues*

To what extent do major programs, as conceived in program requirements, represent sequences of
intellectual growth and increasing
complexity? What are the sources of
the faculty's judgments about sequence, progression, and depth?

There is an expanding body of research on cognitive development in
specific subject areas.

Should faculty members be encouraged to consider such research
in forming judgments about sequence and intellectual development?

Does the chronological organization of some areas of instruction and
the heavy reliance in others on
"standard" textbooks enhance or inhibit attention to issues of sequential
intellectual growth?

Are there new approaches or technologies that challenge prevailing
conceptions of sequence and depth?

Ought there to be self-conscious
connections between introductory,
middle-range, and advanced courses
that make plain to students in what
way Course B exhibits "depth" in relation to Course A?

☐ *Introductory courses*

What ought the introductory course to introduce?

Should the contents of an introductory course be the result of a consensus or debate within the program's faculty? Should these contents be systematically taken up again in more advanced courses?

Should the introductory course focus on what counts as appropriate arguments and strategies within a given field? On domain-specific elements in writing assignments? On major controversies within the field?

Should the introductory course(s) that serve general education needs (through distribution requirements or the like) be separate from the course or courses that introduce the student to study in the field?

☐ *Middle-range courses*

Are middle-range courses organized primarily by subject matter or by some articulated developmental sequence of skills and capacities? Do the assignments and modes of evaluation focus on the students' acquisition of growing knowledge and competence in framing problems? How can middle-range courses contribute more effectively to students' intellectual growth and development?

Ought there to be planned moments of second-order reflection by students about their intellectual and personal progress within a field?

☐ *Advanced work*

The most advanced work in a major program is frequently an individual research project.

What are the expected gains from such research projects? Should students doing research be formally involved in research collaborations? Should they be involved in research collaborations at an earlier stage in their development? Should they affiliate with collaborative research projects over the entire duration of the major?

Are there modes of work other than the research project that are comparably significant in demonstrating an appropriate level of mastery?

Ought there to be common or capstone experiences that provide opportunities for students to reflect on and integrate their work in the major? To reconsider materials studied in previous courses? To consider the nature of the program the faculty has designed and their different experiences of the program?

Students' experiences of connected knowing

How are educational goals of a major made explicit to students? With respect to a program's assumptions about sequence and advancing sophistication? With respect to particular courses? With respect to students' aspirations? How can present practices be improved?

Is there reason to believe that particular fields currently present special obstacles to the participation of discrete groups of students, minorities, women, men? If so, how can the field help remove these obstacles?

Is a capstone project the appropriate moment to attempt some more integrative experience? A senior seminar or capstone course? An occasion which connects the claims of a student's chosen field with the claims of other (neighboring or remote) fields? An occasion in which students reconsider materials studied in previous courses and reflect on their differences in perception?

Should the major encourage reflective enterprises such as an intellectual autobiography or attention to the relationship between competencies in the major field and work experience?

Do our present systems of student assessment focus on sequential intellectual growth? Ought they? How can achievement of intellectual proficiencies or students' understanding of interrelations between constituent elements in their fields be evaluated? Should programs assess students' abilities to connect learning in the major with learning from other fields of study?

Should there be specified occasions for individual students to reflect on their progress in light of individual aspirations and expectations? On values being acquired through study

in a particular field? On relations between fields of knowledge? On relations to extracurricular experiences (that is, work or community service)? Should there be ways of assessing the match between departmental and student expectations?

Connections with other fields
There appears to be a growing sense, in many fields, that the customary disciplinary divisions are no longer self-evident. Customary boundaries are being erased, creating new disciplines and combinations of previously distinct disciplines.

How does this affect the way in which a major program structures its relations with other fields? Required courses? Electives? Joint programs? Team teaching? Integrative seminars with students and faculty in cognate fields?

Ought there to be explicit occasions for students to reflect on competing claims of different fields? On connections across fields?

How much claim on a student's time ought the major to make? Are the customary divisions between the major and the remainder of the undergraduate curriculum still viable?

IDENTIFICATION
OF ILLUSTRATIVE
CAMPUS PROGRAMS
OR PRACTICES

The advisory committee hopes that each task force will identify illustrative or exemplary practices in particular departments or programs that illustrate its recommendations for strengthening study-in-depth. The project staff will provide assistance in eliciting materials from specific departments or programs identified by the task forces.

∎

CHAPTER ONE

BIOLOGY*

INTRODUCTION

Just as "diverse" describes the organisms that have inhabited our planet over the past four billion years, so "diverse" can also describe the backgrounds and objectives of students majoring in the biological sciences in our nation's colleges and universities. The wide range in the academic levels of degrees in biology, coupled with the range of abilities and aspirations among today's students, initially presents a varied picture of the biology major. Further study, however, reveals a high level of uniformity in the biology curriculum, which has changed only slightly in the past three decades. Departments of biology do not appear to be centers of adventurous and futuristic thinking.

The major subjects we teach have remained basically the same over the past half-century. If there has been a shift in what is being taught, it is the new technologies that appear to be driving the changes. We continue to teach courses on evolution, ecol-

ogy, reproduction, genetics, and so on as we have over the past half-century. Now, however, we are able to understand and teach the processes that explain the patterns of biology. Molecular biology, biochemistry, and an ever-increasing number of new technologies have brought a new power and credibility to the biological sciences.

Unfortunately, not all biology majors have access to these new technologies, and what they do come to know about modern biology often still is presented through the lecture method. Most undergraduate biology majors seldom actually use the new technologies; they rarely do science. The predominant approach to student learning is still one in which the professor professes in a large lecture hall three hours per week and students spend several hours in a laboratory in which the highest level of technology is usually the student microscope. Why we continue in this single limited mode of teaching deserves investigation.

Another problem with biology is

the curriculum. When biology faculty members discuss curriculum the conversation often turns to courses and "coverage." Department turf battles are usually about attracting students to individual faculty members and their research interests and not about the knowledge, skills, and values we want students to have when they graduate. "Acceptable coverage," including introductory textbooks and course titles, must reflect the special interests of every faculty member in a department. Consequently textbooks today are becoming impossible to lift, let alone read, and the number of courses taught by departments of biology continues to increase. We also must recognize that while all these additions are being made to the extremely busy biology curriculum, little consideration is given to the courses for the nonmajors who seek a general, broad-based exposure to the nature and importance of the inquiry process. If biology in its more representative state is to be offered to beginning students, entry-level courses must be taught by enthusiastic faculty members with a broad-based understanding of the field who can develop challenging and stimulating courses.

Although we are interested in the courses students complete in departments of biology, that is not the major thrust of this study. Instead we question the methods and processes used throughout the curriculum to bring cohesiveness to the program. What happens to students as they move through departmental requirements for the biology major? Is the biology curriculum cohesive from the student perspective? Are students exposed to the value system of science, and do the courses they take make the connections among science, technology, and society? Are we providing students with real and identifiable models of and experiences with the procedures of biology? Is the biology course for nonscience students presenting a unified picture of the life sciences and improving students' scientific literacy? Is the laboratory in introductory courses a place where both majors and nonmajors can learn how science works? Does the biology curriculum provide a wide range of field experiences for all students?

In addressing these questions we use several resources. First are the results of a survey of more than three hundred senior students and one hundred faculty members from a wide range of college and university departments of biology. We wish to thank those students and faculty members who participated in the survey. Another important reference for this report is an earlier study titled "American College Biology and Zoology Course Requirements: A *de facto* Standardized Curriculum" by Frank Heppner et al. (*BioScience*, No. 2, 1990). This is an account of what courses are presently being taught in departments of biology and zoology. In total, this study is a synthesis of a student survey, a faculty survey, the Heppner report, reports from individual institutions describing several outstanding biology programs, and personal observations. It is intended to assist those who design and plan the curriculum in departments of biology.

The major objective of this document is to encourage faculty members in departments of biology to examine the curriculum for the biology major with an eye to the future. Teaching the body of knowledge we call "biology" through the lecture method simply is not adequate. Students must participate in the doing of science in both the laboratory and the field. Of even greater importance, we want students to leave our departments as biology majors with an understanding of how science can make major contributions to a free society. If we see the biological sciences as an important way of knowing and interpreting the natural world, what we teach and how we teach should reflect our belief system.

THE STATE OF THE BIOLOGY MAJOR

The curriculum

When biology professors examine what takes place over four years in the lives of students majoring in biology, for a variety of reasons they center their inquiry on the curriculum. The faculty survey emphasizes that the curriculum for university-trained biologists is a series of courses, the content of those courses, and the appropriate textbooks. The emphasis is upon courses, bodies of knowledge, and what we want students to know, rather than how we want students to think and what we want them to be able to do, that is, think critically, solve problems, and work collaboratively. The behaviors we want students to emulate are seldom given consideration. What scientists value in the enterprise of free inquiry generally is not mentioned as part of the curriculum review process. Consequently, students are left with the impression that we value textbooks and lecture notes rather than higher order learning.

Not surprisingly, this study revealed that curricula throughout the country are similar, especially in the first two years. The course outlines read like the table of contents in the large compendium-type textbooks.

Programs are more diverse in the

junior and senior years. The upper level diversity follows faculty interest, with a greater range of course offerings in a faculty of twenty members than in one with five.

Most institutions follow a core curriculum, whether or not they use the term. A review of the Commission on Undergraduate Education in the Biological Sciences (CUEBS) 1967 publication titled *Content of Core Curricula in Biology* reveals that course offerings today are closely aligned with the report's recommendations.

Students attending small liberal arts colleges of less than two thousand students were, in general, pleased with the curriculum in the departments of biology. At the same time, biology majors in larger universities were less satisfied with the biology curriculum in their institutions. There probably is some connection between faculty availability in smaller versus larger institutions and the plans among nontraditional students to use the major. Two-thirds of the students attending liberal arts colleges have plans for either graduate school or medical school, while students attending larger and more diverse universities are interested in using their biology major to reach a much wider range of career objectives. Many larger universities offer numerous emphases within the basic major, and these reflect diverse ca-

reer options. Eighty percent of the graduating seniors from all institutions surveyed, however, felt that the major was well organized and that the courses were taught in such a way as to provide a sound overview of the biological sciences.

The student survey indicated that students receive inadequate feedback from professors concerning examinations and written papers. More than 50 percent of all students who completed the questionnaire believed that faculty do not help students learn from their mistakes and fail to devote enough time to reviewing examinations and term papers with individual students.

Less than 40 percent of the students attending large state universities had an opportunity to complete an independent research project or to assist a professor in research, while in the smaller colleges more than 66 percent of all students participated in a research program. With or without the research experience, 60 percent of all graduating seniors felt they were ready for an entry-level position in their chosen career.

In general, the sequence of courses for majors that follow the beginning course reflects the background, training, and interests of individual faculty members. Courses in genetics, ecology, development, systematics, morphology, comparative anatomy, cellular biology, and physiology are being offered under a variety of titles. Practically all the smaller colleges and many of the larger universities identify the very real need for teaching more molecular biology. Again, departments generally express their needs in terms of courses that should be added and rearranged. Much less concern is expressed about a capstone or research experiences for students, exposure of students to the history and philosophy of the biological sciences, better teaching of the values and ethics questions in the sciences, and improved systems of evaluation that will allow students to demonstrate what we want them to know and be prepared to do upon graduation.

Introductory biology courses

The curriculum for the biology major has a tremendous impact on how we design and teach the introductory biology course. Biology majors and faculty members tend to agree that if departments cannot do a better job of addressing the needs and interests of both biology majors and nonmajors, separate courses should be developed. There appears to be a growing trend in both small colleges and large universities toward offering a spectrum of courses to meet the needs of a wide range of students.

Many students who completed the survey felt compelled to comment on their experiences in the beginning biology course. They appeared to feel some sorrow for the nonscience majors enrolled in this first biology course as well as for the students planning to major in biology.

Statements such as "year-long rat race," "course in memorization," and "waste of time" were used by majors to describe their experiences in the beginning biology courses. Student survey responses suggest that little attention is given to making the connections among science, technology, and society in most introductory courses, while the content and vocabulary of biology are presented in rather heavy doses.

A widespread problem is courses designed exclusively for nonmajors. Too often they are watered-down versions of the regular course taught with the aid of traditional textbooks and boring laboratory activities. Unless we can develop courses that present science as an experience in solving problems and thinking critically—courses that teach science as an interesting way of knowing the natural world—the scientific enterprise will continue to be thought of as the enemy of society and not worthy of its financial support. Many students leave their first and only college course in biology with a bad memory of that experience, wondering whether there is any connection between the plants and animals of the natural world and what they studied.

Areas of special interest and concern

Feedback from the student and faculty surveys point to a number of problems in the biology curriculum that deserve the serious and long-term attention of the faculty. The twelve problems identified in this study pertain strictly to the undergraduate curriculum in the biological sciences and must not be confused with the problems surrounding graduate research, faculty publications, equipment budgets, specialized journal holdings, or even the cutting edge of biological information.

Faculty members in many large universities receive few rewards for addressing the issues on our list. Consequently, the reward system must be altered in order to effect educational improvement. The development of a system of equal support for undergraduate and graduate education by private foundations, state governments, and the National Science Foundation would go far toward that goal. Unless specific rewards for strengthening the undergraduate curriculum are created, it is likely that there will continue to be fewer students majoring in the life sciences, and the quality of the experience for those who do major in the sciences will remain inadequate.

The following problems are identified in no special order, but all are subjects we encourage biology departments to address.

☐ The role and importance of the laboratory experience

In 1972, the Commission on Undergraduate Education in the Biological Sciences described the primary role of the laboratory as a place to investigate natural phenomena. A broader definition of the function of the laboratory included:

■ to illustrate objects, concepts, processes, and experiments that have been referred to elsewhere in the curriculum

■ to provide training in laboratory techniques

■ to stimulate intellectually the student and develop appreciation for biology and living things

■ to stimulate discussion

■ to engage the student in the process of investigation.

The vast majority of biology faculty members still support these objectives. For a variety of reasons, however, the laboratory is being lost from the biology curriculum, especially in the introductory biology course.

In many institutions, the reward system discourages faculty members from participating in the beginning biology laboratory. Emphasis on publishing and the need to attract outside research funding has resulted in the nation's best scientists leaving the undergraduate laboratory courses in order to spend more time with graduate students. Beginning graduate students who teach introductory laboratory courses far too often have little or no training on how to design and conduct an investigative laboratory.

Correction of the problem will require major shifts by practically every institution in how faculty members spend their time and in how funds are allocated. The laboratory rather than the lecture must be the focal point of courses for beginning students, and dollars spent must be equalized among beginning courses, upper-level undergraduate courses, and graduate courses. Finally, funding agencies must be certain that what they spend on undergraduate laboratory programs is equal to their spending on graduate research.

Faculties and administrations are encouraged to reexamine the place of the investigative laboratory in student learning. Science educators must take those steps necessary to improve the quality of learning for all students in the introductory biology courses. Prospective biology majors, as well as those students who will not become laboratory scientists but will be voting citizens, must be provided with opportunities to understand the role of the laboratory in a scientific society.

☐ The role and importance of field experiences

The decline and near demise of field experiences in the undergraduate biology curriculum represents a less-than-responsible educational position, especially in this age of increasing environmental problems. There has never been a greater need for and interest in more complete research data in ecology, evolution, and biodiversity. Yet biologists are failing to provide undergraduate students with quality field experiences.

In many colleges and universities, field biology has practically disappeared from the curriculum. Beginning field courses and advanced undergraduate courses in such areas as plant systematics, ecology, limnology, entomology, and ornithology provided an opportunity for small groups of students to study in the field for fifteen afternoons per semester, conducting basic investigations with a faculty member. The field course that allowed many of us to work closely with a professor and that inspired our desire to continue to study and interpret the natural world is unfortunately no longer available to most of today's students.

Has the study of systematics and ecology been starved out of the curriculum? Do graduate students, who will become the future professors of biology, leave the research bench long enough to become acquainted with the flora and fauna of North America? Many younger faculty members come to college teaching with little or no field experience during their years of undergraduate and graduate study, and they are understandably frightened by the idea of teaching a field biology course.

We live in a highly homocentric world, where the ecocentric view is largely unknown and ignored. If biologists are unable or uninterested in acquainting themselves and the millions of undergraduate students with the natural world that controls the destiny of all life on Earth, the value of biology departments to education in the liberal arts stands in question. Biologists must accept responsibility for improving the quality and quantity of field biology courses offered to all undergraduate students.

☐ The role of the faculty in advising

Many undergraduate biology majors never experience quality time with a concerned and knowledgeable advisor. Yet good counseling and advising is essential to the ultimate success with which the students move through the curriculum. Planning for a meaningful biology major must start in one's freshman year, and such planning requires faculty attention. Even very capably run academic counseling centers cannot substitute for good faculty advising.

Again, we found the university reward system to be so directed towards faculty publications and the graduate program that it would be risky for a nontenured faculty member to become heavily invested in advising fifteen or twenty undergraduate students. Because beginning students soon realize the faculty does not have time for them, many students wander through a four-year program. Private liberal arts colleges with no graduate programs have much better success in advising students while, for obvious reasons, large universities are less committed to this important task. In colleges of fewer than two thousand students, many students stated that they know their advisor as a friend and a person they can call on as problems and personal needs develop. This same situation does develop in some larger institutions, but rarely.

It would be wise for all faculty members to devote more time simply to visiting with students if they expect talented undergraduates to be attracted to careers in the biological sciences. Encouraging students to visit animal rooms, greenhouses, field facilities, and faculty research laboratories can send the message that the faculty is interested in beginning students and that exciting and interesting careers are available.

☐ The undergraduate research experience

Although most faculty members recognize the need for undergraduate students to participate in a basic research project, most students majoring in the biological sciences never have this important experience. Students attending liberal arts colleges are more likely to become involved in a personal investigation or actively participate with a faculty member in his or her research, but even in these institutions one-third of the students never have a research experience.

A few very special institutions draw students into a problem-solving experience in their junior and senior years. A small number of colleges require a senior thesis for all students majoring in the sciences. Most of these institutions enroll fewer than two thousand students and do not have graduate programs. Some larger universities, however, have designed strong research programs for undergraduates.

The reasons given in other institutions for not requiring student research or a senior thesis usually are lack of faculty time, equipment, funding, and student interest. Yet faculty members recognize the importance of the research experience, and most students want such participation. The problem is that the faculty agenda gives low priority to the importance of research training for undergraduates. Faculty members in smaller colleges devote so much time to teaching that undergraduate research is crowded out, while university faculty limit their research to the graduate program. The undergraduate research program thus falls between the cracks.

☐ Improving evaluation and assessment in the biology curriculum

In most biology departments, evaluation and assessment of student learning is probably the most misunderstood topic of major discussion. Faculty members simply do not know what, when, and how to assess. Also, they appear to be fearful and somewhat apprehensive of the subject. They often are unprepared when students challenge the grading system. Outside assistance on these issues that is available from specialists in evaluation and assessment is rarely sought.

Students who completed the survey form were most critical of faculty methods of evaluation. A number of students accused the faculty of requiring students to write papers and answer essay questions and then failing to respond critically to students' work. A single grade on a written assignment is not adequate. Substantial written feedback is needed if students are to learn from writing assignments. Evaluation is not just for the instructor to arrive at a grade; it is also for the student. Some students felt faculty members played "dirty tricks" on examinations by teaching and emphasizing one aspect of the subject but testing on subjects never emphasized in the course.

Faculty discussion of the pros and cons of multiple-choice questions, short-answer questions, and essay questions are not adequate today to the knowledge, skills, and values we should be teaching and testing in the undergraduate biology program. Basic research in student evaluation points to a much larger role for performance-based assessment, oral examinations, concept mapping, and research reports in a total program of assessment.

It is especially important that these assessments be made throughout the time in which students are completing the biology major. Benchmark programs of evaluation, following early testing as students enter the biology major, could serve to strengthen the major and send messages to students and faculty members as to where more emphasis should be placed. Certainly no single tool should be used to constitute a four-year assessment.

☐ Textbooks as the curriculum

Textbooks control and define the curriculum in the undergraduate biology program just as they do the K–12 science curriculum. Publishers produce ever-larger and continuously heavier textbooks because that is what faculties select for their courses. It is important to note that faculty members, not students, select textbooks. As long as faculty members insist on broad and total coverage,

continuously adding to the volume without eliminating some subjects, there is no limit to the eventual size of textbooks. This process has led to a lockstep curriculum, taught from a variety of textbooks, all covering the same subjects in almost the same order.

Students noted that practically all textbooks start with molecular and cellular biology, which makes sense to faculty members but throws students into subjects that they find least interesting and in which they have limited backgrounds.

In many biology departments a single textbook and the accompanying laboratory manual are dictated by vote of the faculty. Those choices often represent a compromise that is least offensive. They also make it difficult for individual faculty members to experiment by developing their own readings and laboratory activities. Although this system assures the faculty that all students study similar material, it is extremely limiting for creative teachers.

☐ The capstone course

In a variety of ways, students and faculty members who completed the survey expressed interest in a senior capstone course or a program to pull together the major concepts of biology for graduating seniors. Although there is some evidence of success among departments that offer such courses, this subject has not been studied widely.

Several questions need to be addressed, however, before capstone courses can be implemented:

■ Is any single faculty member qualified to teach a capstone course for all majors?

■ If the capstone course is team-taught, will it become a series of separate faculty lectures? How can we assure integration?

■ Would such a course become a rehash of the introductory biology course?

■ Could this course be taught as a current-literature-of-biology course in which students read and present short summary statements from journal articles?

■ Is there a need in biology departments for a course that teaches the modes of inquiry?

■ Are there other ways—such as senior seminars—of helping students pull together the knowledge and skills they learned in a wide range of courses?

☐ The place of values and ethics education in the biology curriculum

The students surveyed definitely want the faculty to address the ethical implications of the knowledge and skills they teach in the courses offered to biology majors. Faculty members are encouraged by students to discuss in their courses those values that are important to the inquiry process, that is, openness, risk-taking, and honesty. It is important to note that most of the critical problems society faces have a biological component. These problems also challenge human values and belief systems. Such subjects as world population, abortion, birth control, acid rain, and biodiversity are central to biology but also reach into the family, economics, and religion.

If publishing and sharing information are so important to the inquiry process, why do faculties provide so little support for cooperation and sharing among students in laboratory courses? Why are faculties not more open and explicit about what they want students to know and demonstrate in their courses? Are there ethical limits to what science and industry should produce in the way of new technologies? Is the scientific community capable of judging what the limits of new knowledge and publication should be? Can and should society trust the scientific community to regulate itself and provide adequate testing and evaluation of new products? These are the kinds of questions students want biology faculties to address.

☐ Reaching minorities in departments of biology

Departments of biology and the sciences in general have extremely bad records of attracting and retaining minority students. Because of the "Catch-22" nature of the problem,

we have limited numbers of both minority faculty members and students. As a vivid example of our
poor performance, four private liberal arts colleges in the survey have a
total of five minority students out of
a total of more than ninety graduating senior majors.

Meanwhile, women made up 50
percent of the graduating seniors in
these same four colleges. It is interesting to note that women appear to
be more interested in health science
careers and in attending medical
school while male students in higher
percentages plan research careers
and want to enter Ph.D. programs.
The biological sciences are attracting
women in numbers never before believed possible. NSF Special Report
Number 89-318 states that over the
period of 1976–86 the employment
growth rate for women in the biological sciences was more than twice
that for men.

The long-term solution to meeting
the need to attract minorities to the
biological sciences—and other sciences—must start in elementary and
secondary schools. Professors, colleges,
and universities, as well as private
and public funding agencies, all have
key roles to play in this process. Increasing interactions among minority
students and role models and providing experiences that arouse curiosity and foster self-confidence are
effective approaches to correcting

what has become a national disgrace.
The National Science Foundation
must take a leadership role in addressing this problem through programs that reach not only minority
students in schools and colleges but
the teachers who work daily with
these students as well.

☐ Interdisciplinary programs

The most critical problems society
faces are interdisciplinary in nature.
Solving these problems requires the
ability to integrate the knowledge,
skills, and values of a wide range of
intellectual disciplines. Problems related to population, malnutrition,
ecosystem destruction, education,
and health care have a biological
component, but there are also economic, cultural, and religious aspects
to all these issues. Yet the very best
undergraduate students of biology
accuse us of teaching biology in a
vacuum. As one student stated the
problem, "Olin Science Hall reeks
with isolationism."

If professors of biology wish to extend their contributions to the larger
society, they must improve their ability to listen to a wider range of students and faculty members. Some
students just plain don't like us and
choose not to associate with scientists. Many students will do anything
possible to keep from enrolling in a
science course. Perhaps higher education is not totally responsible for
this situation. Some students are

"science haters" long before they enter college. We need to better understand where the problems originated.

The life sciences must become an integral component of a broader interdisciplinary educational scheme that extends beyond the sciences. Our students—those majoring in biology and those whom we advise—want us to assist them in making the connections among the sciences, humanities, and social sciences. If we present a negative picture of the general education program, as though it is of little value and not worthy of the attention of students majoring in biology, we are, in fact, limiting the potential for intellectual growth of those students we most wish to serve.

The data provided by the survey of biology majors revealed a lack of interest in—indeed, almost a disdain for—general-education courses among many older students enrolled in state colleges and universities. Students in four-year private colleges, however, generally enjoyed the courses they took outside the sciences and considered the liberal arts experience extremely valuable to their total education. In this case, the precollege background of students appeared to affect their attitudes toward their total education. Those students attending private liberal arts colleges came from homes where practically all their parents had attended college,

while among students attending state institutions the vast majority of the parents never had attended college. Science professors should be aware of this trend.

☐ The role of the university in the preparation of teaching assistants to become professors

For a variety of reasons the major research universities are not preparing graduate students to take their place in community colleges, liberal arts colleges, and small state universities. The faculty survey provides evidence that in all institutions except the largest state and private ones, faculty members devote more than 70 percent of their time to teaching, with less than 20 percent to research (and this often with undergraduate research activities) and 10 to 15 percent to completing administrative tasks.

Many beginning graduate students are moved quickly into the research laboratory without first demonstrating a broad-based knowledge of science. In their first job assignment, when those new Ph.D.s are expected to take over the beginning biology course and teach everything from molecular biology to the evolution of plants and animals to population ecology, therefore, they wonder why they spent years in the research laboratory rather than complete a wide range of courses across the spectrum of the life sciences. One faculty member suggested that five to six years are required for a young person to learn what it means to be a professor in an institution where the vast majority of one's waking hours will be devoted to being with undergraduates in lectures, labs, the field, and one-on-one discussions.

Experience as a teaching assistant is valuable for graduate students who plan teaching careers, but it falls far short of preparing them to organize and present lectures, structure investigative laboratories, assist students in elementary research activities, counsel and advise students, prepare examinations, select audiovisuals, use the research literature in science education, and organize and conduct field courses for beginning students. These are, for most professors, the basic skills required for survival in biology education, and they should be strengthened while students are in graduate school.

Universities that prepare graduate students in the skills described above will help them to succeed in various types of institutions and will at the same time contribute to the quality of learning for all students as they enroll in their first college biology course.

□ The evaluation of the total program in the life sciences

Departments of biology need to examine carefully what they teach, how they teach, and why they teach

in the present curriculum. We are doing many things right, as a high percentage of our graduating seniors will attest. The flaws in the biology program identified by students, potential students, and faculty members, however, demand our attention. Beyond those students we are reaching, large numbers of students are being overlooked by our methods and actions.

In many institutions the relationship between the biology major and the career objectives of the students is unclear. Approximately one-third of the prospective health professionals, school science teachers, and agricultural specialists are dissatisfied with what we teach and the departmental requirements for the major.

Another problem is that many future science teachers are exposed to poor examples of how to teach. The university model of the large lecture with limited or no laboratory experience is not appropriate for prospective teachers or beginning undergraduate students. This problem should be addressed by departments of biology if we are seriously interested in improving the scientific literacy of the nation. This will require a major redistribution of faculty time and departmental budgets.

There is good evidence that both self-analysis within departments and external review have a role to play in altering what we teach and in changing faculty behaviors. Critical review and revision of a departmental program is almost impossible by those who originally designed the program. It is only when departments take the risks necessary to look within themselves and alter reward systems that we will ever know what is possible.

CONCLUSION

Based on the findings of this limited study, there appears to be a need for a national debate to address these recommendations and other problems confronting the undergraduate curriculum in the biological sciences. This should become a major objective of the American Institute of Biological Sciences.

---

*Members of the task force of the American Institute of Biological Sciences were Jack L. Carter, Colorado College; Charles Chambers, American Institute of Biological Sciences; Frank Heppner, University of Rhode Island; Roy H. Saigo, University of Northern Iowa; Geraldine Twitty, Howard University; and Dan B. Walker, California State University–San Jose. This report is recommended by AIBS as a framework for campus discussion of the major in biology.

ECONOMICS[1]

Economics is a popular undergraduate major, constituting almost 2 percent of the national total. About
thirty-two thousand economics
majors graduate annually from
American colleges and universities.
Enrollments have grown steadily
over the past two decades, perhaps
reflecting a belief that majoring in
economics will improve a graduate's
job prospects.

Most economics majors plan to
continue their education beyond the
baccalaureate level, but fewer than
half actually do. Those who do continue their education are divided almost equally between those in MBA
programs and those in law schools;
less than 3 percent of the thirty-two
thousand annual graduates enroll in
economics doctoral programs. Those
who enter the labor force directly after graduation go into a wide variety
of occupations in a diverse set of in-
dustries, government agencies, and
not-for-profit organizations. Few describe their employment as an
"economist."[2]

PURPOSE OF THE
ECONOMICS MAJOR

Developing students' capacity to
"think like an economist" is the
overarching goal of economics education. All other virtues follow. But
what does it mean to think like an
economist? Do our students understand the diverse approaches of different economists and the limitations
of the prevailing paradigm? How can
we be assured that our students can
really think more like an economist
by the time they walk across the
graduation platform?

Thinking like an economist involves using chains of deductive
reasoning in conjunction with sim-
plified models—such as supply and
demand, benefit-cost analysis, and
comparative advantage—to understand economic phenomena. It involves identifying trade-offs in the
context of constraints, distinguishing
positive (what is) from normative
(what should be) analysis, tracing
the behavioral implications of some

change while abstracting from other aspects of reality, and exploring the consequences of aggregation. It also involves describing the redistributive implications of changes in economic institutions and policies, amassing data to evaluate and refine our understanding of the economy, and testing alternative hypotheses about how consumers and producers make economic choices and how the economic system works.

Thinking like an economist includes several distinctive elements. First, an economist's approach usually emphasizes deductive reasoning: What insights can be derived logically from a set of premises? Second, there is an emphasis on parsimonious models: models which help us focus on the more important behavioral relationships in our complex world. To some people, economists tend to abstract too much from the richness of human behavior and reality; to many economists, the strength of our analysis is the provision of focus and, thus, clarity of thought. Third, the economic approach emphasizes decision-making techniques: perspectives on how choices are made and the consequences of those choices. Finally, while all economic problems involve normative issues, there is a strong bias toward an analytical approach that abstracts from or downplays "values" issues.

Thinking like an economist also involves creative skills. Identifying economic issues and problems, framing them in ways other people do not see, devising novel policy proposals, analyzing both the intended and unintended effects of policies, and devising innovative methods to estimate the magnitude of these effects are all as central to the discipline as is the development of logically coherent theories.

Thinking like an economist is facilitated by breadth and depth of knowledge and by the general forms of human reasoning that cut across the disciplines. An economic argument contains not only logic and facts, but also analogies and stories. Facts and logic alone rarely suffice. Context is important. Our understanding of America's recent economic decline is shaped by the facts of Britain's history, by the logic of playing catch-up, by analogy to earlier civilizations, and by stories of arrogance punished by failure.

The construction of economic arguments can help connect the study of economics with the rest of what students learn. Similar arguments are employed across disciplines. The equilibrium achieved in the world market for copper has striking similarities to the equilibrium achieved in a chemical reaction or the equilibrium achieved in *Hamlet*, act V, scene 2. What is important and what is shared across fields in the liberal arts curriculum is argument.

Economics is particularly well suited for facilitating learning across the curriculum. Positioned methodologically between the sciences and the humanities, economic issues crop up everywhere, largely because the central rationale underlying economics—coping with scarcity—is pervasive. The form of economic argument (frequently quantitative, always parsimonious), however, sometimes inhibits communication across disciplinary boundaries.

In the economics major we share with other disciplines a desire to empower students with a self-sustaining capacity to think and learn. They should know how to pose questions, collect information, identify and use an appropriate framework to analyze that information, and come to some conclusion.

THE REALITY OF THE ECONOMICS MAJOR

Both the structure of the economics discipline and the major itself can be likened to a tree. The major is rooted in the introductory courses which introduce students to economic thinking and its applicability to a variety of issues. The trunk is a core set of principles, analytical methods, and quantitative skills that are widely accepted in the profession. The branches of the tree, extending out in all directions, represent the array of subdisciplinary fields ranging from monetary economics to industrial organization. These subfields reflect the main points of interest and research in economics and generate the problems to which principles and quantitative approaches can be applied fruitfully. These two characteristics of economics—a central core of theoretical and empirical knowledge combined with opportunities to extend that knowledge to a wide variety of topics—differentiate it from the structure of other social science disciplines.

Looked at another way, the economics major is a helix—plowing the same ground repeatedly but at progressively greater depth. It goes beyond a simple accumulation of exposure to successively more topics. Basic principles introduced in the beginning courses are reinforced and refined in intermediate theory courses and then rediscovered and extended in elective courses.

The curriculum for an economics major begins with a two-semester sequence in principles of macroeconomics (the study of aggregate income, employment, and price phenomena) and microeconomics (the study of individual firm, worker, and consumer behavior), or sometimes with a single-semester introductory course combining macro and micro.[3]

After the introductory courses, most majors take two intermediate theory courses (macroeconomics and microeconomics) and a course in basic quantitative methods. In the intermediate theory courses ideas introduced in the first course are reexamined, usually with less restrictive analytical tools.

Intermediate theory courses accomplish three goals. First, they demonstrate how economists use theory, how rigorous thinking can illuminate economic phenomena, and how theory and real-world events interact to produce new knowledge, concepts, and theories about the economy and how it works. Second, they provide basic tools required to undertake economic analyses in elective courses. Third, they offer important signals to students: what the major is like, what content must be mastered, what skills must be developed, and what standards of performance must be met. The quantitative methods course usually emphasizes statistics and hypothesis testing.

Finally, in junior-senior electives—such as international trade, economic history, public finance, labor, and economic development—students acquire substantive knowledge. These courses bring economics principles, analytical methods, and quantitative skills to bear on problems in diverse institutional contexts. Seldom are particular elective courses prescribed.

The typical economics curriculum rarely provides any kind of culminating experience. Some programs (about 7 percent—almost all located in selective liberal arts colleges) require a major research paper or thesis; this experience can be the final stage in a student's transition from neophyte to independent thinker. The comprehensive senior examination is found mainly in small liberal arts colleges and in only a quarter of them. Even less common is the senior seminar offering students the opportunity to integrate the ideas they have gathered from various courses.

Mathematical aptitude and skills are useful to an undergraduate economics major. The relationship between incremental and average values, for example, is pervasive in economics. Mathematics can clarify relationships and improve student understanding. Consequently, economics majors sometimes are required to take calculus to prepare for their intermediate theory courses. The important principles in intermediate macro and micro, however, can be learned without the use of calculus. Though calculus can help some students understand the economics concepts, unfortunately the mathematics sometimes becomes an end in itself rather than a means to facilitate learning economics.

A calculus course that serves economics students well should cover partial and total differentiation, constrained and unconstrained maximization, and integration; and it should emphasize application and interpretation rather than drills in computational skills or formal proofs of theorems. This, unfortunately, does not describe many first-semester college calculus courses.

Similar problems sometimes haunt the quantitative methods requirement, which is intended to foster students' skills in working with real data. These courses are often overloaded and taught at too fast a pace to prepare students adequately for the empirical dimension of elective courses. Frequently data appraisal (for example, survey design, sampling procedures, data accuracy) is squeezed out of the course, and some quantitative methods courses fail to cover adequately the philosophy, appropriate use, and limitations of hypothesis testing and regression analysis.

Economics majors rarely are systematically exposed to conflicting values in their economics classes; this is a feature with mixed blessings. Introductory students are likely to be taught early that economists are concerned with positive and not normative issues. It is said that markets determine who will work and for how much and what will be produced and for whom. Advanced students are introduced to subtleties such as why different people have different productivities, or why income is distributed unequally. While economics courses routinely discuss the sources of poverty and the possible consequences of adopting different policies to alleviate it, usually little is said about what kind of commitment should be made by individuals, groups, or perhaps the government. Economists feel more comfortable describing the origins of the disadvantaged than grappling with the extent of society's responsibility to improve their lot. Since the exposure of students to such problems in other courses is typically value-oriented, economics provides a useful balance, and an alternative, even if a limited, perspective.

Considerable evidence suggests that introductory college economics courses are effective in the sense that students understand economic processes considerably better after taking one.[4] It also appears that the effects persist over time.[5] By contrast, comparable evidence on the major is sparse.[6] Nor do we know whether any real success is achieved in enabling students to learn after they leave college or to equip them to analyze contemporary economic problems they will read about in the press, encounter in their work, or deal with as citizens.

ON TEACHING AND LEARNING IN THE MAJOR

What are the strengths of the economics major and where are the best opportunities for improvement? Its overriding strength is a well-defined and commonly accepted core of analytical principles. This core facilitates communication among students and faculty in different fields within economics. Students can use their common understanding of principles to bridge institutional or chronological gaps. Because there is widespread agreement about the structure and content of the undergraduate curriculum, little faculty energy is dissipated in debates about course requirements. Differences of opinion about the curriculum manifest themselves largely as differences in what is taught in courses of the same title and how it is taught. A laissez-faire attitude toward content and method within courses often results in considerably more variety being offered to economics students than is apparent from catalogue course descriptions. When this variety penetrates the core curriculum, however, it can lead to confusion and frustration in those elective courses which rely on the core to establish a uniform foundation for all students.

Because the basic principles of economics apply to a wide array of problems, majors are usually exposed to different types of inquiry, all within courses that constitute the traditional major. The commonality of the principles offers opportunities to make connections by spanning apparently dissimilar subjects. The sequential curriculum facilitates study at progressively greater depths; the common core of principles, coupled with their wide applicability, allows repetition to reinforce important ideas, making it easier for students to carry their learning forward after graduation.

The economics major is not without problems, however. The major's current popularity, coupled with staffing constraints, has forced class sizes upward. Large classes lead instructors to adopt a lecture approach, emphasizing passive learning, narrow forms of evaluation, and few or no writing assignments.

In our enthusiasm for teaching students how to "think like economists" we sometimes teach as doctrine that everyone should think like an economist, and that such thinking is possible only with the use of marginal analysis. The neoclassical paradigm in economics stresses "marginality," examining relatively small changes while holding other factors constant, even though many problems require solutions involving large changes. The discipline is less well equipped to analyze large changes, and the capacity of students to interact with other disciplines using a broader mind set can thus be limited.

Finally, the amount and type of student writing assignments and oral presentations in many programs not only fail to prepare students for the demands they will encounter after graduation but also limit the ability of students to demonstrate their mastery of economics while still in college.[7]

Class size

In recent decades economics enrollments have climbed faster than teaching staff. Larger classes dictate less than ideal teaching techniques and methods of evaluation.[8] Though classes are smaller at some institutions, the effects of large introductory economics classes at Ph.D.-granting universities still exert considerable impact on the prevailing structure of courses and attitudes of faculty members, most of whom come out of graduate experiences as teaching assistants in large classes. Except in smaller liberal arts colleges, heavy reliance is placed on lecturing, sometimes even when class size permits pedagogical approaches that encourage active participation by students.

It is mainly in smaller classes that economics instructors can expect their students to be more than mere receptors of economic knowledge and manipulators of contrived exercises. The sad fact is that we often expect students to learn to think more like economists without providing them opportunities to learn gradually from the inside how economists go about doing economics. After a lecture on buoyancy, students are thrown into the deep end of the pool and many discover that without practice and encouragement they cannot swim.

Allowing students more opportunity to become active learners will require many more classes of fewer than twenty-five students. In smaller classes there are greater opportunities to mesh pedagogical methods with the needs of various students who are then likely to be more directly and personally engaged in learning, reducing their apathy and frustration.

Instructional methods

Effective learning requires active participation by students. The system of incentives, which is paramount in channeling student energies, should encourage this activity. Exams should challenge students to use what they have learned in new settings and not merely require them to solve mechanical problems or regurgitate the textbook. In field courses, students should be expected to use the tools learned in prerequisite courses. More hands-on experiences, independent studies, and senior theses, for example, should help students perceive order in the economic world and still appreciate its inherent ambiguities.

An innovative approach to teaching economics recently developed at Denison University illustrates the opportunity to engage students actively in the learning process.[9] A lecture/laboratory format rather than the traditional lecture or lecture/discussion format is used to teach most of the economics courses at Denison. In economics laboratories, students use real world data to develop, explore, and test economic theories. The tutorial nature of laboratories creates an apprenticeship atmosphere that draws students more actively into the learning process.

Active learning also can be nurtured through independent research projects. An independent research project offers students opportunities to frame an unstructured problem, pose the appropriate questions, select the analytical methods, gather the requisite information, interpret results, and defend their conclusions to a critical audience.

The textbook remains the principal tool for teaching economics. Good as most are, we question the efficacy of relying so heavily on the array of predigested evidence presented in the usual textbook and its panoply of supplements and teaching aids. Undergraduate economics majors are seldom encouraged to read "real" (vis-à-vis text) books that reflect the efforts of economists to understand difficult real-world problems.[10] Textbooks provide finished (and sometimes dead) knowledge rather than knowledge in the making, and they often represent a superficial yet overwhelming smorgasbord of loosely connected ideas rather than the in-depth development of a coherent theme with related evidence and argumentation.

Packing 450 students into a large lecture hall and sending untrained graduate teaching assistants to meet with smaller discussion groups periodically is not the best way to teach economics in depth or to reach the increasingly diverse population of undergraduates.[11] Yet in many institutions large introductory economics classes are inevitable. Technology can help confront the problem. Computers have been used effectively for some time in the form of computer-managed instruction, where regular computer assignments discipline study effort.[12] Computers can also simulate market behavior and aggregate economic activity.[13] At the least, computers are the pencil and graph paper of today's student.

Writing
Readin', writin', and 'rithmetic are of course central to a liberal arts education. Two centuries ago Edmund

Burke grouped economists with calculators, "in whom," he lamented, "the glory of Europe was extinguished forever."[14] The glory may be less today, but the modern world depends on knowing how large is big. Likewise, a student's ability to read and listen should be sharpened by majoring in economics. Close reading of poetry is no more exacting than close reading of economics, though close economics reading is less self-consciously taught. The middle of the triad—writing—is a particular problem in economics today. Writing and speaking should play a large role in the economics major but usually do not.

While typical class sizes may preclude meaningful writing assignments in most introductory courses, increasing the amount of student writing in intermediate theory and economics electives is both feasible and desirable. Word processing offers an often overlooked opportunity. By reducing the cost of rewriting, word processors allow faculty to work with students to improve writing and argument. This is a marked advance over the traditional approach, in which the instructor laboriously provides detailed feedback at the end of the semester, only to have it completely ignored by the student.

Perspective

Thinking like an economist need not inhibit one from thinking in other ways. But if economics is learned in isolation, other ways of knowing may be devalued. Neils Bohr noted the "precluding feature of knowing": for example, observing that people are sometimes rational in making decisions may preclude remembering that frequently they wander in a fog of indecision. Taking a Western view of the dividing line between the family and the marketplace can make it harder to understand a Moroccan bazaar or an Israeli kibbutz. Moreover, economics can downplay equity and subjectivity, since economists have, as we delight in saying, a comparative advantage in efficiency and objectivity. Such specialization can leave our students unable to cope with the imprecision and ambiguity of the world, choosing unreflectively the hard half of the false dichotomy between hard and soft.

The wide applicability of economics principles often tempts us to overlook the limitations of "thinking like an economist." In our enthusiasm to demonstrate the power of economic analysis we risk becoming doctrinaire. If we really want to foster independent and critical thought by our students we need to demonstrate open-minded self-critical thinking. But criticism must be introduced carefully. Excessive negativism at the beginning may discourage students from grasping any of the ideas of economics. And as Joan Robinson argues, everyone ought to learn at least enough about the popular paradigms of economics to know how to avoid being deceived by economists.[15]

The enthusiasm frequently engendered for specific economic models can also have pedagogical consequences. When enthusiasm crosses the fine line dividing it from dogmatism and when economic models are initially revealed as self-evident truths, debate is stifled and learning is sacrificed. Under such circumstances, is it any surprise that critical discussion of methodology is difficult to stimulate in later elective courses?

The give and take of teaching
Teaching is not simply a matter of stuffing student minds with facts, theories, and empirical techniques. The ability of teachers to convey ideas effectively to students depends on their capacity to understand students' perspectives and orientation, to recognize the experiences of students, and to connect with students' prior knowledge. For example, a nineteen-year-old coming fresh from what often amounts to a socialist community (the family) and with little experience with scarcity or choice may find it difficult to grasp capitalist economics. Moreover, undergraduates of all ages may be at

radically different stages in terms of their capacity to work with ambiguity and abstraction. Numerous studies following the groundbreaking research of William Perry on Harvard students have found across a variety of institutions and student populations that first year college students employ dichotomous thinking—things are either right or wrong, black or white. As students mature, their ability to cope with abstraction and ambiguity often improves, suggesting the need for tailoring instructional strategies to students' stages of development.

The changing mix of students warrants more explicit attention. For example, women now constitute a majority of all persons enrolled in American colleges and universities.[16] In spite of the enthusiasm reflected in their growing matriculation rates, the college experience engenders for many women a "decline in the level of their intellectual and personal aspirations."[17] Many little things, when cumulated, can make the college classroom a chilly place for women to learn. Commonly used examples from sports may be one of these "little things." Textbooks that have few women presented in nontraditional roles is another. Feiner and Morgan found that women are mentioned in fewer than 1 percent of the examples in introductory economics texts.[18] To the extent that the material is devoid of experiential content for half the audience, learning is diminished.

The competitive, aggressive standards of argument that pervade certain disciplines, including economics, also make some women uncomfortable.[19] While the expert-and-client model appeals to some students, others may prefer more cooperative methods of learning. To facilitate learning in a diverse group of students, instructors need to employ an array of pedagogical techniques.

Attention also must be given to evaluation. Based on a large sample of data from Great Britain, Lumsden and Scott found that male economics students do better than women on multiple choice questions and vice versa for written essays.[20] A proper balance of evaluation instruments is necessary to compare properly the achievement of all students.

WHAT AND HOW MUCH DO OUR STUDENTS KNOW?

Little is done, except at a few liberal arts colleges, to assess the impact of the economics major on our students' intellectual development. It is assumed—"hoped" may be more accurate—that climbing the tree of economic knowledge, represented by a succession of progressively higher-level courses, produces graduating majors who can better see and understand how to think like an economist.

A successful assessment program could provide feedback to help a department revise its courses, alter its pedagogy, restructure its major, or in extreme cases rethink its entire undergraduate program. Implementing an evaluation program would be relatively simple if assessment instruments sensitive to the kinds of proficiencies of interest to departments were readily available. Since valid and reliable examinations would be available for use by one department even after being "consumed" by another, and since their preparation entails substantial initial costs, we recommend that the Committee on Economic Education of the American Economic Association assume responsibility for developing exemplary programs that help departments evaluate how well they prepare their majors to think like economists.

An end-of-the-major assessment program, particularly if it involves external examiners, can lead to a constructive change in the learning environment. It can make students and faculty members allies in the common goal of helping students understand economics. As students strive to attain the expected proficiencies, faculty members may see their roles recast along the lines of coaches rather than referees. In short, external assessment holds out the promise of making students and teachers collaborators rather than adversaries in the learning process.

RECOMMENDATIONS

Foundations

The foundations of the major rest on three sets of courses: introductory macro and micro, intermediate macro and micro, and quantitative methods.

☐ Introductory macro and micro

These courses offer breadth to the major and, more importantly, introduce students to the fundamental concepts of economics and methods of applying economic theory to interesting and novel situations. This approach reveals the power of economic analysis and its practical utility. These courses tend to be encyclopedic and all too often oriented toward formalism of theory.

The introductory courses should emphasize the application of a limited number of important concepts and theoretical tools to a variety of problems at the expense of some of the existing formal and detailed elaboration of theoretical constructs or complete coverage of the vast array of topics included in most textbooks.

☐ Intermediate macro and micro

The two semester intermediate theory sequence can be improved in several ways. First, departments have often, by default, relinquished control of these courses to those who teach them.

Departments need to coordinate the content of the intermediate theory courses to insure that they emphasize a foundation of knowledge and skills on which other courses and instructors can rely.

While most intermediate macro and micro courses develop well the rigor and elegance of economic theory, they tend to slight its evaluation. In particular, the "usefulness" of theoretical topics and paradigms, largely assessed by confronting theory with data, applying models to various problems, and comparing the outcomes of alternative theoretical constructs, merits greater emphasis.

These courses should establish explicit connections between theory and its empirical counterparts in order to help students appraise the importance of theoretical constructs, provide a basis for selecting assumptions, and show that theory is relevant.

To achieve the overall objective of the major *the intermediate macro and micro courses must emphasize active student learning, practice in applying what students learn, and the exercise of critical judgment.* Much of this can be accomplished by increasing the number of carefully structured writing assignments that demonstrate the power of application.

Certain practices war against enhancing the effectiveness of the intermediate theory courses. One is the preoccupation with formalism rather than a focus on logically rigorous analysis of economic issues. The intermediate theory courses can reveal the power and excitement of the discipline provided they convey how economists use theory, how rigorous thinking can illuminate economic phenomena, and how theory and real world events interact to produce new knowledge, concepts and theories about the economy and how it works.

☐ Quantitative methods

Economics is an empirically oriented discipline. The focus is on explaining and testing our understanding of economic phenomena. Hence, students need an appreciation for and an ability to deal with empirical matters. Rather than view this as a matter of learning statistics, we need to ask what it is that students must know to function as economists. The foundation in empirical methods depends on:

■ knowing something about the measurement of economic variables (methods of data collection, reliability, and so on)

■ being able to organize, work with, and manipulate data for purposes of comparison

■ the capacity to test hypotheses with empirical data

■ knowing how to interpret the re-

sults of various statistical procedures.

We recommend that the quantitative methods course be reoriented from its almost singular statistical focus to emphasize this wider range of quantitative methods employed by economists.

Breadth requirement

A respectable economics major requires at least five (three-credit-hour) courses beyond the foundations to provide sufficient opportunities for students to develop the art of applying economic principles and concepts in different institutional contexts. *The chosen electives should be distributed to ensure an appreciation for the historical, international, and political context of economics.* Such breadth will help students avoid a narrow, parochial perspective based solely on marginalist thinking and should prepare them to deal sensibly with problems that involve other than atomistic models of individual choice.

Contextual inquiry includes courses in economic history (where connections between economics and history are explicit), history of economic thought (where different modes of thought are exposed), comparative economic systems (where social, political, and cultural dimensions that influence distinctive economic systems are compared), and area studies (where synthetic analyses of countries and regions are explored). Such courses illuminate the importance of context and structure—initial conditions and constraints—and take the edge off narrow thinking about economics.

International courses include not only trade and finance, but also economic development, area studies, and comparative systems; other courses may fit too (for example, the multinational corporation). Such courses place students in a stronger position to use their tools of economic inquiry in a world that is rapidly becoming more integrated.

Public-sector economics courses include not only public expenditure analysis and taxation, but also some offerings in theory (stressing public goods, externalities, collective decision-making, and market failure), labor economics (stressing aspects of regulation), and the like. Such courses simultaneously illuminate and qualify the role of individual, free-market choice, a dominant paradigm in economics. Students should gain greater appreciation for methods of collective choice, including nonmarket options for resource allocation. These dimensions of decision making account for one-third to almost all resource allocations in most countries, and they are just too important to relegate to a few weeks of exploration in the foundation courses.

All elective courses should consciously forge explicit links to both economic theory and empirical methods. Students should be expected to fit theoretical principles to the particular institutions studied in the courses, and assignments should reinforce students' understanding of empirical methods acquired in the core quantitative methods course.

All courses that satisfy the breadth requirement should contain a substantial active-learning component, such as oral and/or written reports, interactive computer simulations, class discussions, or laboratory exercises *and should draw on a broad array of source materials*. Thus, these courses should not rely exclusively on textbooks for assigned reading.

Depth requirement

To complete the process of intellectual maturation, *every student should be required to apply what he or she has learned to an economic problem, and in the process acquire experience really "doing economics."* For a particular intellectual encounter to accomplish this goal, *it should involve considerable responsibility on the student's part for formulating questions, gathering information, structuring and analyzing information, and drawing and communicating conclusions to others in oral and/or written form.* The depth requirement should be implemented in each elective course and complemented through the establishment of "capstone" experiences such as special seminars or traditional opportunities for senior theses, honors research projects, and independent studies.

HOW TO MAKE IT WORK

A respectable economics major that teaches students how to "think like an economist" in a way that has lasting benefits requires considerable instructional resources, especially if, as we argue, students must obtain extensive practice at really doing economics. It requires relatively small classes (twenty to twenty-five students in intermediate macro and micro and elective courses and approximately fifteen students in courses emphasizing writing), oral presentations and argumentation, and research projects.

Deans and chairs will immediately observe that such a major is expensive and, thus, compromises must be made. It is our argument, however, that unless an experience is offered to economics majors of the type described above, the minimum mastery level of understanding how to "think like an economist" is sacrificed. Compromises that significantly reduce this goal invariably result in majors simply being exposed to economics in varying degrees, and as a result the lasting effects of the experience are diminished, if not foregone.

How is it possible to make such a major work? The answer, it seems to us, is painfully simple: ration access to the major to fit the resources available while maintaining quality standards and fulfilling the responsibilities of each college or university. Placing a limit on the number of economics majors will conflict with the philosophy of many institutions. But unconstrained access to a major without concomitant resources, resulting in sufficiently diminished standards so as to compromise the intellectual integrity of the enterprise, is also at variance with prevailing educational philosophy. Responsible educational planning requires living within one's budget of instructional resources, and the issue of how to ration access to the major then becomes paramount.

The method of rationing may vary from school to school, depending on the institution's policies and procedures. Whatever method is used, however, rationing should be educationally sound with respect to the goals of the major. Our own preference is to offer intellectually challenging intermediate macro and micro and quantitative methods courses whose reputation insures that the number of students intending to major does not exceed capacity.

What does and does not constitute "intellectual challenge" in such

REPORTS
FROM THE
FIELDS

courses must be spelled out. It does not require the use of formal (and seemingly difficult or sophisticated) tools (mainly mathematics) that can constitute a barrier to learning; and it does not involve the use of unfair or tough grading standards, unreasonable assignments, or scare tactics as techniques to discourage enrollments. It does involve holding students to the standard of properly applying reasonably sophisticated economic ideas to a variety of unfamiliar problems. This standard is intellectually more demanding than facility with formal tools *per se*, and it is, in fact, the best early indicator as to whether a student has the ability to come to grips with the major—to "think like an economist."[21]

The undergraduate economics major has slipped in quality over the past two decades as large enrollments undermined standards. We see no reason, however, why large enrollments in economics courses need pose a problem. Indeed, offering high-quality introductory economics courses (even if taught in large classes) should be a primary objective of an economics department within a liberal arts college. A related goal is to ensure that economics is one of the most exciting and intellectually challenging majors. Having said all this, we believe the real challenge is to make certain that economics majors understand how

to "think like an economist"—surely a demanding but attainable goal. To accomplish this, tough choices—the hallmark of economics—must be made.

1. The authors of this report are John J. Siegfried, Vanderbilt University; Robin L. Bartlett, Denison University; W. Lee Hansen, University of Wisconsin; Allen C. Kelley, Duke University; Donald N. McCloskey, University of Iowa; and Thomas H. Tietenberg, Colby College. This essay is a condensed version of a report on the economics major to be published in the *Journal of Economic Education* in summer 1991. This report does not necessarily represent the views of the American Economics Association or any of its officers. We thank William Becker, William Damon, Rendigs Fels, T. Aldrich Finegan, Thomas Jeavons, Paul King, Richard Lucier, Keith Lumsden, Robert Margo, Hans Palmer, Michael Salemi, Carol Schneider, William Walstad, and seminar participants at Grinnell College, St. Olaf College, Carleton College, and Wake Forest University for comments on a draft of the report.
2. John J. Siegfried and Jennie E. Raymond, "A Profile of Senior Economics Majors in the United States," *American Economic Review* 74 (May 1984): 19-25.
3. Requirements for the economics major at 546 American colleges and universities in 1980 are reported in John J. Siegfried and James T. Wilkinson, "The Economics Curriculum in the United States," *American Economic Review* 72 (May 1982): 125-42. The typical economics student is described in Siegfried and Raymond, "Senior Economics Majors." Facts relating to the economics major are taken mainly from these sources. Three-quarters of introductory economics students in the U.S. take a two-semester sequence; one-quarter take a one-semester course. See M. Jane Barr Sweeney et al., "The Structure of the Introductory Economics Course in the United States," *Journal of Economic Education* 14 (Fall 1983): 68-75.

4. John J. Siegfried and Rendigs Fels, "Research on Teaching College Economics: A Survey," *Journal of Economic Literature* 17 (September 1979): 923-69; John J. Siegfried and William B. Walstad, "Research on Teaching College Economics," in *The Principles of Economics Course: A Handbook for Instructors*, ed. Phillip Saunders and William Walstad (New York: McGraw-Hill, 1989): 270-86.

5. Phillip Saunders, "The Lasting Effects of Introductory Economics Courses," *Journal of Economic Education* 12 (Winter 1980): 1-14.

6. See, for example, David G. Hartman, "What do Economics Majors Learn?" *American Economic Review* 68 (May 1978): 17-22.

7. In 1980 the typical senior economics major wrote 4.5 term papers of five or more pages in economics courses. The standard deviation of 3.5, however, suggests that almost 20 percent wrote no more than a single term paper in all of their economics courses combined (Siegfried and Raymond, "Senior Economics Majors," 22). In a 1990 survey we conducted in conjunction with this essay, only nineteen of the eighty responding colleges and universities reported that their graduating economics majors usually write more than two major papers. Another nineteen, mostly large universities, reported that the typical economics major did not write a single major economics paper.

8. In 1980 the national average introductory economics class size was 58, with a standard deviation of almost 50. Advanced courses are usually smaller. Average class sizes for intermediate microeconomics, intermediate macroeconomics, and quantitative methods were 34, 38, and 37 respectively, while the size of all other economics courses averaged 29 (Siegfried and Wilkinson, "The Economics Curriculum," 128, 133).

9. Robin L. Bartlett and Paul G. King, "Teaching Economics as a Laboratory Science," *Journal of Economic Education*, 21 (Spring 1990): 181-93.

10. W. Lee Hansen, " 'Real' Books and Textbooks," *Journal of Economic Education* 19 (Summer 1988): 271-74.

11. There is some evidence that training economics teaching assistants enhances their students' learning (Darrell R. Lewis and Charles C. Orvis, "A Training System for Graduate Student Instructors of Introductory Economics at the University of Minnesota," *Journal of Economic Education* 5 (Fall 1973): 38-46; Michael Watts and Gerald J. Lynch, "The Principles Course Revisited," *American Economic Review* 79 (May 1989): 236-41.

12. Allen C. Kelley, "An Experiment with TIPS: A Computer-Aided Instructional System for Undergraduate Education," *American Economic Review* 58 (May 1968): 446-57; Siegfried and Fels, "Research on Teaching College Economics," 942-43.

13. Karl E. Case and Ray C. Fair, "Macro Simulations for PCs in the Classroom," *American Economic Review* 75 (May 1985): 85-90.

14. Edmund Burke, *Reflections on the Revolution in France* (London: Dent, 1955), 73.

15. Joan Robinson, *Marx, Marshall and Keynes* (New Delhi: Delhi School of Economics, 1955), 30.

16. Almost 51 percent of the 1985-86 bachelors degrees conferred in the U.S. were earned by women. Economics has relatively few female undergraduate majors (34.4 percent) in contrast to psychology (69.0 percent), sociology (68.9 percent), biology (48.8 percent), and mathematics (46.5 percent). Among the few disciplines with even fewer female students than economics are philosophy (32.8 percent) and physics (14.6 percent). On the other hand, the proportion of undergraduate economics majors who are women has grown rapidly since 1977-78, when it was but 24.9 percent. National Center for Education Statistics, *Digest of Education Statistics 1988* (Washington, D.C.: U.S. Department of Education, Office of Educational Research and Improvement, 1988).

17. Jean Owens Schaefer, "Teaching Women," *Journal of NAWDAC* 48 (Summer 1985): 11-22.

18. Susan F. Feiner and Barbara A. Morgan, "Women and Minorities in Introductory Economics Textbooks: 1974 to 1984," *Journal of Economic Education* 18 (Fall 1987): 376-92.

19. Julie Kuhn Ehrhart and Bernice Sandler, *Looking for More Than a Few Good Women in*

REPORTS
FROM THE
FIELDS

Traditionally Male Fields (Washington, D.C.: Association of American Colleges, 1987), 7.

20. Keith G. Lumsden and Alex Scott, "The Economics Student Reexamined: Male-Female Differences in Comprehension," *Journal of Economic Education* 18 (Fall 1987): 365–75.

21. Introductory courses should not be used to ration access to the major since such courses should be widely accessible to non-majors and students of diverse backgrounds and goals.

HISTORY*

Historians of the 1990s will carry the past into the twenty-first century. Now is the time for us to rethink our purposes and practices, to seek and accept new commitments, to give the past a vigorous future.

We face a formidable challenge, for contemporary society—with its emphasis on new products and new fashions—ignores the past or reduces it to banalities for popular consumption or political manipulation. The mass media portrays disconnected historical figures and disjointed events, providing few opportunities for explication and analysis.

Schools, colleges, and universities, too, have devalued the past by compromising the place of history in their curricula. Moreover, the history taught in classrooms and presented in books and articles too often lacks energy and imagination. As a consequence, many students not only fail to gain a sense of history, they come to dislike it.

As educational institutions share responsibility for devaluing the past, so also do they have it in their power to restore its value by educating those in their charge to think historically and to use knowledge and understanding of the past to challenge the present and the future. This report is a call to action.

History's essence is in the connectedness of historical events and human experiences. By examining the causes, contexts, and chronologies of events, one gains an understanding of the nature of continuity and change in human experiences. History therefore plays an integrative role in the quest for liberal learning and, accordingly, in a college's offerings. While acknowledging that our discipline does not have all the answers and that vigorous and longstanding disagreements exist among us, we nonetheless share the conviction that knowledge, abilities, and perspectives gained through the study of history are applicable also in other disciplines. We are compelled, therefore, to claim a central place for the study of history in our institutions' programs.

The time is right for us to make

such a claim. Many in the general public can be counted upon to support it, for they appreciate the importance of historical knowledge and display considerable interest in the past. They read books on historical topics and figures, visit historical museums, watch documentary films, and are active in local historical societies and projects. Many of them observe the status of history in schools and colleges and wonder why it does not enjoy more respect. They care about the place of history in the curricula of schools and colleges, and they want to see it strengthened and its influence enlarged.

This report presents recommendations reflecting ideals essential to the study of history. Its purpose is to assist college and university history faculties in their efforts to offer students a coherent curriculum and to strengthen their claims for a central place for history in their institutions' programs. A brief summary of existing conditions and practices sets the context for the recommendations, and the recommendations, in turn, prompt strategic questions for history faculties to address in laying plans for the future.

While focusing on the history major, the report also considers the larger role that history plays in college curricula and in the lives of those pursuing studies in other fields, suggesting ways to enhance

the contribution of history to the education of all students. Because the fate of history in colleges and universities is inseparable from its well-being in elementary and secondary schools, the report proposes measures to be taken in common with those who teach history there.

HISTORY AND LIBERAL LEARNING

The study of history incorporates the essential elements of liberal learning, namely, acquisition of knowledge and understanding, cultivation of perspective, and development of communication and critical-thinking skills; it reflects concern for human values and appreciation of contexts and traditions.

Establishing historical memory requires reconstructing human actions and events, ordered chronologically or topically. This reconstruction depends upon the acquisition of knowledge, incorporating facts, principles, theories, ideas, practices, and methods. Students of history analyze written, oral, visual, and material evidence. Their analyses yield generalizations, interpretations, and understandings, properly qualified and placed in contexts that reveal the process of change over time. Historical understanding is enhanced through connection with studies in other liberal disciplines.

An essential ingredient in knowledge and understanding is perspective cultivated through sensitivity to cultural and geographical differences and awareness of conflicting interpretations of the same occurrences. Perspective, in turn, must be accompanied by a sense of the chronological ordering of events and of simultaneity—of understanding relationships of diverse events at a given moment.

Studying history as a discipline requires one to engage one's mind with the facts, ideas, and interpretations conveyed or suggested by historical evidence; to give contexts to discrete pieces of evidence; and to devise plausible explanations and judgments based on the evidence. The discipline of history equips one to extend facts, ideas, and interpretations into new realms by weighing the validity of arguments, assessing the soundness of historical judgments, and otherwise practicing the art of critical thinking characteristic of discerning minds. Because those who examine evidence typically do not know what they think about it until they see what it leads them to say, written and oral discourse is essential for them to gain historical insights and form interpretations and conclusions.

In coming to know the past, one becomes aware of contrasts between peoples of different times and places and within one's own time and place. These contrasts reflect differing value systems translated into action. Similarly, one becomes sensitive to the artistic interests and expressions of various peoples, demonstrated through their efforts to create and cultivate beauty in forms that help to define them as a people, and to the part science and technology have played in the story of humankind.

Through engagement with the past, students come to recognize the continuing need to rethink the past, reinterpreting it in the light of new evidence and new concerns and using new tools of analysis. If rethinking history is a continuing theme in undergraduate studies, as it should be, students will carry their abilities to inquire, analyze, and interpret into their studies in other fields and into all aspects of their lives and work. They will be equipped to approach knowledgeably, sensitively, and critically whatever careers they choose.

In sum, history is at the heart of liberal learning because it equips students to:

☐ participate knowledgeably in the affairs of the world around them, drawing upon understandings shaped through reading, writing, discussions, and lectures concerning the past

☐ see themselves and their society

from different times and places, displaying a sense of informed perspective and a mature view of human nature

☐ read and think critically, write and speak clearly and persuasively, and conduct research effectively

☐ exhibit sensitivities to human values in their own and other cultural traditions and, in turn, establish values of their own

☐ appreciate their natural and cultural environments

☐ respect scientific and technological developments and recognize their impact on humankind

☐ understand the connections between history and life.

History faculties strengthen course offerings and majors by engaging their students in discussions concerning these purposes and leading them to understand how the content and structure of the courses and majors they pursue relate to these purposes.

EXISTING CONDITIONS AND PRACTICES

A sampling of the policies and practices of history faculties has led the task force to conclude that the design and requirements of history majors in colleges and universities differ on many points. The most notable points of difference include: the purposes of the major, the number of hours or courses required for a degree, specific courses required and the sequence (if any) in which they are to be taken, the balance of lower- and upper-division courses, the fields included, and the concern, or lack of it, for historical method and historiography.

The programs the task force examined reflect the variety of institutions in which they are offered. Even among institutions of a given type— liberal arts colleges, for example, or major research universities—policies and practices vary widely. Programs in history generally seem to be determined by the mission and traditions of each institution; the size, special interests, and competencies of the faculties offering them; the demands of students; the convictions, whims, and prejudices of those who establish and maintain them; and, in many instances, retrenchments or reductions in resources beyond the faculty's control.

We recognize that the history majors in some institutions are very good, but we also believe that in many they are not as sound as they must be if they are to meet the challenges facing the faculties that offer them. The recommendations that follow reflect our judgment that most history programs would benefit from a thorough review of requirements, offerings, and practices. Each recommendation addresses specific aspects of the major that the task force believes should be the subject of concern in history faculties.

RECOMMENDATIONS

1. *The content of the history major should be consistent with the purposes of studying history, and it should include these specific components:*
☐ *a strong foundation course (which may be waived for those with extraordinarily strong backgrounds in history)*
☐ *a course expressly designed to acquaint students with the diversity of the global setting in which they live*
☐ *a course in historical methods*
☐ *a research seminar with a writing requirement*
☐ *an integrating or synthesizing course.*

History is a discipline in which there is no standard content, no prescribed sequence of courses. The coherence of a history major depends upon the success that students and teachers, working together, achieve in developing clear organizing principles for their work. Each recommended component of the major contributes to the development of such principles.

A history major should include a well-designed foundation course, ideally taught in small classes with diverse methods, to establish the bases for helping students understand the historian's approach to the past. This course—whether in American history, world history, or Western civilization—should use a syllabus with principles and practices agreed upon by all who teach it and, if possible, by the entire department. Building on the precollegiate experiences of the entering college students, the foundation course should eschew the "one-damn-fact-after-another" approach to history, centering rather on historiographical or thematic topics. The problems pursued should be amenable to essay-writing requirements. Essay exams, rather than multiple-choice questions, should be required in these courses throughout the term.

The diversity of American society and rapidly evolving global interdependence compel history faculties to move their students beyond the history of the United States and Western civilization and engage them in the study of other cultures. As a matter of highest priority, the course offerings in every field must address this diversity, giving open and honest attention to questions of race, gender, class, ethnicity, and worldwide interdependence.

It is not enough simply to establish separate courses to achieve diversity or topical completeness in the major. Subjects that merit treatment in separate, specialized courses should be integrated into more comprehensive courses as well. Similarly, if a particular approach to history is warranted in a separate course, that approach also should be incorporated into the more general courses.

Instruction in historical methods and historiography is at the heart of efforts to develop organizing principles for a major. As the past grows larger and more formidable, more and more of its content lies beyond the reach of even the most dedicated and competent historians. History faculties therefore are obliged to equip their students to go beyond the content treated in their courses by introducing them to historical methods and historiography, enabling them to understand the value and limitations of various kinds of historical writing.

Consideration of conflicting historical interpretations provides a natural starting point for studying historians' methods. It also may be useful to explore with students the evolution of history as an academic discipline by tracing it from the days, more than a century ago, when it was introduced in colleges and universities as a "scientific" field of study or by examining an idea that has been at the center of many debates over the nature and purpose of studying history, such as historicism.

While offering specific courses devoted exclusively to the study of historical method, history faculties should insist that all courses include instruction in historical method and give attention to historiographical questions. Developing the habit of an inquiring mind requires the habit of maintaining an open mind and, legitimately, of accepting the tentativeness of historical explanations and the necessity for ongoing revisions.

The goal of the senior seminar in a history major should be to "turn students loose" on a research project culminating in a senior essay of some distinction. All history majors, not just honors students, should be required to take the senior seminar.

The other required senior course— a synthesizing, or integrating, or reflective, or capstone course—has a contrasting purpose: to give students the opportunity to seek new insights by drawing together what they have learned in earlier experiences. In such a course, typically built around a broad theme, students are challenged to relate what they have learned in history to their studies in other fields.

A history major, then, is more than a string of courses covering specified time periods, geographic areas, or topical fields and designed simply to transmit knowledge. A sound major is built on the commitment of faculty members to helping students understand more fully the purposes, principles, and methodologies involved in the study of history and grasp essential particulars and universals of societies past and present. By actively engaging students with the content of their courses and with each other, it also explores questions of judgment and interpretation, of good and bad, of right and wrong, leading to a mature view of humankind.

The size and areas of competence of the faculty members offering courses in the major obviously affect the major's content. Small institutions, with history faculties of fewer than seven or eight, probably find it impossible to "cover" all of the standard fields in which their larger counterparts offer specializations. Such faculties have several options. One is to capitalize on their strengths by concentrating their offerings in their fields of competence and stressing the development of research and writing skills that enable students to move knowledgeably by independent study into the fields that are necessarily left uncovered by the faculty.

Another option is to devote resources to the continual retraining of the faculty, enabling them through released time and support for advanced study to move beyond the fields in which they have concentrated their studies into new ones that serve local needs. While this option risks extending faculty members too far, leading to superficial treat-

ment of fields in which they lack expertise, it enables the faculty to offer more comprehensive programs.

Regardless of the size of the faculty, every care should be taken to ensure that the student-faculty "fit" is productive. A small department risks the danger of creating too close a discipleship, and departments of all sizes face the possibility of encouraging anonymity and overspecialized work.

2. *The structure and requirements of the history major should reflect the faculty's understanding of the purposes of studying history.*

The structure and requirements of the major should make the most of the faculty's strengths. Although of necessity it may neglect certain areas, the faculty can assist students in developing skills they need for independent study in these areas. If a history faculty cannot influence its college to incorporate into its general education or distribution requirements those elements the faculty regards as essential to a liberal education—or to a professional education, for that matter—that faculty can build these requirements into its own major and its offerings for the nonmajor.

In designing a comprehensive and well-balanced major, in addition to considering questions that local circumstances prompt, a history faculty should address the following ques-

tions to which we suggest answers:
☐ What are the purposes of the history major?

The general purposes are stated implicitly above in "History and Liberal Learning." In more specific terms, the major prepares students for graduate work in history; for studies in law, business, medicine, and other professions; and for careers demanding the knowledge, understanding, perspective, skills, and sensitivities one gains through studying history.
☐ How many hours should be required?

The major should require about one-fourth of the total hours needed to complete a four-year degree, probably not including six hours in foundation surveys. In addition, to acquaint students with other forms of inquiry, the major should require another six to twelve carefully selected hours in related humanities or social sciences fields. Indeed, the undergraduate major is strengthened and enriched through a coherent interdisciplinary approach.
☐ What should be the relationships and balance between lower- and upper-division courses?

Because learning in history is not necessarily cumulative and does not need to be chronological, the content of lower- and upper-division courses cannot be prescribed. Nor are there approaches that are appropriate at one level and inappropriate at another. The principal distinction between courses at the various levels of study lies in the sophistication of the knowledge and understanding they reflect and the abilities they require of students enrolled in them.

More than half of the credits toward a history major should be earned in upper-division courses. Typically, the foundation courses, carrying the lowest numbers, are followed by those with greater depth and then by the senior-level seminars and colloquia that provide opportunities for students to explore specific topics in depth. While a history major rarely requires all students to take specific courses in sequence, the major can convey a sense of coherence, and implicitly of sequence, by ensuring that courses at each level make increasingly more rigorous demands.
☐ Should there be concentrations within the history major?

Fostering students' depth of knowledge and understanding in one area within the major is desirable. A concentration aimed at developing such depth typically requires at least four courses. Ideally, courses taken in other disciplines also should relate to the concentration. At the same time, to foster students' breadth of knowledge and understanding there should be limits to the concentrations, with no more than half of the courses credited toward the major taken in a single field.

Concentrations within history majors may be arranged by theme, period, geographical region, or some combination of these options. Since the concentration is more likely to be designed and understood by students and their advisors than by those teaching the courses in which they enroll, faculty members should seek to discover how their courses relate to each student's particular concentration.

☐ What matters most in the design and offering of a major?

The best-designed history major is of little value if those who teach the courses in it fail to bring the major to life. The major is of even less value if the way the courses are taught reflects the faculty's lack of commitment to excellence in teaching. Striking a new balance between commitments to teaching and the demands of research may be necessary in some institutions. Conversely, students suffer if all of a faculty member's time and energies are devoted to teaching at the expense of scholarly work.

Here are some additional points to be considered: Historians and students of history find meaning in the past through discovering the connectedness of things. The most effective programs are those that equip students to discover connections, thereby both satisfying and stimulating students' curiosity. The courses in the major, while not necessarily taken in sequence, should cultivate in students a sense of historical chronology, perhaps by faculty members' consciously relating each course in the major to others and concentrating on chronology within each course.

Every course should require students to engage in research and writing at a level appropriate to the course's place in the major. Some of the courses in the major should provide special opportunities for oral presentations that go beyond classroom discussion. The requirements of the major must be flexible enough to allow faculties to address specific student interests. This is particularly true as adult students increasingly populate college classrooms. Acknowledging this, however, and recognizing that adult students enrolling in college after years away from classroom experiences may require special assistance in developing study practices, the task force asserts that significant distinctions should not be drawn between the programs of these students and the ones who have traditionally pursued undergraduate studies.

The history major should have coherence, integrity, rigor, focus, and imagination. Coherence is evident in majors that fit together conceptually and practically. A major with integrity is one with principles and practices that cannot be compromised. Testimony to rigor lies in the significance of the demands the major places on those who offer it as well as those who pursue it. A major with a focus is one with a specific, readily defined purpose. Imagination in a major enables it to capture images of the past, make new images of the past, and play with the past as well as work with it.

3. *The pedagogical methods and instructional materials used to accomplish the purposes of the major should be appropriate to those purposes.*

These issues, among others, must be addressed:

☐ Who should teach the foundation courses?

The purposes of foundation courses are to excite as well as to inform, to engage the minds and imagination of those who may be indifferent to history or even antagonistic to it. It takes an excellent teacher to accomplish these purposes. Obviously, then, only the best teachers should teach foundation courses.

☐ How should the organizing principle of a course be conveyed?

Students should be informed at the outset, and as the course progresses, why the period under study was framed as it was, why the theme of a course makes sense, why certain content is included and other not, why the scope of the coverage is as broad or as narrow as it is.

☐ How can classroom time be utilized most effectively?

Lectures may appear to be efficient, but they do not necessarily accomplish what we like to think they do. Indeed, they are efficient only in the sense that they enable a teacher to deal handily with large numbers of students at the same time. Unless there is time for interaction between teacher and student and among students and, particularly in smaller classes, opportunity for conversations that continue beyond the classroom, lectures simply encourage students' passivity and contribute little to their learning. The use of audio and visual materials may serve good purposes, provided these materials are used as genuine instructional tools and not simply as ways of breaking the routine.

If lectures must be used to accommodate larger classes, history faculties must balance them with smaller classes that employ other methods of teaching. These may be seminars and colloquia that give students opportunities for oral presentations and discussions based on their research and writing.

☐ What are some possible learning opportunities beyond the classroom?

Courses in a history major should include substantial writing requirements related to textual analysis. Starting with the foundation course, students should be required to identify a position in a text and deal with it critically, marshalling the evidence found in the text to support conclusions the students present in writing. Traditional library resources and new research technologies provide students with experiences that go far beyond their immediate application in history courses. Research of this nature, along with the requirements of extensive writing, assumes student competence in using computers and word processors.

In addition to coupling library activities with writing assignments, the history program can create opportunities for students to engage in field research, typically as part of guided research projects. Through research in archives and museums and the use of other community resources, students learn that traces of the past are found in a wide variety of forms.

Advising plays an important part in the teaching of history students, not only as advisors guide students through program requirements but also as they answer questions about related matters—for example, the importance of studying foreign languages and statistics and the career possibilities for history students.

☐ What are the principal considerations regarding instructional materials and the major a history faculty offers?

Textbooks are the old standby, of course, and they may well be essential in some courses. Their use should be limited, however, to reinforcing a framework for the course established by the professor; serving as a handy reference for topics dealt with in class; giving a course continuity and sequence that its in- and out-of-class treatment might not provide; and presenting maps, graphs, tables, and pictures.

Other materials, particularly primary documents, play a vital role, as do monographs, journal articles, book reviews, and maps. Oral histories recorded on tape or film or accurately transcribed, along with photographs, slides, motion pictures, artifacts, and audio- and videotapes serve as good sources for analysis.

4. *The place of history in the programs of studies of nonmajors should be clear and pursued appropriately.*
Students not majoring in history, particularly those in such professional fields as business and engineering, may seem to be only tourists in the foreign country called the past. That does not diminish the value of historical study in such students' academic programs, however, for a grasp of history will be of value to them no matter the careers they pursue.

Most of what has been said so far about the study of history for the history major is applicable also to the nonmajor. In addition, imaginative history professors find ways to relate the study of the past to specific interests of nonmajors, enticing these students to see relationships between their narrower outlooks and the broader dimensions of the past. For all students, the history of women's experiences and of ethnic and race relations provide contexts for understanding the changing nature of gender roles and issues of race and ethnicity.

5. *History faculties should know and address important concerns regarding the training and retraining of teachers and the condition of history in the schools.*

Their commitment to history requires college history faculties to:
☐ provide the best possible history courses for prospective teachers
☐ teach the courses in exemplary ways, since teachers tend to teach in the manner of their most influential teachers
☐ attempt to ensure that prospective teachers major in history rather than education
☐ collaborate with the education professors who teach instructional-methods courses.

The following practices all contribute to the general well-being of history as an academic discipline:
☐ forming alliances with the schools to improve history education

☐ determining and publicizing what high school students should learn prior to their enrollment in college
☐ inviting history teachers from the schools to participate in departmental colloquia or seminars—always ensuring that the relationships that develop are collegial rather than patronizing
☐ offering continuing education and in-service opportunities for teachers, enabling the teachers to remain current with new developments in history
☐ serving as guest teachers in the schools upon invitation.

If collaboration is to occur, someone—probably a member of the college or university faculty—must take the initiative, and collaborating institutions must provide incentives for those who participate in the jointly offered activities.

History faculties should participate in writing state curriculum documents for elementary and secondary school social studies curricula. They must be alert to legislative issues relating to the study of history and to policies implemented by state departments of education because curriculum requirements imposed by legislatures may be treated lightly by state officials responsible for enforcing them.

Teacher certification standards are of special concern to history faculties because the long-standing inclination to increase requirements for education courses while minimizing the importance of studies in the teaching field always threatens to populate precollegiate history classrooms with people who are not equipped to teach their young charges. Where trends seem to be in the opposite direction at the moment, history faculties should encourage such trends. They might, for example, support efforts to require that all social studies teachers have a minor in history regardless of their social studies specialties.

Should legislatures, responding to efforts to strengthen the place of history in social studies curricula, mandate new history courses or proficiency exams for students, legislatures should also provide support for educating teachers to teach the courses.

6. *The needs and abilities of students should be taken into account by those designing and offering a history major.*

Most of the needs of students have been addressed in this document. Additionally, though, a history faculty may help its cause by building a sense of community among students majoring in history. A student organization might sponsor activities that bring together students in common endeavors. Along the same lines, special efforts to provide a supportive environment for persons of color and nontraditional students should

be encouraged.

Students also need to understand the value of a history major in choosing careers and professions. History faculties should address this need in advising their students and in their department's publications; they can demonstrate, for example, that undergraduate studies in history lay a solid foundation for careers in business, law, and government. Opportunities for rewarding careers as teachers in elementary and secondary schools are increasing, and students should be encouraged to consider them, too.

Faculties should advise students interested in pursuing advanced studies in history on how to select and gain admission to graduate programs and about career options in college teaching, museums, archives, historical societies, publishing firms, historic preservation organizations, and public service.

Faculties should work closely with the college's career planning center, not only directing students to the center for information and advice but also helping the center establish the contacts that will enable it to have the latest information available. Professional associations in history should be prepared to provide career planning centers with timely information.

Our knowledge is meager concerning the cognitive abilities of college-age students that equip them to learn history. The task force urges that research on this topic be undertaken. The findings would contribute much to the rethinking of the history major and the manner in which history courses are taught.

7. *The purpose, structure, and content of the history major should be reviewed regularly, along with the effectiveness of those who teach it and the achievements of students pursuing it.*

The majors offered by history faculties in fact are evaluated regularly by both faculty members and the students these majors are designed to serve, but typically these evaluations are informal and off-the-record. Faculty members are not well informed about the students' judgments, and students are in the dark as to what faculty members are thinking. Formal evaluations addressing mutual concerns of students and faculty ideally should occur regularly and for the record.

Evaluation of programs in colleges and universities, often called program review, usually focuses on the purposes, structure, quality, and place of the programs under review; it also considers the resources programs require, the demand for them, and their cost. Evaluation seeks to assess the performance of both teachers and students—the quality of the teaching and the nature and extent of the learning that occurs in

college classrooms and beyond. Such evaluation compels history faculties to identify their criteria for good teaching, to address in specific terms their plans for evaluating the effectiveness of the teaching in their departments, and to measure their students' learning.

Excellent teaching requires, first of all, expertise in the discipline. Beyond this, it requires abilities to define instructional objectives, organize materials and activities for accomplishing these objectives, present materials clearly, and conduct classroom activities purposefully. It also engages students' minds, develops their skills consistent with course objectives, motivates them to perform to the best of their abilities, and evaluates their achievements.

Faculties that take seriously these requirements of good teaching seriously are obliged to establish criteria for measuring the extent to which each of them is satisfied. They must ask, for example, how their abilities to define objectives and organize materials are measured. By review of course syllabi? If so, what criteria are applied in reviewing them? Are reviewers from other institutions invited to participate in the assessment of syllabi, reflecting the practice of reviewing scholarly work?

What do faculties expect of classroom activities? How do they assess presentation of instructional materials? Do they exchange classroom visits? If so, by what criteria do they evaluate what they observe? How is information gathered from students concerning the presentation of materials? Does the faculty use a standard instrument for student evaluation of teaching or are multiple instruments used? Who designs them? How has the validity of the instruments been established? If graduate students teach, are they adequately trained and supervised?

Concerning practices for measuring student achievement—reflecting engagement of minds, development of skills, and motivation—does the faculty review course examinations for clarity, purpose, and effectiveness? If so, before they are administered or after they are graded? Who does the reviewing, and against what criteria?

Beyond periodic and final exams—oral and written—does the faculty administer comprehensive essay examinations to seniors, testing their knowledge of history and their organizational, analytical, and writing abilities as well as their insights and perspectives? Does the faculty require senior research papers in which students are expected to demonstrate these abilities? Does it conduct oral interviews with the same objectives in mind? Does it use portfolios for reviewing seniors' work during the course of their studies?

How does the faculty keep track of graduates and their success in graduate schools and careers?

8. *History faculties should promote the history major effectively within the institution and beyond it.*

History is an attractive discipline that needs better descriptions of its character and purposes for prospective students. History majors typically are described blandly in college catalogues, conveying little of the excitement that the study of history holds. Accordingly, rewriting the catalogues often is a first step in improving the presentation of the major. Publishing brochures that describe the purposes, content, structure, requirements, methodology, and pedagogy of the major also is desirable. So too is the publication of clear statements regarding career and professional options open to individuals with degrees in history. Professional associations in history should be prepared to provide assistance to institutions as they seek to improve their publications.

9. *To improve and advance their offerings and the place they claim in their institutions, history faculties should identify and address questions of strategy.*

The task force suggests that history faculties consider the following strategic questions, among others, as they rethink and redesign their majors and courses in their institutions:

□ How can a faculty foster commitments to excellence in teaching when scholarly research necessarily is a high priority? How can it help its members establish connections between their research and their work in the classroom?

□ What changes in the reward structure are needed to encourage more attention to improving teaching?

□ How can the history major be made to reflect most clearly the purposes of the field and the commitments of the faculty?

□ How can larger departments best address the problems associated with the major?

□ How can history faculties foster interdisciplinary experiences, creating productive ties with other humanities and social sciences disciplines?

□ How can history faculties gain allies outside the classroom to support requirements such as writing in all courses and using writing assignments more effectively?

□ What role should historians play in reshaping an institution's general-education requirements?

□ How do historians deal with questions of citizenship—their own and their students'—in the courses they teach?

CONCLUSION

As noted at the beginning of this report, the historians of the 1990s will carry the past into the twenty-first century. This report provides a rationale, encouragement, and recommendations for carrying it well—that is to say, for looking closely at the condition of history in college and university programs and working swiftly toward improving it. The report, then, is but the first step in what the members of the task force hope will be a vigorous and imaginative nationwide effort by history faculties to rethink, redefine, and redesign the history major and the courses we offer to our students.

*This report represents the judgments and recommendations of the Task Force on the History Major in AAC's Project on Liberal Learning, Study-in-depth, and the Arts and Sciences Major. It is not an official statement of the American Historical Association.

The authors of this report are Edward A. Gosselin, California State University-Long Beach; Myron Marty, Drake University; Colin A. Palmer, University of North Carolina; Lynda N. Shaffer, Tufts University; and Joanna Zangrando, Skidmore College. James Gardner, deputy executive director of the American Historical Association served as liaison with the AHA. Carol Schneider, executive vice president of the Association of American Colleges, provided many helpful suggestions.

The task force sought comments from a variety of individuals. Concerned about issues of diversity, the task force specifically sought the advice of three minority scholars: Albert Camarillo, a Latino scholar from

Stanford University; Nadine I. Hata, an Asian-American scholar, administrator, and two-year college professor at El Camino Community College; and Clara Sue Kidwell, a native-American specialist at the University of California–Berkeley and former dean in residence of the Council of Graduate Schools. Others who commented on various drafts included: J. Sherman Barker, Hotchkiss School; Peter Filene, University of North Carolina–Chapel Hill; Miles Fletcher, University of North Carolina; Lloyd Kramer, University of North Carolina; Don Reid, University of North Carolina; David Kyvig, University of Akron; Marilyn Rubchak, Valparaiso University; James J. Ward, Cedar Crest College. The task force also solicited input through sessions at 1989 annual meetings of the Organization of American Historians, the Community College Humanities Association, and the American Historical Association. Copies also were circulated to Louis R. Harlan, president of the AHA and OAH, University of Maryland–College Park; Mary K. Bonsteel Tachau, AHA Vice President for Teaching, University of Louisville; and members of AHA's Teaching Division.

INTERDISCIPLINARY STUDIES[1]

The charge of AAC's national study challenged the twelve task forces to look at the intellectual rationale, organizing principles, and cognitive practices of particular fields of study. Our report addresses these issues; in addition, it makes observations and recommendations that concern not only the shaping of an undergraduate major but an entire campus whose intellectual life interdisciplinary studies (IDS) programs can stimulate. Our report focuses not on a particular discipline, profession, or subject matter but on the growing and multifaceted phenomenon of IDS majors and minors and courses now offered in almost every postsecondary setting.

The strength of any IDS program is primarily influenced by its institutional setting and support, including support for faculty commitment. Our report, therefore, addresses institutional issues extensively. Furthermore, we found that IDS programs

usually have a service function to the entire campus that extends well beyond providing an academic concentration, and we have sought to address this larger campuswide service as well. Part of such service is challenging the values and practices of existing curricular structures and faculty research patterns driven by the strict disciplinary defines of the professions; for that reason also we have addressed the entire academy rather than restricting ourselves to the IDS major.

THE URGENCY AND DIVERSITY OF INTERDISCIPLINARY PERSPECTIVES

Although educational institutions only devised academic disciplines and professional specializations early in this century, a sense of urgency about the need for interdisciplinary perspectives has developed during the past few decades. There are many reasons, with the most global embodied in various forms of the observation that "Real life, we need to remember, is interdisciplinary."[2] Of course, "real life" always has been interdisciplinary. In the late nineteenth and early twentieth centuries, however, scholars were persuaded that the development of deliberately self-restrictive disciplinary methods and subject matter offered a powerful mode of analysis that would yield not only new insights but a scientific understanding of nature, society, and even culture. College majors in the arts and sciences emerged from this era of disciplinary commitment and expectant scientific optimism.

Now, about a century later, many scholars question this earlier view of the power and reach of disciplinary inquiry. They observe that too often monodisciplinary approaches have produced masses of data that are not useful in the absence of interpretative, interdisciplinary integration. Substantive analysis and problem solving increasingly require collaborative teamwork that brings together several perspectives, disciplines, and specializations and seeks to synthesize them.

This new practical and intellectual ethos has led, in turn, to a striking growth of interdisciplinarity. Many structures within the academy, and a large proportion of research at the frontiers of the modern disciplines,

now are fully and inescapably interdisciplinary. Examples include subjects such as biochemistry, molecular biology, and plate tectonics, as well as the social, linguistic, rhetorical, and textual "turns" that are transforming relations among anthropology and literary theory, history and sociology. Interdisciplinary contributions to the traditional academic departments/disciplines have led several national professional societies to sponsor interdisciplinary subunits and programs expressly designed to advance integration and synthesis among several professional specialties.

These revised conceptions of scholarship and research and the accompanying new pedagogies and epistemologies have contributed to the remarkable growth of academic IDS programs in colleges and universities across the nation. IDS majors, minors, programs, concentrations, and even single IDS courses offer a form of learning that is increasingly sought after and valued. Faculty members, students, and academic administrators perceive IDS as an important resource for overcoming the intellectual constraints imposed by traditional discipline-bound divisions and for integrating knowledge derived from disparate contexts and sources.

The development of vigorous IDS programs provides a campuswide climate of shared discourse and intellectual interaction in which faculty members have the opportunity to expand and extend their own training and research applications. In turn, students become involved in instructional contexts and collaborations that prepare them to graduate into our increasingly diverse and culturally complex world—a world in which political polarizations are becoming more rather than less extreme and in which the ability to analyze and evaluate competing opinions sensitively and fairly is increasingly important.

Not surprisingly, then, IDS enrollments have increased exponentially within the last decade, and IDS assumes many forms reflecting the variety of institutional shapes of American college and university campuses. On many campuses, interdisciplinary education provides a framework for a general education or core curriculum, but its forms across these institutions actually are quite manifold. The major forms include:
☐ interdisciplinary colleges and universities
☐ interdisciplinary training and continuing education in research centers and institutes
☐ undergraduate major and minor programs of study in the liberal arts tradition, more specialized areas, and regional studies
☐ graduate programs in a variety of fields
☐ cluster courses of a multi- or interdisciplinary nature
☐ general education or "core" curricula and honors programs
☐ academic opportunities for independent study and adult degree programs
☐ single courses within disciplinary and professional contexts
☐ courses and programs centered on praxis, such as internships and fieldwork, travel- and work-study, and problem-oriented research teams.

Within such a broad range of programs there is no one "typical" interdisciplinary student. In a growing number of U.S. universities and colleges, students choose interdisciplinary options for satisfying general-education requirements, although undergraduate interdisciplinary majors also may pursue more specialized programs, including:
☐ cybernetic systems
☐ urban studies
☐ human services
☐ multicultural education
☐ regional and ethnic studies
☐ border studies
☐ environmental studies
☐ human ecology
☐ human development
☐ materials science
☐ American studies
☐ women's studies
☐ cultural studies
☐ cognition

☐ science, technology, and society.

IDS reflects an enormous variety of local administrative, pedagogical, social, and cognitive differences, but there are some common structural elements and patterns. William Mayville identifies three significant program models: revolutionary models designed to dispense with the traditional disciplinary apparatus, professional models designed to train specialists by using an interdisciplinary format that acquaints them with the broader and often ethical or social consequences of their chosen profession, and programmatic models designed to broaden the cultural and intellectual frameworks of students.[3] One or another of these models may be predominant in any given situation, and we have not argued here that one of the three is better than another. They are helpful models for understanding why there is such a range of types of IDS programs and majors.

We highlight three basic organizational structures in which the IDS major is likely to be situated.
☐ Established programs with permanent staffs and program budgets. They often act like other campus departments, have a capstone course, or even an established sequence of courses, and function across a large part of the university (for example, the Eugene Lang College at the New School for Social Research and the State University of New York–College at Old Westbury).
☐ Interdepartmental committees, programs, or colleges with independently defined curricula or degree requirements but no faculty members appointed solely by the unit. Such a unit sometimes is called a "cluster program"; it depends upon other institutional units for its existence, although it may have considerable administrative autonomy.
☐ Individually designed majors or other programs and administrative arrangements wherein students or faculty design degree programs on a year-to-year or ad hoc basis. Many campuses provide this option for a small number of student-designed minors or majors at the undergraduate and graduate levels.

Structures may be differentiated further in terms of their individual institutional contexts, which range from large public institutions in which research expectations determine standards of promotion and tenure to small liberal arts schools where teaching is more prominent in the reward system and where a distinct interdisciplinary milieu prevails across the campus.

CRITICAL INTELLIGENCE, SYNTHESIS, AND DEPTH

Whether or not they are structured into major/minor requirements, a series of IDS courses represents superior preparation for contributions to society by liberally educated college graduates. Task force members heard repeatedly of the need for employee flexibility to retrain for new and unanticipated applications of knowledge and synthesizing skills, and we were struck by the fact that in well-designed IDS programs students do indeed learn how to integrate creatively a wide range of information. Certainly the link between IDS and liberal learning is apparent in the disciplined interconnection of intellectual coherence and skills acquisition that marks critical intelligence, creativity, and synthesis.

The metaphor of "depth" as a widely used goal for study in the traditional majors implies the deepening of knowledge along a vertical axis and presumes that interdisciplinarity lies along the horizontal axis of "breadth." The depth versus breadth dichotomy, however, fails to acknowledge the essential third step of synthesis. In IDS, as in an increasing number of traditional majors, the call for "depth" cannot mean merely coverage of one or more disciplines or the mastery of a canon of facts and data.

We prefer to argue that the ideal IDS graduate will demonstrate intellectual facility having depth, breadth, and synthesis. By depth we mean students must have the necessary technical information about and the methodologies necessary for analysis of a given problem. Students should know how to master the complexities involved in obtaining germane research findings and be aware of the methodologies of the disciplinary contexts in which such information is generated. By breadth we mean students should be exposed to a wide knowledge base and trained to organize information in order to make generalizations from particular cases. By synthesis we mean students should be able to apply integrative skills in order to differentiate and compare different disciplinary perspectives, to clarify how those perspectives relate to the core problem or question, and to devise a resolution based upon the holistic interaction of the various factors and forces involved.

Such skills are fundamental to any IDS major or course, the academic integrity of which depends upon clearly defined intellectual abilities and integrative skills. Critical intelligence depends upon utilizing competencies that are typical of IDS approaches:

☐ analyzing and defining problems
☐ generalizing from particular cases and awareness of generic patterns
☐ seeing similarities and differences in situations constructively discerned
☐ responding flexibly to new ideas and situations

□ making sense of ambiguity and contradiction and appreciating that they may not always be reducible
□ developing a critical perspective by taking several sides into consideration before arriving at a rigorously reasoned synthesis.

Acquisition of these integrative competencies will ensure that IDS graduates are able to deal in an informed fashion with ambiguity and paradox, creatively outline possible alternative solutions and options while making comparisons with ethical awareness and sensitivity, and arrive at a carefully reasoned synthesis.

Unfortunately, faculty members teaching many existing "interdisciplinary" courses have not developed clearly defined interdisciplinary core skills and have paid inadequate attention to the integrative process. Too often, IDS programs are merely additive multidisciplinary collections of different perspectives. Interdisciplinary synthesis is achieved not by arraying disparate subjects sequentially before students but by their engaging in strenuous methodological and conceptual work. Therefore, faculty members responsible for IDS must pay attention to curricular design and actual teaching praxis by considering the following questions:
□ How does the major, program, or course bring the techniques and perspectives of several disciplines to bear upon a problem or question? Is

the problem or question carefully defined?
□ Are students helped to understand self-consciously how the various elements in integrative synthesis are obtained and how they interrelate?
□ How and when does a comparative analysis of pertinent disciplinary methods and tools take place? Are there occasions for indicating to students where various types of information can be obtained, including on-line data banks?
□ Are the goals of both specific intellectual and disciplinary depth and broad interdisciplinary synthesis explicitly defined and pursued?[4]
□ Has the faculty considered the danger that fully integrative synthesis may be hindered by the lack of a particular disciplinary contribution that should be added to the IDS program's offerings?

STRUCTURE AND SEQUENCE

Local resources and design lead to a wide range of IDS majors, as we have noted. The content and structure, and to a large extent the actual sequencing, of majors depend upon the size of the IDS program as well as the focus of the major in fields such as women's studies, environmental or urban studies, cybernetic systems, materials science, or Renaissance studies. Individual courses and clusters of courses are integrated most frequently around a theme, topic, or issue; a question or problem; an author, historical period, historical figure, region or nation, or institution; or a particular interdisciplinary field of study or set of integrative methods or concepts.

Since there is such a wide variety of program structure, we cannot stipulate a normative IDS program curriculum or sequence of courses but only can describe here some of the variety. Most interdisciplinary majors rely upon a two-part sequence consisting of lower-level study of the humanities, social sciences, and science and technology—usually conceived as an additive experience of gaining breadth—followed by upper-level capstone work, usually an integrative seminar and/or senior essay or project. Intermediate (junior level) and capstone (junior and senior level) seminars are the most powerful vehicles for increasing critical and methodological sophistication and must be considered a *sine qua non* for an adequate interdisciplinary curriculum.

Such seminars allow students to synthesize the various parts of courses, explore the relationship between various disciplinary perspectives, explore the ethical and praxis-oriented dimensions of disciplinary work, and reflect on how disciplinary relations have changed histori-

cally. At the same time, synthesis can be promoted across the curriculum through good practices we surveyed. Some examples are:

☐ in-depth first-year seminars that provide comprehensive orientation to the nature of interdisciplinary study while probing a single field, issue, problem, or question

☐ advanced seminars that function as integrative capstone courses in which analytical and critical methodologies are refined

☐ courses focused upon second-order reflections on research methods and upon the immediate course work

☐ capstone essays and projects

☐ academic-career portfolios in which students maintain a record of contracts, documented work, and evaluations of their course work, with reflection on interrelationships of the intellectual parts

☐ the use of common living arrangements and shared facilities and equipment

☐ field work, work experience, and travel-study settings

☐ unique courses focused proactively on integrative theories, concepts, and methods

☐ coordinated alignment of parallel disciplinary courses, particularly when accompanied by a formal or informal integrative seminar or discussion group

☐ use of particular integrative strategies, such as systems theory, feminist theory, Marxism, etc.

☐ the clustering of separate disciplinary courses around a common integrative seminar, as at Dominican College in California and in the Federated Learning Communities at State University of New York–Stony Brook.

Sequencing must take carefully into account the increasingly diverse makeup of the student body. No IDS major ought to be regimented in such a manner that a program cannot be adjusted for the specific qualifications, needs, and interests of particular students. Since on a particular campus the IDS curriculum frequently will provide the greatest amount of student freedom to shape a program of studies in a manner that recognizes earlier learning experiences, IDS programs must be designed to be as flexible as possible while maintaining a disciplined emphasis on the integrative core of the programs.

Counseling obviously is an important component in balancing the need for disciplined focus on analysis and integration with the need to adjust sequencing of courses to the interests and experience of returning adults and transfer students. What we see repeatedly is that such balancing is happening and that IDS programs provide an important venue in the academy for "nontradi-tional" students (who today are becoming the norm in many urban settings): returning older students, transfer students, or students who chose their major programs late in their academic careers.

Several IDS majors may serve as exemplary models with respect to sequencing. The curriculum of the Department of Human Development at the University of California–Hayward begins with an initial session in which students identify their educational needs and the possibilities of meeting them within the program. The junior-level core consists of a series of twelve complementary and contrasting modular courses that represent different approaches to human development. Students also have opportunities to appraise their progress in small-group meetings, and their work culminates in a senior-level seminar and essay or project.

The core sequence in Earlham College's Human Development and Social Relations Program—a two-term sequence in psychology and social anthropology—introduces the major theoretical paradigms, methodological strategies, and bodies of empirical data in academic disciplines related to particular problem areas. Los Medanos College, a community college in California, has a three-tiered interdisciplinary general-education program featuring interdisciplinary courses focused upon social and humanistic issues. The first tier is more encyclopedic in nature; the remaining tiers focus upon integrating concepts and establishing the process of ethical decision-making.

In the University of Alabama's interdisciplinary program in women's studies, introductory courses provide a "sample"; other courses bridge two disciplines, such as psychology and sociology of the family; and an integrative seminar focuses upon gender, race, and class. At Shimer College—a four-year liberal arts college in Illinois based on small classes and "great books"—students move from associative generalizations at the basic level to a more rigorous study of interrelationships among the modes and methods of inquiry within various disciplines, then ultimately to synthesis. The Tier II Synthesis developed at Ohio University involves seniors in the final integrative stage of a comprehensive general education program. It stresses the development of a capacity for synthesis, defined as bringing together two or more disciplines to yield patterns or corresponding ideas.

With respect to instructional modes, we found repeatedly that IDS programs are important on-campus sites for pedagogical experimentation and change. In many cases, learner-oriented communities facilitate interaction and integration through small-group work, individualized and self-directed learning, and field work and other applied experiences. On other campuses we found dialogical models of the educational process, active involvement of teachers as co-learners, collective problem-solving, special ways of clustering courses, and opportunities for collaborative research among faculty members. In fact, campus renewal and experimentation in pedagogy are taking place in many campus IDS programs where they clearly represent some of the most potent possible resources for the revitalization of academic instruction.

CAMPUSWIDE ASPECTS OF IDS

A change agent for overall enrichment of academic quality across the entire institutions, IDS programs can contribute a reference base of ideas and concepts that generates a common discourse on campus, liberally educating faculty members and students alike by exposing them to crucial literature and experiments, significant artistic expressions, and modes of analytical comparison and criticism. Presentations, conferences, and programs offered to the entire campus draw well, since IDS sponsors are recognized for their ability to integrate diverse knowledge and refine effective new approaches to scholarship. IDS programs and centers offer exceptional resources for non-classroom and campus and regionwide conferencing, teleconferencing, and workshops and colloquia of importance across academic and professional communities. Such resources should be accessible to non-IDS majors so that they can integrate them into their existing disciplinary requirements.

A number of IDS majors serve multiple functions within their parent institutions. At St. Olaf College, students in the interdisciplinary Paracollege take regular college classes and satisfy the same general proficiencies as other students; regular students, in turn, can take several Paracollege seminars and workshops or transfer in for a one-semester Paraloop. The Hutchins School of Liberal Studies at Sonoma State University offers an interdisciplinary major in liberal arts and a minor in integrative studies, as well as serving as an alternative general-education program for lower-division students. The School of Interdisciplinary Studies at Miami University (Ohio) is integrated into the larger university curriculum in the sense that students take a substantial part of their upper-level course work outside the program but in tandem with special seminars and a senior essay or project within the school itself.

Interdisciplinary programs can allow a college to meet student needs quickly and flexibly when a major political change or technological innovation suddenly modifies what students need to study. Courses that are not likely to be fully subscribed within one department or school—yet are of importance to a wide range of students—can be supported. Short academic terms—such as interim terms in January or May or summer semesters—also permit interdisciplinary additions to the overall curriculum that involve faculty members or off-campus instructors who are not available during the fall/spring academic year.

An IDS program center, advising office, or library/lounge area can ground the identity of the IDS major in a physical place while facilitating collegial dialogue. Such a center also can provide important employment information. Jobs that make extensive use of IDS perspectives are not always so advertised, and part of the IDS program design should involve helping prospective graduates identify likely options as well as contacts with previous graduates who will have networking possibilities.

FACULTY MEMBERS IN IDS

Often an effective IDS major can be identified by faculty commitment to and administrative support for regular, continuing faculty-to-faculty and faculty-to-student interaction outside the classroom. We found repeatedly that the best programs featured the development of learner-oriented communities whose bounds went far beyond the walls of the classrooms but often included an informal campus IDS center on campus. Discussion groups, workshops, and conferences held in conjunction with IDS programs offer powerful opportunities for cross-campus dialogue and ongoing faculty development; sometimes such special programs are what both faculty members and students remember the most about IDS involvement. Likewise, faculty members frequently speak of returning to more traditional disciplinary teaching with revitalized teaching interests.

A faculty member interested in teaching IDS courses is not automatically prepared to do so. While most IDS programs involve extensive faculty participation in their planning and design, preparation for interdisciplinary teaching itself often is limited to a preliminary orientation, a workshop, or sitting in on a course the semester before assuming the instructional mantle. In most cases there is little use of the now-extensive IDS literature, and as a result a teacher's graduate-school disciplinary training, rather than interdisciplinarity, may predominate in the actual classroom exchange. IDS programs should insist that instructors have at least some acquaintance with the academic literature on interdisciplinarity and IDS and should provide workshops for training new faculty members and advancing the interdisciplinary skills of existing faculty members.

Faculty members will be more inclined to participate in IDS if they know that their institution rewards such efforts when awarding tenure, promotion, and salary increments. Although official institutional statements frequently promote undergraduate teaching and interdisciplinary work, the realities often belie the promotional rhetoric. Several of the programs reviewed by task force members lack a healthy mixture of younger and older faculty members because younger faculty members pursue interdisciplinary teaching only at a real risk to their academic careers. Yet apart from service on a few cross-campus committees or projects, IDS teaching may be one of the few truly cooperative enterprises in which contemporary faculty members may be engaged.

ASSESSMENT

While well-known national instruments claim to be appropriate for assessing IDS, most assess the liberal arts tradition broadly conceived or focus entirely upon specific details of disciplinary knowledge rather than upon the relationships among depth, breadth, and synthesis. These instruments seldom take into account the fact that many IDS programs and courses are rooted in particular clusters of disciplines; hence, they are insensitive to the particular needs of many IDS curricula.

Obviously, assessment should not mean just testing or questionnaires. Informal critical incident and qualitative assessment approaches, including in-depth interviews with both present and former students, are more likely to produce usable evaluative information than questionnaires administered without regard for the program context or distinctiveness. Any instrument or set of assessment strategies devised for IDS should focus upon the care and rigor with which students' integration and application of knowledge are developed throughout the program. It should include evaluation of the usefulness of the academic degree to graduate programs and to a wide range of employers.[5]

Beyond careful attention to the integrative process itself, any assessment strategy should highlight as well:

☐ personnel (Who has been teaching repeatedly? Who might be added or placed in rotation?)

☐ tracking procedures (Who advises? Who helps students keep clear records of progress expected? What postbaccalaureate tracking is done?)

☐ transcript patterns within the IDS program (How different are the closest parallels in the traditional disciplinary majors? What seems to be unique about patterns in the IDS courses elected?)

☐ developmental issues (When are specific competencies such as evaluation, analysis, and integration most likely to be produced? Is there evidence from student work that these competencies actually are developed?)

☐ general-education issues (How do IDS students compare with others in terms of writing across the curriculum? Are objectives clearly defined in classes? Are they actually achieved? Do courses incorporate the content and goals of the campus general-education design? Has the IDS faculty considered how to offer course courses in areas in which faculty members have unique experience and expertise?)

☐ teaching effectiveness (In what ways are student and peer evaluations shared with instructors? When are workshops on effective IDS teaching most likely to be helpful?)

In conducting assessment, evaluators should be alert to unique problems at the faculty, student, and program levels:

☐ Younger faculty members—who may be the best equipped to venture into new areas—may fear evaluation from persons whose skills or sympathies do not lie within interdisciplinary work. We observed repeated cases in which publications in refereed interdisciplinary journals were disallowed or discounted in favor of more traditional disciplinary publications. In other cases, student evaluations were critical sources of assessment for IDS faculty members and in some institutions were weighted more heavily than those of faculty peers.

□ Periodic reviews of student performance as a whole and exit reviews of individual graduating students can provide useful self-criticism and reassessment. Student feedback regarding the planning and methodologies of teaching and presentation of their own and faculty members' research is crucial if IDS students are to learn to own their education. Establishing ongoing tracking of recent graduates also can provide important nurturing of one another and assisting new graduates in finding employment opportunities.

□ Programs that do not incorporate frequent student feedback and administrator/faculty reviews are not likely to succeed. Periodic reviews at least every five years ought to provide information for administrative support of the program and for negotiations with the campuswide curriculum/instruction committee that reviews degree requirements and ap-

proves new courses. Persons outside the program, and from off campus, ought to have a voice in evaluating IDS programs. Retrospective reviews by alumni, as well as follow-up of graduates, should be built in, and reviews of course textbooks and syllabi should be undertaken by both faculty members and students.

Assessment provides a means for faculty members and administrators to remain alert to the fixity that would limit the flexibility toward disciplinary boundaries that often has been the rationale for beginning IDS programs. Assessment ought to be conceived broadly enough that it looks both inward—toward the performance of the IDS program—and outward—toward analysis of society's present and future needs. When designed correctly, exernal and internal evaluation can provide an important feedback mechanism for all those concerned with IDS.

RECOMMENDATIONS

Despite the growing attractiveness of IDS approaches in research and education, the task force members found a widespread lack of institutional financing and administrative support for sustaining them. On the basis of our reviews of programs and our consultations with interdisciplinary educators, we list here actions that can be taken to advocate IDS within institutions of higher education and to assure the quality of offerings.

Recommendations to IDS program directors and faculty members

☐ IDS programs should insist upon formal preparation of instructors working in the field and encourage continuing reevaluation of the common IDS enterprise.

☐ We recognize the wide variety of existing structures of IDS programs and hence the inappropriateness of our recommending a particular sequence of courses for all majors. We do recommend, however, that any IDS program or major be planned carefully by faculty members and administrators with a view toward balancing depth, breadth, and synthesis. The sequence that is stipulated must be conveyed clearly and repeatedly to both students and faculty members, and possibilities for exceptions must be spelled out carefully. Wherever possible, an ombudsperson should be available for both students and faculty members.

☐ Regular review of IDS aims and program procedures must be held to ensure that instruction is truly integrative and not merely additive and that student performance is being improved consistently.

Recommendations to academic administrators and faculty curriculum committees

☐ Attractive faculty development programs, seminars, and institutes originating in IDS contexts should be integrated into campuswide academic planning, activities, and funding.

☐ Administrative structures must provide secure budgetary lines in hard money, seek funding for IDS public/community programming, perform periodic reexamination of the entire university curriculum to assure that existing structures respond adequately to the needs of contemporary society and research communities, and ensure that there are no penalties for faculty members who engage in IDS research or teaching and provide safeguards for faculty members who teach in both an IDS program and a specific discipline. Contracts or letters of agreement should stipulate precisely how the IDS teaching or administration is to be ranked in tenure, promotion, and salary considerations.

☐ Administrators should assist IDS program directors' access to other campus resources such as community outreach, nontraditional-degree programs, adult degree programs, business-community and education-community groups, international studies, and honors. Such support can sustain efficient utilization of available funds for speakers, workshops, and media resources.

Recommendations across the academic campus

☐ Involvement in and support for national IDS organizations and clearinghouses for information is vital. They provide start-up information, good practice examples, bibliography, and knowledgeable and experienced consultants who can help a campus avoid costly mistakes and unnecessary wheel-spinning.

☐ Persons concerned about IDS on an individual campus should develop support committees and systems for IDS programs and activities on campus. Seldom do directors of women's studies, international studies, and other IDS programs sit down together to address common problems, issues, and resources; the result is a further fragmentation of the campuswide interdisciplinary enterprise.

☐ Campuswide advisers ought to be kept aware of IDS majors and programs and asked to help students learn how to satisfy academic interests and needs that can be satisfied only through IDS courses and programs. Advisers also can help students identify graduate or profession-

al schools that welcome IDS majors.

☐ Everyone involved in IDS must work to see that all granting agencies—national as well as local—do not discriminate against IDS-oriented projects and to ascertain that local support for individual and group IDS applications remains as strong as it is for other projects.

☐ Library budgets should include provisions for ordering IDS materials that do not fit allocations for the traditional disciplines and departments. A reference bibliographer trained to support interdisciplinary research can be a valuable resource.

---

1. An expanded version of this report provides an orientation to the essential literature on interdisciplinary studies and relevant professional associations, a historical overview of interdisciplinary studies in American education, and a sketch of the variety of interdisciplinary programs. It is published along with a bibliographic survey, a directory of programs, and materials on curricular development and administration of programs as a special issue of the journal *Issues in Integrative Studies* (see appendix).

The Society for Values in Higher Education task force that prepared this report comprised Alice F. Carse, SUNY–College at Old Westbury; William G. Doty, University of Alabama–Tuscaloosa (chair and scribe); Julie Thompson Klein, Wayne State University; Edward Ordman, Memphis State University; and Constance D. Ramirez, Duquesne University. The report of the task force on interdisciplinary studies is a statement recommended by SVHE as a framework

REPORTS
FROM THE
FIELDS

for campus discussion of interdisciplinary studies.

2. Project on Redefining the Meaning and Purpose of Baccalaureate Degrees, *Integrity in the College Curriculum: A Report to the Academic Community* (Washington, D.C.: Association of American Colleges, 1985), 30.

3. See William Mayville, *Interdisciplinarity: The Mutable Paradigm*, AAHE-ERIC Higher Education Research Report No. 9 (Washington, D.C.: American Association for Higher Education, 1978), 31.

4. See Ernest Lynton, "Interdisciplinarity: Rationales and Criteria of Assessment," in *Inter-Disciplinarity Revisited: Re-Assessing the Concept in the Light of Institutional Experience*, ed. Lennart Levin and Ingemar Lind (Stockholm: Organization for Economic Cooperation and Development, Swedish National Board of Universities and Colleges and Linköping University, 1985), 149.

5. See Lynton, "Interdisciplinarity."

MATHEMATICS*

MATHEMATICS
IN HIGHER EDUCATION

In 1970, total undergraduate mathematics enrollment exceeded three million students; at that time, U.S. mathematics departments produced twenty-four thousand bachelors' and twelve hundred doctoral degrees a year. But then the bubble burst; the numbers of mathematics bachelors' degrees dropped by more than 50 percent in ten years, as did the number of U.S. students who went on to a Ph.D. in mathematics. Total undergraduate mathematics enrollment, however, continued to climb as students shifted from studying mathematics as a major to enrolling in selected courses that provided tools necessary for other majors.

Today mathematics is the second largest discipline in higher education. Indeed, more than 10 percent of college and university faculty members and student enrollments are in departments of mathematics. More than half of this enrollment,

however, is in high school-level courses, and most of the rest is devoted to elementary service courses. Less than 10 percent of the total postsecondary mathematics enrollment is in post-calculus courses that are part of the mathematics major. Even in these advanced courses, many students are not mathematics majors; they enroll to learn mathematical techniques used in other fields. As a consequence, the mathematics major has suffered from neglect brought about in part by the overwhelming pressure of elementary service courses.

We are especially concerned in this report with how students' experience in the major contributes to the education of the great majority of students who do not pursue advanced study in the same field in which they majored. This study, therefore, is not as concerned with curricular content required for subsequent study or careers as it is with the quality of students' engagement with their collegiate major.

GOALS AND OBJECTIVES

Mathematics shares with many disciplines a fundamental dichotomy of instructional purpose: mathematics as an object of study and mathematics as a tool for application. These different purposes yield two quite different paradigms for a mathematics major, both of which are reflected in today's college and university curricula. The former paradigm focuses on a core curriculum of basic theory that prepares students for graduate study in mathematics; the latter focuses on a variety of mathematical tools needed for a lifelong series of different jobs.

Certain principles articulated in 1981 by CUPM make explicit areas where *Integrity*'s objectives for liberal learning and those of the mathematical community align:

☐ The primary goal of a mathematical sciences major should be to develop a student's capacity to undertake intellectually demanding mathematical reasoning.

☐ A mathematical sciences curriculum should be designed for all students with an interest in mathematics, with both appropriate opportunities for average mathematics majors and appropriate challenges for more advanced students.

☐ Every student who majors in the mathematical sciences should complete a year-long course sequence at the upper-division level that builds on two years of lower-division mathematics.

☐ Instructional strategies should encourage students to develop new ideas and discover new mathematics for themselves rather than merely master the results of concise, polished theories.

☐ Every topic in every course should include an interplay of applications, problem-solving, and theory. Applications and interconnections should motivate theory so that theory is seen by students as useful and enlightening.

☐ Students majoring in mathematics should undertake some real-world mathematical modeling project.

☐ Mathematics majors should complete a minor in a discipline that makes significant use of mathematics.

Emphasis on coherence, connections, and the intellectual development of all students are evident in these principles. As broad goals, the prevailing professional wisdom concerning undergraduate mathematics matches well the intent of *Integrity*.

Diverse objectives

Once one moves beyond generalities and into specifics of program development, however, mainstream mathematical practice often diverges from many of the explicit AAC goals. Most students study mathematics in depth not to achieve broad goals of liberal education but for some professional purpose—for example, to support their study of science or to become a systems analyst, teacher, statistician, or computer scientist. Others study mathematics as a liberal art, an enjoyable and challenging major that can serve many ends. It is as true in mathematics as in any other field that the great majority of undergraduate mathematics majors do not pursue advanced study that builds on their major.

Since department goals must match institutional missions, it would not be right for any committee to recommend uniform goals for individual departments. There will always be considerable room for debate about strategies for achieving the several different (but overlapping) objectives common to majors offered by the twenty-five hundred mathematics departments in U.S. colleges and universities:

☐ Advanced study: preparation for graduate study in various mathematical sciences or in other mathematically based sciences.

☐ Professional preparation: skills required to pursue a career that requires considerable background in mathematics:

■ Natural and social sciences: background for careers in science or engineering, especially in the physical, life, and social sciences.

■ Business and industry: preparation for careers in management, finance, and business.

■ School teaching: preparation for teaching secondary school mathematics.

■ Liberal education: general background for professions that do not directly use mathematical skills.

Because so few U.S. students pursue graduate study in the mathematical sciences, many mathematicians believe that the mathematics major should be strengthened in ways that will prepare students better for graduate study in mathematics. Indeed, national need requires greater encouragement for students to continue their study of mathematics beyond the bachelor's level— whether as preparation for school teaching, for university careers, or for government and industry. In some institutions, this encouragement may arise from a thriving program that points toward graduate study; in others it may evolve from an emphasis on the major as liberal education. In all cases, departmental objectives must be realistically matched to student aspirations and to institutional goals. Wherever faculty and students share common objectives, mathematics can thrive.

Achieving depth
Each student who majors in mathematics should experience the power of

deep mathematics by taking some upper-division course sequence that builds on lower-division prerequisites. It is neither necessary nor wise, however, to require that all mathematics majors take precisely the same sequence.

Despite institutional diversity, there is striking uniformity in mathematics curricula: all mathematics majors begin with calculus for two, three, or four semesters; most introduce linear algebra in the sophomore year and require one or two semesters of abstract algebra; virtually all require some upper-division work in analysis—the "theory of calculus." Nowadays, most require some computer work as well as some applied work among electives.

Beyond this core, however, students pursue many, varied programs. Most mathematics departments resolve the dilemma of diverse goals for the major with some sort of track system that offers different routes to achieving depth. Tracks within the major are a sensible strategy to respond to competing interests of students, faculty members, and institutions.

By its very nature, mathematics builds on itself and reinforces connections among related fields. A student who progresses from calculus to probability to operations research sees as many connections as does one who moves through the more traditional sequence of advanced calculus and real analysis. Although the focus of each student's work is different, the contributions made by each track to the general objectives of study-in-depth are comparable and equally valuable.

Emphasizing breadth

Every student who majors in mathematics should study a broad variety of advanced courses in order to comprehend both the breadth of the mathematical sciences and the powerful explanatory value of deep principles.

Breadth is as important as depth as an objective of a mathematics major. Students introduced to a variety of areas more readily will discern the mathematical power of connected ideas; unexpected links discovered in different areas provide more convincing examples of a deep, logical unity than do the expected relationships in tightly sequenced courses.

For the many majors who will teach (either in high school or college), it is vitally important that their undergraduate experiences provide a broad view of the discipline—since further study generally is more narrow and specialized. For those seeking their niche in the world of mathematics, a broad introduction to many different yet interconnected subjects, styles, and techniques helps pique interest and attract majors. And for the many students who may never make professional use of mathematics, depth through breadth offers a strong base for appreciating the true power and scope of the mathematical sciences. Graduates of programs that emphasize breadth will become effective ambassadors for mathematics.

Effective programs
Effective programs teach students, not just mathematics.

Departments of mathematics in colleges and universities exhibit enormous variety in goals and effectiveness. For example, the percentage of bachelors' degrees awarded to students with majors in mathematics ranges from well under one-half of 1 percent to more than 20 percent. Mathematics programs that work can be found in all strata of higher education, from small private colleges to large state universities, from average to highly selective campuses. The variety of such programs reveals what can be achieved when circumstance and commitment permit. Exploration, experimentation, and innovation—along with occasional failures—are the hallmarks of a department committed to effective education. When faculty resolve is backed by strong administrative support, most mathematics departments easily can adopt strategies to build vigorous majors while meeting other service obligations.

One successful department builds

strength on a foundation of excellent introductory instruction. "We put our best teachers—and the most interesting material—in the introductory courses." Another department that has had great success in attracting students to major in mathematics bases its work on two articles of faith: "We believe that faculty should relate to their students in such a way that all students in the department will know that someone is personally interested in them and their work. We believe that careful and sensitive teaching that helps students develop confidence and self-esteem is far more important than curriculum or teaching technique."

Regular, formal recognition of student achievement at different stages of the major serves to build students' confidence and helps attract students to major in mathematics. Students know mathematics' reputation for being challenging, so recognition of honest accomplishment can provide a tremendous boost to a student's fragile self-esteem.

CHALLENGES FOR THE 1990s

Changes in the practice of mathematics and in the context of learning pose immense challenges for college mathematics. Many issues pertaining directly to course content and curricular requirements are under review by other committees within the mathematical community. We focus here on a set of challenges that transcend particular details of courses and curriculum.

☐ learning: to help students learn to learn mathematics

☐ teaching: to adopt more effective styles of instruction

☐ technology: to enhance mathematics courses with computer methods

☐ connections: to help students connect areas of mathematics and areas of application

☐ variety: to offer students a sufficient variety of approaches to match the enormous variety of student career goals

☐ self-esteem: to help build students' confidence in their mathematical abilities

☐ access: to ensure that women and minority students have access to advanced mathematical study

☐ communication: to help students learn to read, write, listen, and speak mathematically

☐ transitions: to aid students in making smooth transitions between major stages in mathematics education

☐ research: to define and encourage appropriate opportunities for undergraduate research and independent projects

☐ context: to ensure student attention to the historical and contemporary context in which mathematics is practiced

☐ support: to enhance students' motivation and enthusiasm for studying mathematics.

These challenges have more to do with the success of a mathematics program than any curricular structure. Successful mathematics programs differ enormously in curricular detail, but all respond effectively to these broader challenges. The agenda for undergraduate mathematics in the 1990s must focus at least as much on these issues of context, attitude, and methodology as on traditional themes such as curricula, syllabi, and content.

Learning

Undergraduate students should learn not only the subject of mathematics but also how to learn mathematics.

Undergraduate mathematical experience should prepare students for lifelong learning in a sequence of jobs that will require new mathematical skills. Departments of mathematics often interpret that goal as calling for breadth of study, but another interpretation is just as important. Because mathematics changes so rapidly, undergraduates must become independent learners of mathematics, able to continue their own mathematical education after they graduate.

Most college students do not know how to learn mathematics, and most college faculty members do not know how students actually learn mathematics. It is a tribute to the efforts of individual students and teachers that any learning at all takes place.

Effective programs pay as much attention to learning as they do to teaching. First-year students need special attention. Typically, they bring a high school tradition of passive learning that emphasizes bite-sized problems to be solved by techniques provided by the textbook section in which the problem appears. By maintaining this traditional teaching format, college calculus teachers typically exacerbate the problem.

Calculus should be taught as the intellectual equivalent of a first-year seminar in which students learn to speak a new language and in which there is a great deal of emphasis on one-to-one communication between student and teacher. In too many institutions, however, calculus is taught in large impersonal settings that make meaningful dialogue unrealistic. Many of the efforts now under-way to reform the teaching of calculus emphasize student motivation and styles of learning as a primary factor in reshaping the course.

Teaching
Those who teach college mathematics must seek ways to incorporate into their own teaching the findings of research on teaching and learning.

The purpose of teaching, and its ultimate measure, is student learning. As students must learn to learn, so teachers must learn to teach. Although there is no formula for successful teaching, there is considerable evidence that certain practices are more effective than others. Those who study cognitive development criticize standard teaching practices for failing to develop fully students' power to apply their mathematical knowledge in unfamiliar terrain. Teachers who study this research and the alternative practices suggested by it can benefit enormously.

Most mathematics majors never move much beyond technical skills with standard textbook problems. Passive teaching and passive learning result from an unconscious conspiracy of minimal expectations among students and faculty members, all of whom find advantages in a system that avoids the challenges of active learning. Both the curriculum and teaching practices must correct this habit of intellectual malnutrition.

Research shows that formal learning by itself rarely influences real-world behavior; many students continue to use their flawed intuitions instead of the concepts learned in the artificial classroom environment. Additional research on how young adults learn mathematics—or more often, why they fail to learn—shows the importance of a supportive environment that emphasizes constructive teamwork in a context of challenging problems. Research-like experiences that enrich traditional classroom and textbook learning also improve student motivation and self-reliance. Students whose minds and eyes become engaged in the challenge of true discovery are frequently transformed by the experience.

Too often mathematicians assume with little reflection that what was good for their own education is good enough for their students, not realizing that most of their students, not being inclined to become mathematicians, have very different styles of learning. College faculty members must begin to recognize the proven value of various styles of instruction that engage students more directly in their own learning.

Technology
To ensure an effective curriculum for the twenty-first century, undergraduate mathematics must reflect the impact of computers on the practice of mathematics.

Computing has profoundly changed the practice of mathematics at every level. It provides many students with natural motivation; helps link the study of mathematics to study in other fields; offers a tool with which mathematics influences the modern world and puts mathe-

matical ideas into action; and alters the priorities of courses, rendering certain favorite topics obsolete and making others, formerly inaccessible, now feasible and necessary. As computation becomes a third paradigm of scientific investigation—along with experimental and theoretical science—mathematics itself becomes in part an experimental science.

Technology forces mathematicians to ask anew what it means to know mathematics. College faculty members no longer can avoid the challenge posed by computers: once calculations are automated, what is left that can be taught effectively to average students? Early experiments that make significant use of computing in undergraduate mathematics courses show that as the balance of student work shifts from computation to thought, the course becomes more difficult, more unsettling, and less closely attuned to student expectations.

The transition of mathematics from a purely cerebral paper-and-pencil discipline to a high-technology laboratory science is not inexpensive. Space must be expanded for laboratories. Classrooms and offices must be equipped with computers and display devices. Support staff must be hired. Faculty members must be given time to learn to use and teach with computers and to redesign courses and curricula so they reflect the impact of computing. Colleges must recognize in budgets, staffing, and space the fact that undergraduate mathematics is rapidly becoming a laboratory discipline.

Connections

Dealing with complex, open-ended problem situations should be one of the highest priorities of undergraduate mathematics.

Connectedness is inherent in mathematics. It is what gives mathematics its power, what establishes its truth, and what reveals its beauty. Although widely recognized as the language of physical science, mathematics is truly the language of all science: physical, biological, social, behavioral, and economic. Yet even as the connections between abstract ideas of mathematics and concrete embodiments in the world have multiplied, the internal connections within the mathematical sciences have proliferated. Key theorems and deep problems that link separate mathematical specialties provide a force for vast growth in interdisciplinary research.

At its best, mathematics overflows with connections, both internal and external. But one must be honest; undergraduate courses do not always show mathematics at its best. Many lower-division courses, through which both majors and nonmajors must pass, reveal mathematics as a bag of isolated tricks instead of a discipline that requires real understanding of fundamental principles. Undergraduate mathematics courses must introduce a greater variety of authentic examples amenable to a variety of approaches. Such problems should be pregnant with ambiguity, ripe with subtle connections, and open to multifaceted analysis.

Variety

Mathematics departments should take seriously the need to provide appropriate mathematical depth for students who wish to concentrate in mathematics without pursuing a traditional major.

Although most colleges equate study-in-depth with the major—a circumstance reflected also in this report—it is important to recognize that for some students the major may not achieve the objectives they have for study-in-depth. For these students, curricular structures other than the traditional major may better approach their goals for study-in-depth.

One popular alternative is a joint major. In mathematics and biology, for example, senior students can employ mathematical models based on lower-division mathematics to simulate biological phenomena and then test and modify the model based on laboratory data. Although shallowness is an ever-present danger of joint majors, which may be more like two minors than one major, joint majors can effectively meet some of the objectives of study-in-depth.

Another common alternative is teacher education. Prospective secondary school mathematics teachers generally pursue an undergraduate degree that includes a major in mathematics, often constrained in special ways to ensure breadth appropriate to the responsibilities of high school mathematics teachers. The appropriate mathematical preparation of prospective elementary and middle schoolteachers—who commonly teach several subjects and sometimes teach the whole curriculum—however, is subject to much debate. Many national studies have recommended that these teachers, like secondary school teachers, major in a liberal art or science rather than in the discipline of education. The traditional mathematics major, however, is generally inappropriate for teachers at the elementary and middle levels, and today there appears to be virtually no example of a viable alternative.

Self-esteem

Building students' well-founded self-confidence should be a major priority for all undergraduate mathematics instruction.

One of the greatest impediments to student achievement in mathematics is the widespread belief that mathematics is for geniuses. Many facets of school and college practice—timed tests, intercollegiate competitions—conspire to portray mathematics in "macho" terms, where only bright, aggressive, and arrogant students can succeed. Those who do not instantly understand—including many thoughtful, reflective, creative students—are made to feel inadequate.

Fortunately, there is a growing recognition in the mathematical community that individuals bring different but equally valuable strengths to the study of mathematics. A multiplicity of approaches that encourage student growth in many dimensions is far more effective than a single-minded focus leading to a linear ranking in one narrow dimension of "brightness." These more effective instructional strategies—including open-ended problems, team work that builds diverse problem-solving skills, undergraduate research experiences, and independent study—emphasize active learning and enhance students' self-confidence.

Access

To provide effective opportunities for all students to learn mathematics, colleges must offer a broader spectrum of instructional practice that is better at-

tuned to the variety of students seeking higher education.

Data from many sources show that women and members of certain minority groups often discontinue their study of mathematics before they are prepared for jobs or further school. Black and Hispanic students drop out of mathematics at very high rates throughout high school and college, and only a tiny fraction complete an undergraduate mathematics major.

Evidence from various intervention programs, however, shows that the high drop-out rates among minority students can be reduced. Appropriate expectations that provide challenges without the stigma of remediation, together with assignments and study environments that reinforce group learning, have proved successful on many campuses. What becomes clear from these programs is that the tradition of competitive, individual effort that dominates much mathematics instruction does not provide a supportive learning environment for all students. Mathematicians must learn that the teaching strategies they recall as being successful in their own education—and in the education of a mostly white male professional class—do not necessarily work as well for those raised in vastly different cultures within the American mosaic.

Programs that work for under-prepared students are built on the self-evident premise that students do not all learn mathematics in the same way. Classroom methods must fit both the goals of the major and the learning styles of individual students. These methods, which have been successful with students of color, need to be extended to all students.

Communication
Mathematics majors should be offered extensive opportunities to read, write, listen, and speak mathematically at each stage of their undergraduate study.

College graduates with majors in mathematically based disciplines often are perceived by society as being verbally inept. The stereotype of the hacker who cannot communicate except with a computer has permeated the business world and tainted mathematics graduates with the same reputation. Recognizing the legitimate basis for this stereotype in the incomprehensible writing of their own upper-division students, many mathematics departments are beginning to emphasize writing in mathematics courses of all levels.

In industry, one of the most important tasks for a mathematician is to communicate to non-mathematicians the mathematical formulation and solution of problems. Each student's growth in mathematical maturity depends in essential ways on continual growth in the ability to read, write, listen, and speak mathematically. Students must learn the idioms of the discipline and the relation of mathematical symbols to English words. They need to learn how to interpret mathematical ideas arising from many different sources and how to suit their own expression of mathematics to different audiences.

Transitions
Smooth curricular transitions improve student learning and help them maintain momentum.

As students grow in mathematical maturity from early childhood experiences to adult employment, they face a series of difficult transitions where the nature of mathematics seems to change abruptly. These "fault lines" appear at predictable stages:
☐ between arithmetic and algebra, when letter symbols, variables, and relationships become important
☐ between algebra and geometry, when logical proof replaces calculation as the methodology of mathematics
☐ between high school and college, when the expectation for learning on one's own increases significantly
☐ between elementary and upper-division college mathematics, when the focus shifts from techniques to theory and from solving problems to writing proofs

☐ between college and graduate school, when the level of abstraction accelerates at a phenomenal rate
☐ between graduate school and college teaching, when the realities of how others learn must take precedence
☐ between graduate school and research, when the new Ph.D. not only must solve a serious problem, but learn to find good problems as well.

Students experience real trauma in making these transitions; many drop out of mathematics as a consequence. College mathematics departments should concentrate on ways of supporting students during these critical points of transition.

Research
Undergraduate research and senior projects should be encouraged wherever there are sufficient faculty members to provide appropriate supervision.

Among mathematicians there is little consensus about the objectives, feasibility, or benefits of requirements for capstone courses or senior projects. Many mathematicians believe in coverage as more crucial to understanding: standard theorems, paradigms of proof, and significant counterexamples in all major areas must be covered before a student is ready to advance to the next level of mathematical maturity. In this view, learning what is already known is a prerequisite to discovering the unknown.

Because of mathematics' austere definition of "research," many mathematicians believe that except in very rare cases, undergraduates cannot do research in mathematics. Moreover, in most areas of mathematics, students cannot even assist in faculty research, as they do quite commonly in the laboratory sciences. The exceptions in mathematics are principally where computer investigation—the mathematician's laboratory—can aid the research effort. As a consequence, many mathematicians believe that further coursework not only better serves the goals of integration (because the higher one progresses in mathematics, the more internal links one can see) but also helps advance the student toward better preparation for further study or application of mathematics.

Others feel that encounters with substantial problems can provide legitimate and rewarding undergraduate research experiences. Indeed, many colleges have used summer experiences with undergraduate research to recruit students for careers in the mathematical sciences. Applications, computing, education, industry, and scientific investigation can supplement traditional theory as fruitful domains for undergraduate research experiences.

Research projects enable students to integrate mathematics they have learned in several different courses; to experience the role of mathematical models; to extend their mathematical repertoire beyond what has been taught; and to establish mathematical concepts in a context of varied uses, applications, and connections. The range of opportunities for independent investigation is so broad and the evidence of benefit so persuasive as to make unmistakably clear that research-like experiences should be part of every mathematics student's program.

Context

All mathematics students should engage in serious study of the historical context and contemporary impact of mathematics.

Mathematics courses—especially those taken by majors—traditionally have been taught as purely utilitarian courses in techniques, theories, and applications. Most courses pay no more than superficial attention to the historical, cultural, or contemporary context in which mathematics is practiced. Today, however, as mathematical models are used increasingly for policy and operational purposes of immense consequence, it is vitally important that students learn to think through these issues even as they learn the details of mathematics itself. Examples abound of mathematical activity that leads directly to decisions of great human import. Mathematical models of global warming, computer-controlled trading of stocks, and epidemiological studies of AIDS illustrate how mathematics really matters in important decisions affecting daily life.

It is easy to adapt a modeling project or course to problems of significant societal impact. In such a setting students could undertake original investigation; gain experience in reading, writing, listening, and speaking about mathematically rich material; explore historical antecedents and contemporary debates; and practice team work to address complex, open-ended problems. For many students a capstone project on a public policy issue would be a fitting way to relate their mathematics major to liberal education.

Social support

Mathematics departments should exert active leadership in promoting extracurricular activities that enhance peer group support among mathematics majors.

The abstract, austere nature of mathematics provides relatively few intrinsic rewards for the typical undergraduate trying to balance academic and social priorities. The social support provided by departmental activities helps build mathe-

matical self-confidence and enhances the intrinsic rewards of mathematical achievement. Often such activities tip the balance when students choose majors. Virtually all successful mathematics departments initiate and support a variety of extracurricular activities.

MECHANISMS FOR RENEWAL

Constant vigilance is needed to maintain quality in mathematics, where the subject is constantly evolving; where external departments impose their own often-conflicting demands; where so much teaching effort is devoted to remedial, elementary, and lower-division work; and where the ability of the discipline to attract sufficient numbers of students to careers in the mathematical sciences is now in serious doubt. We focus here on five mechanisms of renewal. Each of these mechanisms requires listening—to students, colleagues, friends, and critics. Departments that listen—and learn—will thrive.

Dialogue

It is important for mathematics departments to help faculty members and students recognize their own perspectives on mathematics and understand the perspectives of others.

Mathematicians often know very little about their students' views of the undergraduate mathematics major and the expectations of colleagues in cognate disciplines for the mathematical preparation of students with other majors. The three interested parties—mathematics professors, science faculty advisors, and students—rarely discuss goals or objectives, focusing only on credit-hour requirements. In the absence of good communication, misunderstandings flourish.

Students must recognize that the practice of mathematics is quite different from their image of it. Often students expect of college mathematics merely advanced topics in the spirit of school mathematics: a succession of techniques, exercises, and test problems, each explained by the instructor with sufficient clarity that the student need only practice and memorize. Such expectations do little to foster creativity, criticism, perspective, and the ability to work on new problems—the more important goals of liberal education.

Announcing or publishing department goals is not sufficient to achieve effective communication. A process that engages all students in significant and repeated discussion of individual goals throughout their undergraduate study of mathematics is required. In particular, careful and individualized advising is crucial to students' success because it builds an atmosphere of mutual respect between faculty members and students. Courses, career objectives, motivations, fears, and celebrations are all part of advising and of special importance in the long, slow process of building students' self-confidence.

Assessment

Assessment of undergraduate majors should be aligned with broad goals of the major; tests should emphasize what is most important, not just what is easiest to test.

Goals for study-in-depth can be effective only if supported by an assessment plan that relates the work on which students are graded to the objectives of their education. Assessment in courses and of the major as a whole should be aligned with appropriate objectives, not just with the technical details of solving equations or doing proofs. Many specific objectives can flow from the broad goals of study-in-depth, including solving open-ended problems, communicating mathematics effectively, closely reading technically based material, contributing to group efforts, and recognizing mathematical ideas embedded in other contexts. Open-ended goals require open-ended assessment mechanisms. Although difficult to use and interpret, such devices yield valuable insight into how students think.

Because of the considerable variety of legitimate educational goals, it is widely acknowledged that ordinary paper-and-pencil tests cannot by themselves constitute a valid assessment of the mathematics major. Although some important skills and knowledge can be measured by such tests, objectives such as facility in oral and written communication require other methods. Some departments are beginning to explore portfolio systems in which a student submits samples of a variety of work to represent his or her capabilities. A portfolio system allows students the chance to put forth their best work, rather than be judged primarily by evidence of weakness.

Faculty development

To ensure continued vitality of undergraduate mathematics programs, all mathematics faculty members should engage in public professional activity, broadly defined.

The relationship of research and scholarship to faculty vitality is one of the most difficult issues facing many departments of mathematics, especially in smaller institutions. Professional activity is crucial to inspired teaching and essential to avoiding faculty burn-out. Mathematical research in its traditional sense plays only a small role in maintaining the intellectual vitality of a mathematics department: only about one in five full-time faculty members in departments of mathe-

matics publish regularly in research journals, and fewer than half of those have any financial support for their research. Clearly the community needs to support a broader standard as a basis for maintaining faculty leadership both in curriculum and in scholarship.

The first step requires broadening the definition of professional activity from "research" to "scholarship," including activities such as applied consulting work, software development, problem-solving, software and book reviews, expository writing, and curriculum development. These activities serve many of the same purposes as research: they advance the field in particular directions, engage faculty in active original work, serve as models for students of how mathematics is practiced, and provide opportunities for student projects.

Teaching in new areas is also a form of scholarship in mathematics. Unlike disciplines in which faculty members rarely teach outside their own areas of specialty, mathematicians are generally expected to teach a wide variety of courses. Learning and then teaching a course far outside one's zone of comfort is an effective way to build internal connections. A teacher who is still an active learner exhibits to students the true meaning of scholarship.

A second step is to insist on greater communication about professional activity in mathematics so that it becomes public. Only the bright light of public scrutiny by colleagues in various institutions—not only on one's own campus—can affirm the quality and value of professional work. "Public" need not mean merely publication. Lectures, workshops, demonstrations, and reports can serve the same objective. What matters is that the results become part of the profession and be evaluated by the profession.

Departmental review

Both external reviews and informal feedback are needed to assure quality in departments of mathematics.

More than any other academic discipline, mathematics is constrained to serve many masters: the many sciences that depend on mathematical methods; the demand of quantitative literacy that undergirds general education; the need to educate teachers; the need of business and industry for mathematically literate employees; the expectation of mathematical proficiency by faculty members and students in natural sciences, business, engineering, and social sciences; and the requirements of the mathematical sciences themselves for well-prepared graduate students. It is an enormous challenge for a department of mathematics, one that very few are able to fulfill with distinction in every dimension.

Because of these diverse demands, it is especially important that departments of mathematics undergo regular review, with both external and internal mechanisms to provide evaluation and advice. External requirements mandate periodic review of all departments in many colleges and universities, especially in public institutions. But in other institutions, department goals are often defined implicitly, without self-reflection or benefit of external perspectives. At worst, the goals of such departments are defined by coverage of standard textbooks. Often it takes a crisis— such as when the engineering or business school complains about certain courses—for departments to step back and examine their objectives. Reviews should take place regularly, not just when some crisis threatens the status quo.

Reviews provide a strategic opportunity to document the accomplishments of a department; give a structured and neutral forum for mathematicians to discuss issues of common concern with those who use mathematics; and encourage faculty members to think about the department's program as a whole, rather than only about the courses they teach. Such discussions make it more likely that the curriculum will remain responsive to student needs and to the changing demands of the mathematical sciences. Reviews provide an ideal mechanism for the department to assert control over its own program.

Graduate education

Renewal of undergraduate mathematics will require commitment, leadership, and support of graduate schools.

Even though relatively few mathematics majors subsequently receive a graduate degree in the mathematical sciences, the health of college mathematics is inextricably linked with the status of graduate education. As the sole providers of advanced degrees, graduate schools are responsible for preparing college mathematics teachers; as the primary locus of mathematical research, graduate schools shape the nature of the discipline and, hence, the curriculum. Much of the responsibility for renewing undergraduate mathematics rests with the graduate schools, since it is they who provide the primary professional education of those responsible for undergraduate mathematics: college faculty members.

There are many indications that the match between undergraduate and graduate mathematics education serves U.S. interests poorly. Too few U.S. mathematics majors choose to enter graduate school in a mathematical science. U.S. mathematics students do less well in graduate school—and drop out more often—than foreign nationals. Many students finish graduate school ill-equipped for the breadth of teaching duties typically expected of undergraduate mathematics teachers. Relatively few who finish doctoral degrees in mathematics actually go on to effective research careers in mathematics.

In the 1970s, as the number of U.S. students applying to graduate school in mathematics began to decline, the graduate schools responded by increasing the number of international students, most of whom had completed a more intense and specialized education in mathematics than would be typical of American undergraduates. Hence the level of mathematics expected of beginning graduate students gradually shifted upward to an international standard that is well above current U.S. undergraduate curricula. Consequently, the failure or dropout rate of U.S. students increased, creating pressure for more international students and even higher entrance expectations.

It is time to break this negative feedback loop by encouraging better articulation of programs and standards between U.S. undergraduate colleges and U.S. graduate schools. Such cooperation is needed both to enhance the success of U.S. students and to enable the graduate schools to match better their programs with the needs of the colleges and universities that employ a majority of those who receive advanced degrees.

SUMMARY

Among the many majors from which students can choose, mathematics can help ensure versatility for the future. Habits of mind nurtured in an undergraduate mathematics major are profoundly useful in an enormous variety of professions. The challenge for college mathematicians is to ensure that the major provides—and is seen by students as providing—not just technical facility, but broad empowerment in the language of our age.

---

*This report summarizes a larger study (see appendix) prepared by a joint task force convened by AAC and the Mathematical Association of America to address issues concerning undergraduate mathematics majors as a sequel to the AAC's 1985 *Integrity in the College Curriculum: A Report to the Academic Community*. The task force worked under the umbrella of the MAA's Committee on the Undergraduate Program in Mathematics (CUPM), which has provided leadership and advice to the mathematical community for more than thirty-five years. Task force members from MAA were Jerome A. Goldstein, Tulane University; Eleanor Jones, Norfolk State University; David Lutzer, College of William and Mary; Uri Treisman, University of California–Berkeley; Alan C. Tucker, State University of New York–Stony Brook. Lynn Arthur Steen, St. Olaf College, was chair and scribe.

The AAC-MAA task force operated in the context of other ongoing studies that will provide detailed advice to the mathematics community about requirements for the undergraduate major; hence, it dealt only with broader questions of context and priorities.

The report has benefited enormously from many external reviews, and we believe that it now represents a consensus of the informed mathematical community concerning issues of importance to the undergraduate mathematics major. The report was endorsed unanimously by the Board of Governors of the Mathematical Association of America as a statement about the undergraduate mathematics major. We hope that widespread discussion of this report will help focus the efforts at reform already underway on many campuses.

CHAPTER SIX

PHILOSOPHY[1]

Socrates said that the unexamined life is not worth living. Philosophy is the practice of the kinds of reflection he exemplified. It has grown and changed immensely since his time, but it is still concerned with ideas and issues arising across the entire spectrum of human life. Its raw materials come from every phase of life, and its arguments and explanations range over every subject worthy of disciplined reflection.

HISTORICAL SKETCH OF THE PHILOSOPHY MAJOR

Formal philosophical study in the Mediterranean region of Europe began at least as early as Plato's Academy. (It had other beginnings—in some cases earlier—in China, India, and Africa.) Many of the earliest philosophical writings, including many of Plato's, remain central to philosophical education. Philosophy continued throughout ancient times under several movements, notably Platonism, Aristotelianism, Stoicism, Epicureanism, and Skepticism. Students used philosophy then much as they do now: a few intended to make it a career; others used it to illuminate the foundations of—or to expand—learning in another field; and many pursued it as a cultural or civic accomplishment or out of intellectual fascination.

During the long decline of the Roman Empire and into the early Medieval period, philosophical and theological education were commonly combined. Philosophical texts were regularly introduced both in the quadrivium (arithmetic, geometry, astronomy, and music) and the trivium (grammar, logic, and rhetoric). With the rise of the Medieval universities and the recovery of Greek texts in the twelfth and thirteenth centuries, the great philosophical works of antiquity and Medieval Islam were transforming; students eagerly absorbed these works. In this period and the fourteenth century, the systematic works of the great Medievals (especially

Aquinas, Scotus, and Ockham) were written. Philosophy (or philosophical theology) was the centerpiece of university education.

With the Renaissance, the success of Copernican astronomy, and the development of mathematical physics, came the rise of Modern Philosophy and the "canonical" texts of Descartes, Spinoza, Leibniz, Locke, Berkeley, Hume, and Kant. Along with ancient and late Medieval texts, they were standard fare for the universities of Europe. Kant was a bridge between earlier Modern Philosophy and the major figures of the nineteenth century, notably Hegel, Mill, Kierkegaard, Marx, and Nietzsche. In the late nineteenth and early twentieth centuries, America contributed the great Pragmatists: Peirce, James, and Dewey. In the twentieth century the great figures of so-called "analytic" philosophy emerged, including Russell, Moore, the Vienna Positivists, and Wittgenstein—as well as the towering continental figures of Husserl and Heidegger.

The earliest American universities gave a central place to philosophy (along with philosophical theology). The nation's founders were educated in the classics and familiar, especially, with major works in political philosophy. As American colleges and universities organized into recognizable departments, philosophy was separated from "natural philosophy" (physics and biology) and, later, from psychology (arguably giving birth to the latter). Though continuous with earlier philosophical education, the organization of the study of philosophy into the "major" is a fairly recent phenomenon, having been initiated in America only in the last quarter of the nineteenth century.

For a decade or so after World War II, American philosophy was heavily influenced by Vienna Positivism. Taking an ahistorical interpretation of physical science as its model for philosophy, Positivism emphasized empiricism and logical techniques. It excluded from philosophy whatever resisted treatment within the positivist paradigm: competing philosophical approaches, traditional humanistic concerns, and large speculative issues.

In the 1960s and 1970s, American philosophers began to reclaim the traditional roles of philosophy, especially in discussing normative and cultural issues. The 1980s have seen increasingly diverse philosophical developments, including (to name just a few) renewed discussion of metaphysics; a revival of American pragmatism; reinvigorated discussion of public policy issues; much dialogue with continental philosophers; cooperative research between philosophy of mind and psychology, linguistics, and neurobiology; the integration of history of science with philosophy of science; and the articulation of feminist perspectives in philosophy.

BASIC ELEMENTS FOR A MAJOR IN PHILOSOPHY

Like other fields, then, philosophy has seen many developments. Change in the field, however, need not translate into irreconcilable disagreements about what should be taught in philosophy departments or even about the core of what should be required of philosophy majors. Throughout its history, philosophy has willingly confronted challenging alternatives, encouraging and thriving on criticism. Some of the great philosophers have begun by explaining why all philosophy before them has been fundamentally misconceived. Such debate is essential to a well-structured course of study.

Perhaps the leading unifier among philosophers of the most disparate interests and persuasions is philosophy's unique relation to its own history, conceived not as a record of past error gradually yielding to present truth nor as a repository of sacrosanct masterworks, but rather as a set of responses to questions—responses to be understood in context, applied to current concerns where appropriate, and challenged by argument. Through these texts and issues, philosophers of any school,

even if they know little of one another's specific traditions, can communicate in a common discourse. These texts and issues include certain philosophers—Plato, Aristotle, Descartes, Hume, and Kant, to name some that most philosophers would think every undergraduate major should confront—and various problems central in major fields, such as (in alphabetical order) epistemology (theory of knowledge), ethics, logic, and metaphysics (ontology). These philosophers and philosophical problems should generally be encountered relatively early in the philosophy major. They can be studied in courses organized in a variety of ways, for example historically, by problems, or by fields; and they can be introduced in considerably less than half the twenty-seven to thirty semester credits typically allotted to a major (for example in a logic course, an ethics course, and two historical courses emphasizing metaphysics and epistemology: one in ancient Greek Philosophy and one in seventeenth- and eighteenth-century Modern Philosophy).

An almost limitless variety of different major programs is consistent with this recommendation and can be built from the elements it prescribes. For example, a course of study might go on to emphasize the relation of Western to Eastern thought; or applied philosophy, including applied ethics; or the inter-face between philosophy and some other discipline; or the challenge of postmodernism; or logic and philos-ophy of science. As philosophers trained in diverse traditions, we val-ue this variety and would resist any attempt to impose an orthodoxy on major programs. Indeed, we recog-nize that institutions as well as indi-vidual faculty members and students may have interests or needs that re-quire divergent applications of our recommendations. There are also wide differences between schools of other kinds, for example secular and sectarian or research-oriented and vocational. Our recommendations are compatible with disparate institu-tional missions and circumstances.

It is important that any full set of major requirements incorporating the recommendations have a clearly articulated rationale. This statement and the accompanying recommenda-tions are written partly in order to help departments in developing such a rationale.

ALTERNATIVE CONCEPTIONS OF THE PHILOSOPHY MAJOR

Any student majoring in philosophy should develop some knowledge of the history and current state of the discipline, a grasp of representative philosophical issues, a capacity to apply philosophical methods to intel-lectual problems, and a sense of how philosophy bears on other disciplines and on human life in general. Com-pletion of a good philosophy major should develop in the student a criti-cal mind; a balance of analytic and synthetic abilities; a proficiency in doing focused research; a knowledge of the history, problems, and meth-ods of the field; and a capacity for the imaginative development of both abstract formulations and their con-crete applications.

The goals of philosophical study are sought in different ways by dif-ferent programs, but there are some reasonable models which, though they can and frequently should be combined, are often individually dominant in some schools or in the teaching of some faculty members. These models may inform either in-dividual courses or major programs as a whole, and they apply to any level in undergraduate teaching.

☐ The historical model emphasizes the history of philosophy. As applied to the major as a whole, it usually begins with the pre-Socratics or Pla-to; it traces and critically discusses certain views, problems, or methods; and it sometimes places philosophers or their ideas in a broad cultural setting.

☐ The field model stresses coverage of major fields and, so far as possi-ble, subfields. Typically, ethics, histo-ry of philosophy, logic, metaphysics, and the theory of knowledge are taken to be the basic fields, and their subfields—together with major areas such as aesthetics, philosophy of religion, and philosophy of science—often have the strongest secondary role.

☐ There also is a problems model. Here, understanding major philosophical issues is central, usually including at least the mind-body problem, the challenge of skepticism, the free will issue, and the problem of objectivity in ethics.

☐ A close relative of the problems conception of the major is the activity model. According to this view, doing philosophy is primary; hence, methodology is stressed and the main aim is to learn how to approach a philosophical problem or text. Resolution of problems need not be achieved; the process of inquiry is considered more important than the product.

Philosophy major programs quite properly vary a great deal with the kind of institution offering them; with the orientation, size, and scholarly commitments of the faculty; and with the needs and interests of the students. But many programs pursue goals associated with these four models. All four express worthy ideals, and a strong major program should reflect each of the models in some way.

THE STRUCTURE AND REQUIREMENTS OF A MAJOR IN PHILOSOPHY

Philosophy major programs should (and commonly do) require courses in the basic fields and historical courses in Greek Philosophy (usually including Plato, Aristotle, and the pre-Socratics) and in Modern Philosophy (typically including the great seventeenth-century rationalists—Descartes, Leibniz, and Spinoza—the great empiricists of the seventeenth and eighteenth centuries—Locke, Berkeley, and Hume—and, at the end, Kant). Additional requirements can fill in historical gaps, for example in the Stoics and Epicureans, in Medieval Philosophy, and in nineteenth-century philosophy (including at least Hegel, Kierkegaard, Marx, and Nietzsche). Several of the great philosophers should be studied in depth, for example Plato and Aristotle for their metaphysics of form and matter and their ethics of virtue, Aquinas for philosophical theology and natural law ethics, Descartes for skepticism and his opposing rationalist epistemology, Hume for his empiricist account of causation and his bundle theory of the self, Kant for his ontology of the noumenal and phenomenal and his deontological ethics, and Mill for his radical empiricism in epistemology and his utilitarianism in ethics.

Whether through historical studies like these or independently, major philosophical problems should be discussed. How, for example, is thought related to its bodily, historical, and linguistic contexts? Is it a brain phenomenon? Is it historically conditioned? And does it require language?

In addition to addressing the history of the subject, a philosophy program should attend to basic fields; we stress, however, that there is no necessity to cover them in courses bearing the names of those fields. A program arranged around the study of historically influential texts could hardly escape traversing basic philosophical fields since many of those texts are studies in these fields. Moreover, basic fields can be explored through the philosophical problems associated with them—say, ontology in relation to the mind-body problem or ethics in relation to moral objectivity.

Here is a schematic example of one kind of pattern a good program might have.

☐ First two years (or the sophomore year for the many students who do not begin philosophy courses earlier): an introduction to philosophy (often historically organized) and an introduction to logic

☐ Second year: a two-semester sequence with (ancient) Greek Philoso-phy in the first term and (modern) seventeenth- and eighteenth-century philosophy in the second, together with at least one less-comprehensive course, such as aesthetics, ethics, philosophy of mind, political philosophy, or philosophy of religion

☐ Third year: intermediate to advanced courses, often in required fields, such as ethical theory, metaphysics, or theory of knowledge

☐ Fourth year: moderately specialized courses, often seminars and possibly restricted to senior majors. These might range over fields or subfields, say metaethics (the theory of ethics), philosophy of language, philosophy of mathematics, philosophy of history, or the pragmatism of Peirce, James, and Dewey. They might address special topics, such as the relation between morality and law or between reason and society; the importance of gender, class, and race for social justice; the structure of perception; non-Western thought; the nature of universals; the problem of personal identity; the relation between faith and reason; the distinction between facts and values; mentalistic explanations of action; the criteria of aesthetic evaluation and interpretation; and feminist theories in epistemology and social-political philosophy. And they might focus on major figures not usually treated in detail in required courses, for instance Augustine, Reid, Frege,

Husserl, Whitehead, Russell, Heidegger, and Wittgenstein.

A department may offer capstone courses for majors, perhaps as senior seminars. There may be little or no distinction, however, between junior and senior levels, and many Ph.D.-granting departments combine part of the upper end of their major program with first-year graduate offerings. Additional variability occurs because many students who major in philosophy do not select it until their sophomore or even junior year. This may call for special advising to determine in what order students should meet requirements. Moreover, given how little precollege exposure to philosophy most undergraduates have and how late many decide to concentrate in it, philosophy major programs should be completable within two-and-a-half to three years.

Honors programs and thesis requirements may enhance a good major in philosophy, but they are not necessary for it. A thesis may also be required as part of a capstone course for all majors or simply on a tutorial basis. Oral exams may be held on a thesis or as comprehensives, and written comprehensives may also be given, with or without providing students a list of questions for study beforehand from which some (or all) of the examination questions are derived. Similarly, a joint major, such as one in philoso-phy and religion, permits many curricular patterns. The combinations possible in joint majors can also be educationally rewarding, but even in a joint program the "basic elements" of a philosophy major, as described earlier, should be required.

Students majoring in philosophy should complement their philosophy courses with a balanced selection from other departments. Particularly in their first two years, philosophy students need a strong liberal arts background. This provides greater general knowledge, increased academic strength, and more to philosophize about.

Philosophy is, in part, a *meta-discipline*, as indicated by the long—and open-ended—list of "philosophy of" courses. It is concerned, for example, with methods, theories, and results in other fields. Hence, philosophy students should explore some other disciplines in depth. An interest in philosophy of science, for instance, should be complemented by courses in certain of the sciences; philosophy of language can be informed both by linguistics and by the study of foreign language; philosophy of mind is complemented by courses in psychology, biology, and literature; aesthetics should be supported by courses in the arts, including literature; an interest in feminism or African philosophy can be complemented by literature or political theory or psychology.

Requiring a minor can also help students explore another field or discipline in depth. The required minor, however, does not replace the value for students of a wider set of appropriate courses that complete and extend the philosophy major.

COGNITIVE DEVELOPMENT IN THE PHILOSOPHY MAJOR

Sequencing of courses can help to give depth to a major program, but there is no single way—and probably no best way—of ordering philosophy courses to guarantee that those who complete the sequence will achieve depth. Major philosophers should be read at every level in the curriculum; indeed, it may be impossible to achieve depth in the treatment of, say, Aristotle and Kant, at the senior level if the instructor cannot presuppose that they have been studied earlier. While it is useful for students to be acquainted with some of the major texts by Plato, Descartes, Berkeley, Hume, and Kant before beginning the general study of metaphysics—so they can place ontological issues in historical context—it is equally useful for them to have first acquired a generic overview of metaphysics as an aid to understanding the positions of these philosophers. In general, no one kind of philosophy course—for example historical,

field, problem, or activity—must logically precede study of any other. The relationships among these kinds of courses are dialectical, not developmental.

The study of philosophy is interactive in the sense that provisional criticism of one philosopher is often part of provisional sympathy to another. Philosophical education introduces, at every stage, all of the main kinds of knowledge some developmental psychologists reserve for the end stages of learning. This approach is unavoidable in working with traditional philosophical texts because of their content. Moreover, one reason why philosophy is stimulating and challenging is that it resists fragmentation of learning into separate stages or steps. For instance, any good philosophy course stresses both "separate" and "connected" knowing, as in drawing distinctions to mark differences and analogies to capture likenesses. Philosophical maturation is not a climb through discrete strata but a progressive integration of appreciative and critical approaches to problems and texts such as those commonly encountered in the student's first philosophy course.

A recent (nonscientific) survey confirms that most students of philosophy recognize that philosophy is taught integratively. Of the philosophy majors surveyed by AAC for this project (covering a limited but significant group of undergraduates), 83 percent said their philosophy courses usually emphasize ways to connect different kinds of knowledge. This compares with 55 percent of the total student population surveyed answering the same question about their major.

Quite apart from the structural device of systematic sequencing, philosophy major programs can apparently engender coherence through their overall content as well as their modes of instruction. Although only 44 percent of the philosophy students reported that their more advanced philosophy courses required information from earlier courses (as compared with 60 percent of the total of students surveyed) and only 50 percent reported that their more advanced courses required skills learned in earlier ones (as against 59 percent for the disciplines overall), 74 percent of philosophy majors responding to the project's informal survey reported a good understanding of what they were expected to learn and why, while only 57 percent of the total population of students surveyed made the same response. And 57 percent of the philosophy students (as compared with 43 percent of the students overall) said their course of study had helped them develop an overview of the discipline.

Perhaps most students who major in philosophy prefer cognitive endeavors that integrate different modes of learning to those that separate it into discrete steps. Philosophy majors may also be more academically confident than those in some other disciplines; in the AAC survey, 52 percent of philosophy majors reported having an overall college GPA of "A" (compared to 32 percent of the total group of students surveyed). This suggests it may be inadvisable to shift the burden of creating coherence away from the interaction between philosophy teachers and students in the belief that curricular structure alone suffices for, as opposed to merely supporting, the desired intellectual ends.

Moreover, as stressed earlier, students often come to philosophy late: fewer than 10 percent of the philosophy majors surveyed by AAC had declared that major as first-year students (compared to nearly 25 percent of the students overall). Accommodating so many students who enter philosophy at a more mature stage of their college careers would reduce the impact of rigid sequencing of major courses, even if sequencing were enforceable once the major is declared.

DIMENSIONS OF DEPTH
IN THE PHILOSOPHY MAJOR

Cognitive development in the philosophy major should ultimately lead to philosophical depth, which is a main goal in any sound major program. It is both traditional and reasonable to delineate the development of that depth in terms of a growing sophistication in treating philosophical periods, problems, or texts. Introductory work should introduce students to skills necessary for doing philosophy—specifically, the abilities to recognize a philosophical question and grasp a philosophical argument; read a philosophical text critically; engage in a philosophical discussion; and write a philosophical paper that uses skills of interpretation, argument, and library research. These skills can be developed in courses organized in any number of ways (historically, by problem, by field), but they require contact with original sources (not only textbooks), opportunities for discussion (not just lectures), and experience in writing papers (not only examinations). The primary aim of an introductory course, then, should not be "coverage" of a period, field, or set of problems, let alone of all of philosophy.

At the middle level, which presupposes that students have begun to develop the skills mentioned above, courses should generally be devoted to basic fields of philosophy, historical periods, areas where philosophy interacts with other fields of human experience and inquiry (for example philosophy of the arts, philosophy of history, philosophy of religion, philosophy of science), and areas where philosophy illuminates fundamental human or practical concerns (for example social justice, including such topics as race and gender, and applied and professional ethics, extending to areas such as environmental, medical, and business ethics).

Upper-level courses should pursue issues and texts of the sort just mentioned in more detail and with increasing sophistication. No part of philosophy is inherently more advanced than any other; many major texts can be read at any of the three levels. Students in advanced courses should also be encouraged to reflect on the nature of the discipline itself and on the varied paradigms and methods that challenge one another. For instance, depth in philosophy is promoted by students' discovering how similar philosophical problems arise in very different philosophical traditions and in fields as disparate as philosophy of language and ethics.

This suggests that students need access to a variety of courses in which this kind of discovery can occur. The more sophisticated the level of philosophical study, the more variety can be expected in students' approaches to the issues, both within a single class and within the major as a coherent course of learning. Consider, for example, the critical dimension. In lower- and middle-level courses, it is often introduced largely through one philosopher's critique of another, for instance Aristotle's of Plato, Kant's of Hume, and Heidegger's of Husserl. In upper-level courses, students are often asked to develop their own critiques. The latter courses also tend to rely on students' being able to place texts or problems in wider historical and conceptual contexts. Since both of these differences presuppose prior philosophical experience, it is important at the advanced level that students have the opportunity to take courses in which all or most of those enrolled have completed fairly extensive study in the discipline. Since amount of prior study presupposed, rather than specific content, is what defines upper-level work in philosophy, a prerequisite *number* of philosophy courses may be desirable even where no specific prerequisite courses are required.

There is inevitably some trade-off between depth and breadth, but within reasonable limits depth should have priority. From a good, even if narrow, foundation one can build and spread out; but too much coverage at the surface encourages dilettantism. A good understanding of a few of the great philosophers is better than a mere acquaintance with all of them. Depth should be achieved within an intelligible framework that connects importantly similar phenomena without obscuring fundamental differences. A philosopher too eager to subsume related phenomena under a wider category is prone to miss truths distinctive of each; one too preoccupied with distinctions may fail to achieve theoretical insight or generalizable knowledge. Intellectual growth should be cumulative and integrated, not a collection of isolated analyses of texts or issues.

Philosophers often have emphasized a distinction between knowing *that* and knowing *how*. Both are crucial to depth in the major program. Knowledge of ideas and texts has limited value without the capacity to use it in resolving problems; and a capacity to use philosophical methods, when isolated from knowledge of the history and problems of philosophy, is needlessly narrow in application and may sometimes result in wasted energy used to reinvent the wheel. To be sure, one may retain the methodological and technical know-how acquired in a good major long after forgetting the labors from which it was gained. We can remember how to identify and assess argumentation in a text without remembering the works that served as models, and we can learn to frame hypotheses even if the process is so automatic that we are unaware of having ever learned it. But such know-how is unlikely to be gained apart from achieving—at least once—a thorough knowledge of the kinds of writers and problems that provide the raw material for acquiring it.

The dimension of knowing how—of competences—is multifarious. The major in philosophy should stress the capacities for effective and critical reading, writing, and speaking. The study of philosophy teaches the interpretation of texts, the balanced exposition of issues, the appraisal of arguments, the criticism of doctrines, and the construction of explanatory theories. Through the selection of readings and problems, through the painstaking criticism of students' writing, and through dialogue with them, philosophy majors can be given practice in exercising all of these capacities. Particularly as they advance in the program, they should be asked to read and reread, to write and rewrite, and, in class, to question and argue. For these aims to be realized, small classes are immensely helpful and sometimes essential.

After completing a philosophy major, then, students should possess developed skills in formulating questions; reading philosophical texts; extracting, inventing, and evaluating

philosophical arguments; and discussing philosophical ideas. They should have a reasonably extensive knowledge of at least some major figures, fields, and problems; and they should have engaged in some self-conscious reflection on philosophy, its methods, and its role in human culture. There is, however, no one kind of product that should emerge from the philosophy major, any more than there is some single subject or style appropriate for all good painting.

There is a further dimension of depth, one that is not teachable in any prescribed way and must be modeled. It is imagination. Without it students cannot make creative contributions or move from facts to insights. That deficiency is especially crippling in philosophy, but imagination is a highly general capacity needed for success in any complex endeavor.

A major in philosophy should develop students' imagination in at least three areas. First, there is the critical domain of counterexamples to falsehoods, of inferred consequences of a claim that reduce it to absurdity, and of analogies which highlight defects that might otherwise pass unnoticed. Second, there is the realm of responsiveness to concrete cases; here, imagination is needed to give discriminating and illuminating phenomenological descriptions of experience. Students should be drawn into the world of a text or theory and learn how it feels to live there. Third, there is theory building. It takes constructive imagination to frame accounts of the nature of explanation, freedom, intentionality, justice, justification, meaning, necessity, obligation, truth, and valuation, and to unify positions in one area with those in another (for example ethics with ontology). Students should be encouraged to strike out on their own and risk creative theorizing. Nothing stimulates imagination in philosophy like exposure to faculty members doing what they are excited about from their own research, and it is essential to a good major program that instructors be allowed to teach in areas of their own philosophical work.

A good major program will stimulate the imagination in both expository and critical tasks. Particularly in advanced courses, students should learn to develop their own positions. While they appropriately may begin with important texts, they also should extend, refine, or even replace others' positions. For some, especially in their last two years, it may be desirable to assign a long-term research project carrying three to six credits, with early drafts criticized, expanded, and polished. More than one instructor might participate in guiding these projects, and they can be designed

both to complement students' interests in the major and to enhance their understanding of fields related to their project.

Student research can also provide a way to judge the success of the major, and it may be useful in this context to compare writings done by students at various stages in the program. Certainly this kind of test of mastery, based on a student's sustained efforts, is the appropriate sort of measure. Philosophical learning is not properly judged by multiple-choice tests, nor is there any certifiable content that every reasonable department of philosophy must agree should be covered in examinations.

The philosophical activities that can yield depth in the major are aided immeasurably by the development of a philosophical community: a group of students and faculty members engaging in cooperative inquiry. Students of philosophy should not be mere observers of it but participants in the dialectic of interpretation and argument. Departmental activities such as informal discussions, as well as presentations of lectures and papers, help immensely in developing a philosophical community. The existence of such a community can make philosophy much more attractive to students who otherwise might not pursue it. This applies particularly to students from groups now underrepresented in philosophy. In addition to structuring courses in a way that helps minority students see the bearing of philosophy on the full range of human experience, faculty members can interact with them individually and provide occasions for all interested undergraduates to come together for discussions and other activities. For this purpose, a common room where informal discussions develop among students and faculty members is often of inestimable value. Initiative in the development of a philosophical community may have to come from the faculty; momentum may have to come from students. Philosophy applies in countless ways to the world outside the classroom; it should be practiced accordingly.

THE PHILOSOPHY MAJOR IN A LIBERAL ARTS PROGRAM

Philosophy is a basic field of inquiry. The discipline is not part of or reducible to any other; no other discipline uses the same set of techniques and methods; and there is a distinct, though open-ended, range of important problems that philosophy treats. As traditionally conceived, philosophy differs from the sciences both conceptually and methodologically; but even if the distinction should lie only in the greater generality of philosophical questions and the rela-

tively indirect way in which empirical data bear on them, philosophy would remain a basic field. As such, and because of the importance of the ideas and problems it addresses, it is essential in a liberal education. Ignorance of it is a deficiency in such an education; excellence in philosophy fulfills a leading ideal of liberal education.

A liberal education is best understood in contrast with vocational training. The former develops capacities important for life as a whole; the latter develops chiefly skills required for some kind of work. In preparation for life as a whole, philosophy has an important role: properly studied, it equips one with critical and theoretical capacities—such as those developed in logic—applicable to any subject-matter whatever; it acquaints one with major problems—such as those in ethics—confronting every civilization; and it enhances the capacity for self-expression, the taste for exchange of ideas, and the ability to go on learning as new problems and new solutions—or pseudosolutions—arise. Socrates died for the ideal of respect for law. How is one to decide whether that ideal, or any other, is worth this price? This is one of the basic existential questions that the intensive study of philosophy can help one to answer.

If we distinguish between a narrowly vocational education—one directed toward a specific job—and a broadly vocational one—an education valuable in a career—then a good philosophical education is in this second way excellent vocational preparation. Many of the capacities it develops are important in any job and particularly in the professions: the ability to communicate effectively, to solve problems, and to assess proposed plans of action; the capacity to process new information and to separate the irrelevant or misleading from the essential; and the imagination to devise new approaches to life's unpredictable challenges. If this century has brought increasing specialization to the jobs awaiting college graduates, it has also taught us that specialized education is quickly outdated and that the only solid preparation for a rapidly changing world is the capacity to learn as one goes and to apply sound principles to new problems. The mastery of philosophy achieved in a good major can contribute distinctively and substantially to developing this intellectual resilience.

Just as a sound liberal education, directed toward a range of knowledge and capacities, is excellent preparation for a career, it is important for the tasks of citizenship. This is a period in which political participation by Americans is often insufficiently informed, highly manipulable by the media, and vulnerable to demagoguery. A good philosophical education, though it provides no guarantee that its recipients will be responsible citizens, enhances their capacity to participate responsibly in political and community affairs.

RECOMMENDATIONS

Given the conception of philosophy sketched above and the role of philosophy in a liberal education, a number of recommendations are appropriate. These apply differently to different institutions. Properly applied, however, they can help both in achieving depth in the major and in integrating it into a sound general education.

☐ Balance. *A good philosophy major will draw appropriately on the models described above*—the historical, field, problems, and activity models—without allowing any to exclude the main virtues of the others. It should, therefore, achieve historical adequacy, with emphasis both on major periods and on evoking a sense of historical connectedness among authors, issues, and positions; examine basic fields, including at least epistemology, ethics, logic, and metaphysics (though not necessarily in courses so named); produce a knowledge of philosophical problems, especially those—like the grounds of moral obligation and the nature of the good life—which are at once central in philosophy and important to educated people; and develop in students a solid capacity to do philosophy in relation to an appropriate range of authors, problems, and general topics.

☐ Breadth. *The major should not be devoted mainly to preparing students for graduate work in philosophy,* though a good major in fact will do this. It is often appropriate to recommend or require for the major courses that also figure in a service program, such as introductions and some more advanced courses in areas of wide interest—for example philosophy of religion, philosophy of art, philosophy of science, and social-political philosophy. Even courses chiefly for majors should be taught with a sense of the wider values of the subject, not only as preprofessional education. This constraint need not diminish rigor and is compatible with an emphasis on contemporary issues or on the history of philosophy.

☐ Diversity. *The major should take account of diversity in various forms*: in the philosophical points of view appropriately given curricular prominence; in the range of students taught, with their differences in talents, interests, ethnicity, gender, and race; and in the selection of courses for majors. Within the limits of faculty interests and expertise, the offerings should be wide, extending

beyond any one philosophical tradition and beyond Western philosophy. The major requirements should be structured so that the program serves not only students planning graduate work but also those pursuing philosophy out of intellectual interest or as part of a double major.

☐ Unity. *A good major hangs together.* It develops a sense of historical continuity or, if appropriate, discontinuity; it compares and contrasts different philosophers; it treats certain central problems in relation to different thinkers and different periods, methods, or collateral fields; it seeks to explain similarities and differences within a comprehensive framework; and it develops a conception of the methods and goals appropriate to the overall field of philosophy.

☐ Integration. *The major should be internally integrated by patterns of content, by methods of teaching, and by pacing, and externally integrated with the nonphilosophical curriculum by complementary courses in related fields*—say, in the arts (including literature) and the sciences, history and religious studies, languages and mathematics, economics and psychology. This integration with other fields should place philosophy in a coherent vision of the liberal arts. Such integration may be associated with a required minor in another field and may be achieved more or less prescriptively, for example by designating certain courses as appropriate collateral studies or simply by advising an appropriate set.

☐ Structure. *Structure should be provided mainly by instituting the first five recommendations in a reasonable way tailored to the special goals of the program.* Sequencing may help in this but cannot by itself provide adequate structure; and while we have sketched some patterns, there is no single pattern we recommend for all programs.

☐ Requirements and electives. *The major program should leave room for electives both in and outside of philosophy, and the department's electives should be planned in a way that complements the requirements*, for example by supplementing rather than simply reinforcing required courses and by providing, at different levels—particularly the advanced—exposure to topics not treated extensively in the required curriculum. Especially if the requirements are permissive, advising may be crucial; but advising is in any case an important part of a good major program, particularly in philosophy, which is immensely broad and less hierarchically structured than a number of other disciplines.

☐ Depth. *A desirable outcome for philosophy majors is depth.* They should, for example, achieve an articulate understanding of at least some of the great philosophers, representing more than one period; of at least several major philosophical problems; and, in those contexts, of selected methods of philosophical inquiry. They should emerge able to read philosophical works, research intellectual problems, critically appraise philosophical arguments, and frame some philosophical explanations of their own.

☐ Communication skills. *Special emphasis should be given to developing students' writing skills*; specifically, in addition to essay examinations, instructors should assign papers and comment on them in detail. Critical as well as expository writing should be taught, with due emphasis on how to do both in a single essay; and some courses should require students to consult the literature and document a paper accordingly. Speaking in class should also be encouraged; advanced students, at least, generally benefit from giving class presentations, even if they are brief responses to an assigned question or part of a research team effort by a small group of students. Small classes are important for these and other goals of the philosophy major.

☐ Programs and resources. Given that philosophy is a dialectical discipline and that many of its rewards come from developing ideas through discussion, *students should have the opportunity to hear papers presented and appraised.* Ideally, some of these papers would be designed for an undergraduate audience and distributed for study beforehand. It can be especially valuable for students and faculty members to have visiting philosophers as resources on important topics or on subjects not adequately covered in their own department. *Panels and debates are also desirable.* They can enhance ongoing courses and enrich the kind of philosophical community that may contribute immeasurably to philosophical growth. ☐ Review and rationale. *Both the major requirements and the advising system should be periodically reviewed in relation to one another.* Departments should provide a statement of rationale for their major and bear it in mind not only in introducing and advertising their courses but also in constructing them and in patterning them from the introduction(s) through intermediate and advanced offerings.[2] There are many ways to adapt the foregoing recommendations to the needs of specific students, faculties, and institutions, and it is the responsibility of each department to justify its major program as a selection from the myriad possibilities suggested above.

CONCLUSION

Philosophy is a basic field of inquiry, and a major program in the subject should produce students who are competent in using its methods and have a general knowledge of its history, subfields, and problems. Its range encompasses ideas and issues in every domain of human existence, and its methods apply to problems of an unlimited variety. The major in philosophy can develop not only philosophical capacities but also critical and constructive abilities that are readily applicable to pursuits in other academic areas and indispensable in careers far removed from philosophy. These abilities to interpret positions, critically appraise ideas and issues, synthesize disparate strands of a problem, and frame alternative solutions are also incalculably useful in everyday life. A successful program of philosophical study should profoundly affect both the thinking one does and the kind of person one is.

1. The task force that prepared this report included Robert Audi, University of Nebraska–Lincoln; Gary Iseminger, Carleton College; Anita Silvers, San Francisco State University; Laurence Thomas, Syracuse University; and Merold Westphal, Fordham University.

Earlier drafts were presented at the three 1989–90 divisional meetings of the American Philosophical Association. The committee is grateful for the comments and suggestions received on those occasions, as well as from the APA Board of Officers at its meeting in October 1989 and others attending AAC's task force meeting in February 1990. The document is not, however, an APA Board statement, and while the authors have adopted suggestions from many sources, the final product represents their own work.

Special thanks are due to George Bailey, Baruch Brody, Albert Casullo, Byron Haines, David Hoekema, Philip Hugly, Jaegwon Kim, Hugh McCann, Martha Nussbaum, Philip Quinn, Thomas Satre, Carol Schneider, Charles Scott, and particularly Robert Turnbull, who contributed greatly to the historical sketch.

2. The American Philosophical Association's *Philosophy: A Brief Guide for Undergraduates* addresses this need.

CHAPTER SEVEN

PHYSICS[1]

THE CURRENT SITUATION

The physics major builds in a highly sequential manner on a calculus-level introductory course. Students must take this introductory course early in their college careers in order to complete a physics major in four years, though they need not declare their major until later. Students in other technical fields, such as chemistry and engineering, also must begin early. In fact, preparation for success in these fields begins well before college. Those who do not participate in high school mathematics and science programs that prepare students for college study rarely succeed in the physics major. Most college-bound high school seniors are not prepared adequately to succeed in the typical introductory physics course. Less than 20 percent of entering college freshmen have taken high school physics and are prepared to take calculus as a corequisite in college.

In the 1960s and 1970s the number of bachelors' degrees in physics dropped by almost 50 percent. In the 1980s the number of students graduating each year with a bachelor's degree in physics began to recover, from a low of forty-four hundred to fifty-two hundred. About 15 percent of the bachelor's degree recipients are women. Black students represent 3.5 percent, Hispanics 1 percent, and Asians 4.4 percent of all physics majors.[2] About one-third of all physics majors go to graduate school in physics. Another 20 percent go to graduate or professional school in some other area such as engineering, law, or medicine. About 40 percent obtain civilian sector jobs: 25 percent in industry, 11 percent with government agencies, 4 percent in high school teaching.[3] Seven percent enter military service. These percentages have been remarkably stable over the past decade, even while the number of majors has increased by almost 20 percent. In spite of the recent increases in the number of students majoring in physics, a severe shortage of physicists is likely in the next decade as many retire from industrial and teaching positions at all levels.

GOALS OF THE PHYSICS MAJOR PROGRAM

The physics major program provides depth through sequential study. Some of the goals of the physics major can be stated in terms of the curriculum described in the next section. Other goals, stated more generally, include:

☐ Understanding the nature of scientific reasoning in considerably greater depth than can be achieved in a single course. The physics student should understand that progress in science depends on disciplined search and discovery, false starts, inspired guesses, accidents, controversy, and available technology. Changes in the theories and models of physics fit within a well-defined framework, after they have been tested against a large body of experimental results.

☐ Understanding the concepts and methods of physics. Students should be able to use these concepts and methods in fairly sophisticated ways to solve both theoretical and experimental problems.

☐ Being able to connect concepts and representations (such as graphs, diagrams, and equations) to objects in the real world; to make quantitative models of real-world processes,

whether from physics or not; and to deduce reasonable numerical estimates for quantities from the information at hand.

THE PHYSICS MAJOR CURRICULUM

There is remarkable uniformity in the undergraduate physics major program, not only in the United States but around the world.[4] A one- or two-year introductory course surveying five basic subjects begins the major. These subjects—the roots of which lie in the late nineteenth and early twentieth centuries—are mechanics, heat, electricity and magnetism, optics and waves, and quantum physics. Students take six to twelve additional semester courses, which constitute 25 to 35 percent of the credits for the degree.

For the physics major in either a research university or a small college, a curriculum leading to the bachelor of arts or bachelor of science in physics includes a core of intermediate courses in these same five areas. There may be a difference of emphasis, but these five subjects are always there.[5]

Additional topics in required or elective courses may include acoustics and the physics of mechanical waves, computational physics, relativity, advanced experimental techniques, atomic physics, solid state physics, nuclear physics, elementary particle physics, lasers and modern optics, and fluid dynamics. The fact that textbooks for these courses exist and are widely used attests to the uniformity of the physics curriculum.

The structure of the physics curriculum is often referred to as a spiral. The five core subjects are revisited at least twice and often a third time in the elective and specialty courses. Each course in the sequence is necessary for courses at the next level. The intermediate and advanced courses address the core subjects with increasing conceptual complexity and mathematical sophistication, synthesizing from all that have gone before. Prior study of the core is a necessary prerequisite for the elective courses.

In order to have the mathematical proficiency to complete the courses in their own field, physics majors study calculus through multivariable calculus and vector analysis, differential equations, and linear algebra. More advanced physics courses also require mastery of partial differential equations and complex variables. Although many of these topics may be treated in physics courses as well, the typical student majoring in physics takes at least five or six semesters of mathematics courses.

The introductory course for the major

The calculus-based introductory course is a gateway to careers in physics, the physical sciences, and engineering. (Only one in thirty students completing the introductory physics course majors in physics.) In addition to serving as the basis for the physics major, it is often required of majors in other physical sciences and engineering and some premedical and biological science majors.[6] Having a single, introductory, calculus-based course gives students the option of majoring in many different fields, even after completing the course.

Having only one course leading to further work in physics creates difficulties for some students, faculty members, and institutions. It is a hurdle that some students fail to cross; those who do not complete it successfully cannot continue in physics or in many other fields. The small fraction of students going on to major in physics suggests that the introductory course often acts to select students who already have developed some skill in a certain kind of reasoning. The introductory course may sharpen these skills, but it cannot claim to have developed them. Regardless of the reason, a disproportionate number of underrepresented minority students do not succeed in these courses.[7] Relatively few women choose to continue in physics. Students may have difficulty because of inadequate mathematics and physics preparation or because of poor study habits. Other students may be discouraged from taking additional physics courses because they are not attracted by the limited presentation of physics in this introductory course or its limited choice of topics.

To the extent that the introductory course serves as a barrier, it can be a critical problem for physics departments in smaller institutions that may not have enough majors to justify staffing of the major curriculum or to maintain faculty and student morale.

While the five basic subjects in the introductory course have remained the same over the last few decades, there have been changes in emphasis and presentation. Changes have resulted from many efforts at discussion, revision, and development of the introductory courses at local and national levels and from recent advances in physics.[8] Modern discoveries often enter the course as changes in emphasis, as additions to traditional topics, or as applications or illustrations of basic principles and concepts.

Modern computers, word processing, and computer-aided instructions have not yet had a widespread influence on the way physics is taught

nationally.

Direct experience with physical phenomena is an essential part of learning physics. Physics inherently involves observation, measurement, modelling, and abstraction of the natural world. The purpose of demonstrations and laboratory experimentation is to form the basis of organized experience upon which students can test models and explanations of nature. Students also must learn how to record, measure, and analyze the behavior of natural systems. Because there always is an imperfect match between theories and the real world, which students should appreciate, it is clear that simulation of experiments (now possible with computer software) does not provide an adequate experience. However, computer-aided data acquisition and computer-aided analysis and presentation of results can free students from tedious calculations and allow them to address methodologies and concepts in experimentation.

Intermediate and advanced laboratory experience

Every undergraduate physics major program must provide laboratory experience at the intermediate and advanced levels. This instruction is more difficult, more time consuming for students and instructors, and more costly than laboratory instruction in the introductory course. Pressures to substitute cheaper devices and cheaper methods or less direct faculty involvement must be resisted. They would trivialize an essential portion of the complex teaching and learning experience for the students.

In addition to the goals of the introductory laboratory, the goals of the advanced laboratories are to ensure that students experience classic physics experiments and phenomena and are introduced to advanced technologies so that paradigms in courses and instrumentation used in research are not strangers. Advanced physics students must have additional direct contact with the problems associated with measuring physical phenomena: choosing appropriate measuring techniques, getting equipment to work, assuring proper calibration, making measurements, analyzing data to extract desired information, and inferring explanations of the behavior.

Specialization

An important aspect of the physics major is that it encourages a broad view of the discipline rather than a specialized concentration. Bachelor's degrees ordinarily are given in physics rather than any subspecialty such as nuclear physics or condensed matter physics. Specialization in physics begins only in the second or third year of graduate study. Any pressure for early specialization in physics undergraduate curricula should continue to be resisted. The hallmark of the physicist must continue to be broad training and the ability to synthesize models and methods from a wide range of experience with the natural world.

The range of six to twelve semester courses for the major provides for varying degrees of preparation for different kinds of careers. While those clearly directed to graduate school may choose to take still more advanced course work and research, these options are not available at all colleges and universities. It is recognized increasingly that such additional courses are not essential for admission to graduate programs.

CONNECTIONS WITH OTHER FIELDS

There are many connections between physics and other fields. Many students who receive bachelor's degrees in physics go on to postbaccalaureate study in other disciplines such as mathematics, astrophysics, geophysics, atmospheric sciences, oceanography, materials science, engineering, chemical physics, and so on. Many departments in smaller institutions use colloquia and visitor programs to enrich the education of their students about related fields; research universities could well do the same thing.

The use of mathematics in physics courses provides a strong link between physics and mathematics and requires that physics students take several college mathematics courses. Students and faculty members would be better served if there were increased dialogue between physics and mathematics faculty members. Discussions could lead to more coherent design or revision of courses and prerequisites. Physics faculty members need to enrich their courses with a greater appreciation for and presentation of the mathematical mode of approaching problems.

Usually there is nothing in the curriculum about the history, philosophy, and social implications of physics. There are three ways to include these topics: as part of an existing course, as additional courses in physics, or as courses in other departments. History and philosophy of physics often are best taught by professional historians and philosophers of physics.

INTEGRATIVE EXPERIENCES

There is a unity and a logical structure to physics, a set of intimate connections among its branches. Indeed, unity has been, perhaps, the dominant theme in the attempts to understand the physical universe since

Newton (to oversimply his accomplishment) demonstrated that terrestrial objects such as apples obey the same natural laws as do moons and planets. A century and a half later Oersted showed that electricity and magnetism are but two manifestations of the more basic phenomenon called electromagnetism. Later, Maxwell showed that light is a special example of electromagnetism. Often this unity is mathematical. Even introductory students learn that light waves and sound waves obey equations identical in form; what differs is the interpretation of the symbols.

Often only in the introductory course is there an attempt to survey the entire field and call attention to the unity of physics. As we have pointed out above, while later courses are topically more specialized, they remain related to the core because of the spiral structure of the curriculum. A capstone course, therefore, is not as appropriate for a physics curriculum as it is for those curricula which have either a pyramid structure or a tree-like structure that branches early into specialized subfields.

There are other approaches to integration, such as senior comprehensive examinations and undergraduate research. Many departments require a senior comprehensive examination, with the same examination usually taken by all seniors. The success of such examinations in persuading students to make a contemplative survey of their undergraduate experience varies widely among institutions. At some, the examination receives only perfunctory attention from students and faculty members. Elsewhere, tradition leads to its being taken more seriously. In some colleges and universities, more or less formal departmental structures exist to get senior majors together with each other, and perhaps with faculty members, to review for the examination. In such settings, senior comprehensives may stimulate mature insights into the multiple connections that exist within physics.

Quite a different sort of integration often is available in the form of research experience.[9] This may range from "helping out" in a professor's laboratory to a summer job in an academic or industrial laboratory to a year-long project for substantial credit culminating in a significant thesis, a public presentation by the student, and an oral "thesis defense." Such experiences may or may not provide an overview of the connections that pervade physics, but they do require integration of the skills and knowledge acquired over the years of undergraduate study. If properly structured they provide introductions to what practicing physicists do, introductions more honest and accurate than those usually provided through ordinary courses.

Pressures exist to eliminate research experience for undergraduates. If, for example, a senior thesis experience is sufficiently intense and prolonged to provide a genuine introduction to what research really is like, it may take valuable slots from possible advanced courses that some may see as providing immediate payoff in terms of subject matter coverage or enhanced graduate school opportunities. The benefits of a senior thesis project are sufficient that these pressures should be resisted.

In some physics programs, no integrative experience is offered. Though the unity of physics may be grasped by the more perceptive student or pointed out from time to time by professors, departments that do not offer such experiences would do well to add them, even if that means offering fewer conventional courses. The change would benefit all their students: those who proceed to graduate study and those who do not.

WRITING AND SPEAKING

The importance of writing and speaking in the experience of students is widely recognized. There seem to be profound connections between analytical thinking and the ability to express ideas clearly. Students need practice in speaking and writing about physics. They need experience presenting ideas to specialists and nonspecialists. Many students have opportunities to make oral reports in advanced laboratory courses or in seminars. Students who have been involved in research experiences often have opportunities to present their work in formal oral presentations. Yet physics students generally do not have sufficient opportunity for oral presentation. Faculty members should modify their courses to provide this experience.

Only a handful of individual physics professors, furthermore, take it upon themselves to try to improve the writing of their students—insisting on clear, well-organized prose, assigning occasional papers, and including essay questions in examinations. There are at least a few institutions where clear writing is a recognized departmental responsibility. Many professors, however, are reluctant to criticize students' writing; some believe it is "inappropriate" for physicists to evaluate, let alone improve, the quality of their students' prose. The result, almost everywhere, is that the physics undergraduate rarely is asked to compose a paragraph or even a complete sentence except in writing a "lab report" whose evaluation is left to an unprepared and largely unsupervised teaching assistant. Physics has a major problem, but also a major opportunity, in this area.

RESEARCH ON HOW STUDENTS LEARN PHYSICS

During the past decade, physics faculty members and others have begun investigating student understanding in physics with the goal of improving physics instruction. They have identified some common conceptual and reasoning difficulties that students encounter in the study of physics—especially in mechanics, but also in other areas. Results from these investigations have been used to design instruction to address specific difficulties. This work is beginning to affect the teaching of introductory physics in high schools and colleges.

It is important that work on understanding how students learn be incorporated effectively into the training of physics faculty members and teaching assistants, that it be used to revise the methods of instruction in advanced courses in physics, and that it be used in the training of students intending to pursue careers as teachers. Further work needs to be done to help physics students understand the way physics is learned. There is growing recognition that improving the physics preparation of students entering college requires intervention in the preparation of precollege teachers. For physics majors preparing to teach, it is of great importance that their undergraduate study and the way they are taught reflect this research.

UNDERREPRESENTED AND UNDERPREPARED STUDENTS

Students who take introductory college physics without sufficient preparation in high school physics and mathematics have a very low success rate. As a result, the introductory course is a barrier to some majors. Physics, more than most fields, has a poor record of attracting underrepresented minorities and women as majors. This poor record may be linked substantially to the sequential nature of the physics curriculum and to the preparation required for students. Both social experiences and lack of science and mathematics preparation in high school can place women and minority students at a disadvantage.

Some programs have been developed that help underprepared students succeed in introductory physics courses. The students' difficulties go beyond mathematics. The development of conceptual understanding requires experiences on which the student can build the abstracted models of reality that physics requires. The difficulties that these students experience are no different in kind than those of all students; they differ only in magnitude.

Successful programs for these students require many additional hours of student-teacher contact each week for the first year or two of the students' college career.[10] Where programs involve additional preparatory course work, students invariably require more than four years for completion of a physics major.

To overcome this barrier it is important to design physics curricula that are more open to students with diverse preparations. In many institutions various introductory physics courses are designed to serve students with different career goals or disparate mathematics preparation. Unless there is a way to move from these courses into the major, however, students with weaker preparations may be excluded from any practical hope of pursuing physics majors. Role models and mentors—who can be peers—are needed in introductory and advanced courses to help women and underrepresented minority students recognize physics as a possible career.

OPTIONS IN THE MAJOR

Resources provided by the National Science Foundation in the 1960s allowed the physics community to examine its undergraduate curriculum systematically.[11] The curriculum recently has been reexamined at a conference sponsored jointly by the American Physical Society and the

American Association of Physics Teachers.[12] Both earlier and more recent deliberations recognized that preparation of students for graduate study in physics requires a somewhat different curriculum than does preparation for employment upon graduation or for graduate study in other disciplines.[13] These differences have been accommodated in some cases by different tracks within the major and in other cases by judicious choices of electives. However, they have not been implemented generally. The curriculum should provide some flexibility for students pursuing many different careers. This flexibility may include the ability for "late starters" to major in physics.

Some faculty members worry that students from smaller colleges do not do as well on the Graduate Record Examinations as those from major research universities and that preparation for the GRE constrains the curriculum. This worry is unfortunate. Research experience gives an undergraduate excellent preparation for graduate school and often is taken into account by graduate admissions committees.

REVIEW AND CHANGE OF THE CURRICULUM

The content of the major changes constantly but slowly. Changes usually do not require the introduction of new courses; repackaging of the standard components is more common. Details frequently change—as reflected, for example, in the increasing emphasis on symmetries and conservation laws. The quantum physics taught in 1990 is very different from that taught in 1965. Chaos in dynamical systems and computational physics are entering the curriculum in ways not imagined five years ago. The five basic areas always remain, however.

Several forums exist in which changes in the major are discussed at the national level. Local and regional organizations of physics faculty members meet with varying frequency. The American Association of Physics Teachers publishes two journals that include physics education as important parts of their content: *The American Journal of Physics* and *The Physics Teacher*. AAPT holds two national meetings each year at which aspects of the physics curriculum often are discussed. The American Physical Society, while concerned primarily with physics research, is interested in the undergraduate major. The American Institute of Physics and its other member societies also are involved with physics education.

THE ROLE OF COMPUTING IN PHYSICS

Access to powerful computing facilities for undergraduates is bringing great changes in physics. Here physics faces a dilemma. Analytical mathematical techniques—introduced in the seventeenth century and being refined even today—made possible the modern development of physics. These techniques allowed physics to progress without excessive dependence on detailed numerical calculation. Now that the technology for easy calculation exists, it is important that the analytical characteristics of physics be preserved at the same time that students become proficient using the computer to enlarge and improve their understanding of physics. The computer can be used for collecting and analyzing data, for complex calculations, for exploring the nature of the analytical solutions to problems, for complex simulations, and for attacking whole new classes of problems that were not solvable in the past. How to accomplish the integration of computing into the undergraduate major is an important question for the profession.

RECOMMENDATIONS

In the course of preparing this report the panel identified several areas in which it believes further action is desirable. These are identified in the following recommendations.

☐ In the 1960s there was a series of conferences and workshops, involving many members of the United States physics faculties, on the nature of the undergraduate physics curriculum.[14] More than a quarter of a century has passed since the recommendations of those extensive studies were published.

It is recommended that the physics community seek funding for a new national review, with similar detailed study and with similar broad participation.

☐ Some physics departments have studied their undergraduate curricula and prepared formal statements of goals which then are reviewed regularly.

It is recommended that all physics departments should consider the goals of their undergraduate programs and establish procedures for regular review.

☐ Revisions proposed for the introductory physics course are numerous and frequent. There is a tendency for such proposals to focus entirely on what physicists see as new, interesting, and central to their subject.

It is recommended that particular care be taken to ensure that the needs and requirements of the physics "clients" be taken fully into account.

☐ Integrative experiences for undergraduates, such as those described earlier in this report, are part of many undergraduate physics programs.

It is recommended that such experiences be made available to all physics majors and that students be encouraged to participate even if that requires some reduction of formal course work.

☐ While it is common in small physics departments in liberal arts colleges to enrich the students' knowledge of physics and closely related fields through participation in colloquia and seminars, this is less common in larger institutions.

It is recommended that such exposure to ideas outside the classroom be a part of every undergraduate physics program.

☐ Substantial progress has been made in clarifying student understanding in physics and associated learning problems.

It is recommended that the results already obtained be incorporated at all levels in the undergraduate physics program and that further research be extended to additional branches of physics and to later stages in the undergraduate program.

☐ There has been a shortage of high school teachers trained to teach physics for many years.

It is recommended that physics departments increase their direct participation in teacher training and, especially, that the physics component of that training include the results

mentioned in the preceding recommendation.

☐ The studies of the undergraduate physics curriculum of the 1960s emphasized the importance of providing in the undergraduate program for those graduates—a majority even then—who do not continue in physics graduate studies but proceed instead to employment or to other graduate and professional education.[15] Though some physics major programs do accommodate the needs of such students, many do not.

It is recommended that all undergraduate physics programs allow sufficient flexibility to help those students who might build, on a sound basis in physics, the preparation for work and study in related fields. We also recommend that it be possible for a student to choose the physics major as one element of a liberal arts degree.

☐ The advent of inexpensive, powerful, and convenient computers offers great opportunities for physics.

It is recommended that there be careful study of how such tools can be incorporated into the undergraduate physics program so as to enhance students' learning without separating the student from direct experience with the physical world.

☐ The ability to express ideas in writing is an important part of understanding physics.

It is recommended that frequent writing be required of physics students in a variety of physics contexts. This should involve more than writing laboratory reports graded by assistants who themselves have not been trained to judge writing. Students should be asked to express the ideas of physics in writing: in tests and examinations, in written papers, in graded class work.

☐ Oral presentation is an important part of the work of most physicists.

It is recommended that undergraduate physics courses be modified to provide much more opportunity for oral presentation by students.

☐ The traditional strong link between physics and mathematics, once very prominent in undergraduate physics programs, has eroded in recent decades.

It is recommended that physics faculties work to increase their dialogue with mathematics faculty members.

☐ Physics instruction, traditionally, has relied heavily on lectures and on separate laboratories.

It is recommended that there be consideration of alternative methods of presentation such as those now being developed on a few campuses.

☐ Both women and minority students are underrepresented among physics graduates.

It is recommended that more colleges undertake programs to encourage and assist students in these groups to prepare and to succeed as physics majors.

☐ The participation of underrepresented groups in the physics major appears to be related to insufficient high-school preparation in mathematics and physics.

It is recommended that undergraduate physics programs be made more flexible so that it is easier for students to enter the major after the freshman year and still complete degree requirements in four college years.

---

1. The panel that prepared this report included James B. Gerhart, University of Washington, (chair); Neal B. Abraham, Bryn Mawr College; Russell K. Hobbie, University of Minnesota; Lillian C. McDermott, University of Washington; Robert H. Romer, Amherst College; and Bruce R. Thomas, Carleton College.

Two of the organizations that provide forums for the discussion of the physics major in the United States are the American Association of Physics Teachers (AAPT) and the American Physical Society (APS). All the members of this panel belong to both organizations and have consulted broadly with their colleagues. Drafts of this report have been circulated to various committees of AAPT, the APS Committee on Education, and the American Institute of Physics. This report, however, represents the views of this panel.

2. Susanne D. Ellis and Patrick J. Mulvey, *Enrollment and Degrees*, AIP Pub. No. R-151.26 (New York: American Institute of Physics, 1989). This report is issued annually.

3. The number of students going into high school teaching declined sharply when fewer jobs were available. There is some evidence of renewed interest in a high school teaching career.

4. A detailed description of the curriculum and differences in approach is found in AAPT *Guidelines for the Review of Baccalaureate Physics Programs* (1987), prepared by the Committees on Professional Concerns and

on Undergraduate Education of the American Association of Physics Teachers, 5112 Berwyn Road, College Park, Maryland 20740.

5. For example, heat may be approached from the viewpoint of classical thermodynamics or statistical physics; the examples emphasized in quantum physics may differ.

6. Various courses that do not require concurrent calculus usually are available for students in still other majors. Occasionally physics majors begin their study in such courses.

7. African-American, Hispanic, native American, and Alaskan native students are underrepresented in science and engineering.

8. A number of efforts to revise parts, or even the whole, of the introductory college physics course are underway. The *American Journal of Physics* published seven articles, four editorials or guest comments, and twelve letters devoted to the calculus-level introductory course in 1988 and 1989. One well-publicized effort that is promoting controversial and vigorous discussion of the introductory course is the Introductory University Physics Project.

9. Research participation, which is of great benefit to the student, also may be a significant help for faculty members in spite of the expense in faculty time.

10. See, for example, L. C. McDermott, M. L. Rosenquist, and E. H. van Zee, "Strategies to Improve the Performance of Minority Students in the Sciences," in *New Directions in Teaching and Learning No. 16*, ed. J. H. Cones III, J. F. Noonan, D. Janha (San Francisco: Jossey-Bass, 1983); L. C. McDermott, L. K. Piternick, and M. L. Rosenquist, "Helping Minority Students Succeed in Science: I. Development of a Curriculum in Physics and Biology; II. Implementation of a Curriculum in Physics and Biology; III. Requirements for the Operation of an Academic Program in Physics and Biology," *Journal of College Science Teaching* (January, March, May 1980).

11. "Denver Conference," *American Journal of Physics* 30 (1962), 153; "Ann Arbor Conference," *American Journal of Physics* 31 (1963): 328; "Princeton Conference," *American Journal of Physics* 32 (1964), 491.

12. M. N. McDermott and J. M. Wilson, eds., *Physics for the 1990s: AAPT Conference of Department Chairs in Physics* (College Park, Md.: American Association of Physics Teachers, 1989).

13. "The Undergraduate Curriculum for Non-graduate Bound Majors," report of the department heads meeting, group G, in McDermott and Wilson, *Physics for the 1990s*.

14. "Denver Conference," *American Journal of Physics* 30 (1962): 153; "Ann Arbor Conference," *American Journal of Physics* 31 (1963): 328; "Princeton Conference," *American Journal of Physics* 32 (1964): 491.

15. *Ibid.*

POLITICAL SCIENCE[1]

The first premise of our report is our belief that the goal of liberal education is to develop students' general intellectual abilities—curiosity, powers of critical analysis, aesthetic appreciation, and creativity—thus equipping them "to master complexity," "to undertake independent work, and [to attain] critical sophistication."[2] Students' college programs, including their disciplinary major, should foster their intellectual growth along the nine dimensions listed by AAC in *Integrity in the College Curriculum* as constituents of liberal learning:

☐ inquiry, abstract logical thinking, critical analysis
☐ literacy: writing, reading, speaking, listening
☐ understanding numerical data
☐ historical consciousness
☐ science
☐ values
☐ art
☐ international and multicultural experiences
☐ study-in-depth.[3]

Our second premise is our conception of academic disciplines as distinct, principled, ordered, and unique bodies of knowledge and related methodologies. We believe, as AAC also has argued, that study-in-depth in a discipline entails sequential learning, "building on blocks of knowledge that lead to more sophisticated understanding and...leaps of the imagination and efforts at synthesis."[4] Depth of understanding cannot be reached "merely by cumulative exposure to more and more... subject matter." Such exposure "results in shallow learning unless students also grasp the assumptions, arguments, approaches, and controversies that have shaped particular claims and findings."[5]

The political science major "program," therefore, is not merely the roster of whatever courses happen to be in the college catalogue, the sum

REPORTS
FROM THE
FIELDS

of answers to questions such as, "What courses (and how many) will be offered? What will be the relationship among the courses (subgroupings, course levels, and sequencing)? Which courses (if any) will be required of all majors? What study in cognate disciplines (if any) should be required?"

Answers to questions about the formal structure of a program must rest on clear conceptions of the character of the discipline: its content, its methodology, its philosophical premises about the character and use of "knowledge" and how its knowledge relates to that of other disciplines, and the aims and objectives of educating undergraduate majors in those matters. Only such conceptions can guide and justify the curricular decisions entailed by college definitions of course- and credit-hour bookkeeping.

It is always tempting to respond to such questions by trying to design the ideal curriculum. Curricular decisions, however, are constrained by the college's general curricular structure and by limits imposed by the institution's and the department's human, financial, and material resources. Institutional characteristics such as size, sectarian or religious character, quality of faculty and student body also shape—even if they do not constrain—departmental program decisions. Figure 1, summarizing the character of political science programs and faculty size of 667 American institutions, indicates the great variety of institutional contexts of political science programs.

Clearly, it would be impossible to devise a detailed model political science major program that would be

FIGURE 1
TYPES OF POLITICAL SCIENCE DEPARTMENTS

DEGREE PROGRAM, FACULTY SIZE, ETC.	NUMBER
Ph.D.-granting departments with 21 or more faculty members	52
Ph.D.-granting departments with 20 or fewer faculty members	43
M.A.-granting departments with 11 or more faculty members	61
M.A.-granting departments with 10 or fewer faculty members	86
Undergraduate departments, public institutions	75
Undergraduate departments, private institutions	172
Undergraduate combined social science departments	172
Data not given	6
Total number of institutions	667

SOURCE: APSA Departmental Services Annual Report, Survey of Departments 1987–1988.

usable in more than a handful of departments. We have sought instead to examine common practices in the light of our conceptions of the goals of liberal education, the character of knowledge, and the state of the discipline of political science. Our recommendations should be read as suggested procedures for working toward the goals of liberal education in political science, not as a blueprint or outline for a political science major program.

THE PRIMARY TASK
OF THE MAJOR
IN POLITICAL SCIENCE

The first comprehensive statement of the aims and objectives of political study was the report of an American Political Science Association Committee on the Advancement of Teaching, published in 1951 as *Goals for Political Science*.[6] Although the committee gave some attention to the training of college teachers, it concentrated mainly on the discipline's undergraduate program. Its four-year study surveyed curricular practices of 252 institutions by questionnaire and by campus visits. The purposes of political study set forth in that report all serve the primary goal once called "civic education." They include, principally, "education for citizenship," "education for public service," and [correction of "woeful

public ignorance of] international relations."

Although we think sound political study is invaluable for American citizens, our emphasis is on its utility to citizens of any country in their social roles more broadly conceived. We think the goal for study in a political science major is to maximize students' capacity to analyze and interpret the dynamics of political events and governmental processes and their significance. The primary purpose is to equip them to cope with political events and governmental actions. "Cope with" in this context means not merely to understand actions and events, or to manage their effects, but also to evaluate and seek to shape them.

Particularistic knowledge of political problems, structures, and processes is insufficient for that purpose. Students also need the accumulated basic general knowledge of political science and related disciplines: knowledge about the impact of governmental actions on the world in which they live, what shapes and determines those actions, and what governmental actions can and cannot be expected to accomplish; and knowledge about the behavior of citizens, politicians, statespersons, and bureaucrats that affects governmental actions and their consequences. The use of such general knowledge requires students to develop analytic skills with which knowledge may be applied to particular political systems (their own and others).

In sum, the major in political science should be neither a preprofessional program to train political scientists nor a program to produce "good citizens." It should aim at turning politically interested and concerned students into politically literate college graduates, whatever their career plans or their other interests. In other words, it should aim at political education "in depth" for those liberal arts students who have a particular interest in things political, whatever their occupational and professional goals and whatever their other talents and interests.[7]

POLITICAL SCIENCE AS A DISCIPLINE

Some will say political education in depth, as we describe it, is an inappropriate goal because political science is too diversely conceptualized, organized, and taught to be considered a discipline. Admittedly, undergraduate political science programs today collectively present a picture of disparate and unstructured practices aptly described by the *Integrity* report's characterization of contemporary major programs in general: "As for what passes as a college curriculum, almost anything goes.... Today's majors are not so much experiences

in depth as they are bureaucratic conveniences."[8]

One indication of this diversity is the character and role of the introductory political science course in the major program. The 1987–88 APSA survey of 667 American institutions offering undergraduate degrees found that a general introduction to politics and government (comparable to, say, introductory psychology or physics) is required in only 50 percent, recommended in only 12 percent, and not offered in 37 percent of them.[9] At the same time, the list of other, more specialized, introductory-level courses required in one or another department is surprisingly long. Figure 2 summarizes the picture.[10]

The content knowledge a political science department hopes to impart usually is defined by distribution requirements. But the plasticity of definitions of subfields for this purpose is extraordinary. The earliest study of political science programs (the APSA's Haines Committee, 1912–16) divided the field into only four subfields: American government, comparative government, elements of law, and political theory. The only "official" list of subfields, provided by the APSA to the War Manpower Commission during World War II for its registry of scientific and specialized personnel, identified eight.[11] The Dimock Committee, in its survey on which *Goals for Political Science* was based, listed seventeen subfields.[12] The APSA Biographical Directory for 1961 listed eight in what Greenstein and Polsby described as "a last glimpse of a parsimonious, staid set [of sub-fields]."[13] The 1968 APSA Biographical Directory list grew to twenty-seven, while that for 1973 displayed sixty subfields organized into eight major categories.[14] APSA data show that, in 1988, collectively, eight subfields were available at the 667 institutions surveyed. Each of these was either required or recommended by between 64 percent and 97 percent of them (see Figure 3).

The most common distribution requirement today is for at least one introductory-level course plus other courses in at least two, three, or four (and occasionally more) subfields. In those cases where the requirement is stated in terms of required introductory-level courses, the number required (including a general introduction, if there is one) varies from none at all (only 2 percent or so of the departments) to seven (again only 2 percent), with 39 percent requiring either two, three, or four.[15] The content of the introductory courses varies widely, not only from school to school but frequently even from one instructor to the next in the same course.

The discipline's amorphous conceptualization is reflected further in the structure of programs beyond the introductory level. Although most differentiate—at least by course

FIGURE 2
**PROPORTION OF POLITICAL SCIENCE MAJOR PROGRAMS
REQUIRING AND OFFERING VARIOUS INTRODUCTORY-LEVEL COURSES**

COURSE	REQUIRED OF ALL STUDENTS*	NOT OFFERED
Introduction to American Politics	90%	8%
Introduction to Comparative Government	60%	35%
Introduction to International Politics	65%	30%
Introduction to Political Theory	59%	36%
Introduction to Political Behavior	16%	77%
Other introductory-level courses:	2–6%	NA
Scope & Methods, Analysis		
State & Local Government		

*In many—perhaps most—instances, "required of all students" was interpreted to mean ". . . all students wishing to take higher-level courses in the same field."

SOURCE: APSA Task Force Survey of 200 Political Science Programs

number—between introductory, mid-level, and advanced courses, the distinction often seems to be of little practical consequence. As Figures 2 and 3 taken together indicate, subfield introductory courses appear to be required primarily for purposes of "coverage" of the whole field of politics and government. In many cases they are not actually prerequisite to midlevel or advanced courses in a subfield. On some campuses, free choice above the introductory level is the rule beyond the first or second year, regardless of a course's formal level. This very loose and loosely applied structure permits few political science students to experience much "sequential learning" or to complete their work with any sense of having mastered any "common core" of knowledge that they share with other majors.

Few major programs provide opportunities or incentives for students to integrate the disconnected sets of knowledge they acquire in their courses. Some kind of capstone experience at the end of the students' four years would seem an appropriate way to promote such integration, but not all programs that do require end-of-program experiences such as senior seminars, papers, or theses appear to use them for this purpose. The failure to provide intellectual order—that is, the minimal sequencing of students' work, minimal exposure to core subject matter, and minimal integration of students' knowledge—seems to be more common at larger institutions with sizable faculty resources and numerous course offerings than at smaller ones with fewer faculty members but heavier teaching loads.

FIGURE 3

SUBFIELD REQUIREMENTS IN POLITICAL SCIENCE MAJOR PROGRAMS

COURSE	REQUIRED	RECOMMENDED	NOT REQUIRED OR RECOMMENDED
(Intro. to) American Government	87%	10%	3%
Public Law	16%	49%	35%
All other American Government & Politics	29%	53%	19%
Public Administration	17%	49%	34%
Public Policy	13%	51%	35%
Comparative Government & Politics	62%	31%	7%
International Relations	62%	32%	7%
Political Theory	67%	28%	5%
Methodology	56%	25%	20%

SOURCE: APSA Departmental Services Survey, 1987-88.

Although we have been emphasizing the fragmented and heterogeneous character of political science, we nevertheless think there is substantial agreement, diffuse though it may be, on the domain of empirical phenomena to which all political science inquiries relate. We suggest below how that fact may be used to redirect a department's program toward the goal of study-in-depth in ways that fit its particular institutional situation and needs.

STRUCTURING THE POLITICAL SCIENCE CURRICULUM

The task force believes that political science faculty members on each campus can and should shape political science curricula that are appropriate for their students, realistic in terms of faculty strengths and capacities, and intellectually coherent. We have no model curriculum to offer. Program design requires the conscientious efforts of faculty members who are familiar with their own institution's resources, capabilities, and limitations and willing to undertake serious collective reconsideration of the ultimate objectives of undergraduate political education and the state of their discipline. We do suggest, however, some goals, standards, and criteria that we think should guide political science program deci-

sions in any institution. Obviously, they must be interpreted and, we hope, applied by concerned faculty members who adapt them to the specific capabilities and needs of their own institutions and students. We believe it is possible, working within the resources and the curricular structure of institutions as they are now, to develop political science programs that provide educational experiences genuinely serving the purposes and goals of political education "in depth." We do not think it can be done simply by tinkering with the formal structure of the political science major as it is now procedurally defined in college catalogues and departmental brochures. We offer the following recommendations as helpful guides to departments' evaluation and collegial decision making.

At some time in the four years, every political science major should be introduced to a common set of core topics.

Departments might well formulate not only their own list of such topics but also their rationale for it. We offer the following list (in no particular order) as a starting point for discussion.

☐ ethical dimensions of government: public policy issues, political practices, constitutional questions, war and peace

☐ understanding, on their own terms, of those political systems (including, of course, their own!) that are most influential in world affairs and most affect U.S. citizens and national interests

☐ law and its role in different civilizations and cultures; major legal traditions of the world

☐ relations between and among nations; war, peace, and diplomacy

☐ the sociopolitical ideas, values, and customary practices that affect present-day politics in the U.S. and in foreign countries

☐ the bases of human political behavior in diverse political settings and roles

☐ major political philosophies, Western and non-Western, and the political context of their origins.

All political science majors should acquire the knowledge and skills necessary to read and comprehend contemporary political analyses and develop their own analytic capacities.

These include knowledge (and use) of:

☐ philosophic foundations of, and relations between, normative and analytic inquiry

☐ diverse and alternative methods of inquiry, including: competing theories of the common good; comparative political systems analysis; elements of research design, methods, and analysis

☐ basic statistics

☐ writing skills

☐ computer use (for both data analysis and word processing)

☐ oral presentation skills (formal, not merely conversational; academic and professional as well as general).

Providing many of these skills should, of course, be the responsibility of the entire liberal arts program, not necessarily or particularly that of political science departments alone. The department should maintain larger curricular requirements in relation to these general goals.

The program should provide for sequential learning.

Students should utilize and build upon concepts, information, and skills they have learned earlier in other courses and other fields. How this can be done will vary greatly among institutions, depending on size of faculty, number of majors, teaching loads, and other local factors. Merely requiring lower-numbered courses in a field as prerequisites for higher-numbered courses, however, is unlikely to accomplish it.

Study should begin with a general introductory course giving students an overall grasp of the components, boundaries, methodologies, and major issues of the discipline as a whole, preferably by concrete example rather than in abstract formal terms. Where it is not possible to offer both a general introductory and an American government introductory course, a comparatively taught introductory American government course—that is, one explicating basic principles, institutions, and practices of U.S. government by contrast and comparison with other major governments, both representative and nonrepresentative—can effectively serve both purposes.

There should be a capstone experience at the end of the senior year that requires and assists students to survey their whole learning experience, to recognize the interconnections among its pieces, and to comprehend the limitations of our collective knowledge as well as the gaps in their individual knowledge. Such integrative efforts could be promoted through one or more of the following, to mention only a few of the many possible and commonly used devices:

☐ a senior seminar (or seminars) aimed specifically at integrating what students have learned, by focusing on problems cutting across all or most subjects studied or by more formal survey

☐ a research paper on a topic cutting across courses or fields. This can be done through a senior seminar or through individual faculty guidance.

☐ a series of colloquia, each focusing on a major problem or topic cutting across diverse fields and courses

☐ a senior thesis on the kind of problem or topic just described.

Such papers might well be presented and discussed in a colloquium series.

☐ comprehensive examinations, but only if they are carefully designed and sequenced to require students to integrate materials and only if follow-up conferences or group discussions focus on that (see "Evaluation" below).

All students should have the opportunity not only to observe but actually to experience at least one, and preferably several, kinds of real-life political situations off campus.

Examples include:

☐ internships in legal and administrative agencies, political parties and interest group organizations, legislative agencies and legislators' offices, and other political contexts accessible to the department

☐ Washington and state capital seminars

☐ political participation (in political campaigns, conventions, or journalistic coverage of such events)

☐ study-abroad programs.

Students constantly need to be reminded that the subject they study is to be found all around them in their cultural and social environment, not only in textbooks, lecture notes, or the library. The experiences suggested here can serve, like laboratory experiences required in the natural sciences, as devices for keeping students' conceptions realistic. To be most effective, however, we think

they should include adequate brief-
ing and instruction by competent
faculty members, proper direction
and supervision off campus by competent personnel with close liaison
between agency and supervising faculty, and a final formal report or research paper based on the work.
Wherever possible, an invaluable
way to conclude such activities is
with a seminar or colloquium at
which reports and experiences of all
participants are discussed.

*Departments should prepare and dis-
tribute regularly to all prospective and
enrolled majors a concise and regularly
updated "Majors' Handbook."*
The handbook should describe the
program's goals, objectives, structure,
and requirements in language that
students can understand. It should
aim at keeping students' attention focused throughout their academic careers on the goal of an integrated
program rather than on disconnected individual courses. The handbook might include examples of
different integrated programs that
address different students' interests.

MODES OF INQUIRY

More than once in the discipline's
history, political scientists have
squabbled over the "right" conception of or approach to political
study. Their arguments once centered on the propriety of describing

it as "science" and later on the
supposed conflict between "the institutional" and "the behavioral" approach, to name just the two most
contentious issues. While no longer
rent by such bitter disputes, political
science still lacks consensus on basic
epistemological assumptions: that is,
on the basic questions it should address, the concepts that should guide
and organize research, and what
methods of analysis to apply and
when.[16]
The lack of a body of empirical
theory, the lack of consensus about
both the desirability and the content
of a general introductory course, the
heterogeneity of other introductory
courses and of higher-level courses,
and the loose programmatic structure tying them together constitute
formidable problems that must be
addressed when considering the political science curriculum. They also
are problems that make successful
teaching of politics especially challenging and difficult.
They also offer an unusual opportunity, however. Students who develop an understanding of the breadth
and depth of the field also learn
about a much wider range of phenomena and, more important, their
interconnectedness. Students who
develop an understanding of the different forms and modes of inquiry
used by political scientists become familiar with most forms of inquiry

used in all disciplines. In effect, this feature of political study logically entails accepting the defining criteria of liberal education espoused by AAC. Unfortunately, our data suggest that few political science curricula now require majors to recognize diverse forms of inquiry or to question the appropriateness of different applications of them.

Given the very wide range of questions—normative and empirical, descriptive and historical, and others—that political scientists address, considerable variety in modes of analysis is justifiable and inevitable. We believe that the only justification for any mode of analysis is its appropriateness to the question to be answered. Students therefore must be led to ask, "Which particular mode of analysis is appropriate to this particular question?" and not, as if it were a public-opinion survey question, "Generally speaking, what is the best mode of analysis for all questions?" It follows that they also must become skilled in applying not just one but all potentially applicable analytic modes. We therefore make the following recommendation.

Every political science major should gain familiarity with the different assumptions, methods, and analytical approaches used by political scientists and by cognate disciplines (for example, economics, history, psychology, law, and others).

Attention should be given to this in subject-matter courses, as well as in "scope and method," "analysis" or "political inquiry" courses (if any). It is particularly important that students become familiar with the problems of normative inquiry as well as those of empirical analysis and learn to combine the two appropriately (for example, in analysis of political value issues in public policy conflicts).

COGNATE DISCIPLINES

Most political science programs require students to minor in one or more related fields, usually in social sciences such as economics, history, psychology, sociology, and anthropology, although philosophy, law, and others often are acceptable. Most programs also offer students fairly free rein to devise course packages of their own choice. The admonition or requirement that the minor be "related to" the student's own program in the major frequently is only nominal. Joint majors, too, often comprise courses more or less freely self-selected within political science and other departments. In too few cases would current minor or joint-major programs constitute, or contribute much to, "study-in-depth."

Most political scientists probably would agree that understanding politics and government presumes familiarity with some basic geographic, historical, and economic information and some grasp of historical movements and economic institutions and principles. We have the strong impression that few political science students acquire such knowledge. For example, political theory and comparative politics courses deal freely with conflicts among communist, socialist, and capitalist systems and differences in their economic policies. Few political science students, however, appear to choose courses in economics to learn the basic principles of economic functioning that underlie the economy of every society, whatever its ideological system. Relatively few political science courses on "political economy" appear to require students enrolling in them to take courses in economics. The "geographical illiteracy" of students often is lamented, but even in that declining number of institutions where geography courses are still available, they are not often recommended to political science majors as minor courses.

Few political science programs today alert their students to major advances in non-social sciences disciplines, which are amassing fundamental knowledge relevant to understanding human society, political behavior, and the social and physical environment. Examples of important

intellectual developments too often ignored in political science programs include:

☐ the ongoing "cognitive revolution" in experimental and cognitive psychology, including findings that are crucial to the study of political attitudes and behavior

☐ the new (neo-Darwinian) evolutionary biology that has revolutionized thinking about the formation of social aggregates by primates and hominid ancestors of modern humankind and that is already being applied in important ways to the study of human cultural and political evolution

☐ modern primate ethology, which is advancing fundamental knowledge about human behavior that is directly relevant to important classes of political behavior such as violent aggression, leadership, and voting. The rapid advance in knowledge across a broad range of the biobehavioral sciences threatens to make political science obsolete if it does not take these advances into account and equip its students accordingly.[17]

Departments should reexamine their conceptions of "minor field" and "cognate disciplines" and seek to ensure that students' minor-field courses do in fact contribute to their political understanding and analytic competence and important knowledge from other disciplines is not ignored.

In particular:

☐ If history "core" requirements for all students are inadequate, political science departments should establish appropriate departmental minor-field requirements and encourage instructors to treat adequately the historical dimensions and aspects of topics covered in their courses.

☐ Unless already called for by college requirements, political science departments should require at least minimal training in fundamental economics for all their majors.

☐ Until geographical education can be obtained from elementary and high school programs and from college departments of geography, political science departments should encourage instructors to incorporate in each of their courses the teaching of whatever facts and principles of geography are essential to mastery of the course materials.

☐ Political science departments should encourage faculty members' reeducation in biobehavioral sciences and other disciplines offering knowledge essential to their subject and incorporate relevant knowledge from them in their courses.

THE CONTEXT
OF POLITICAL STUDY

It is incumbent on political science educators to give students a realistic awareness and understanding of the rapidly growing, intricate, global interdependence of the lives and activities of all the world's nations and people. Students must become aware that what people do in Africa; East, South, and Southeast Asia; Europe; the Americas; or anywhere else, and what happens to them, unavoidably has both short- and long-range effects on the lives of others elsewhere. Even though political science itself has been developing on other continents, and despite a veritable explosion of literature on foreign polities and societies—mostly but not only European—many American political science programs appear to be excessively parochial (that is, U.S.-centered) and still tend to reflect the economic and political power realities of a bygone era.[18] In the extreme case, government and politics in the United States are treated not only as distinctive (every political system is, after all, distinctive) but as an especially distinctive system. Basic textbooks on American government, for example, rarely draw comparisons with other governments, even for purposes of illustrating or explicating particular features—for example, comparing the role of Congress in the American presidential system and Parliament in the British parliamentary system. The U.S. government sometimes is presented, implicitly if not explicitly, as the appropriate model for all democratic governments. When it is compared with other systems, there often is a tendency to exaggerate the relative weaknesses of others and minimize shortcomings in American performance.

For most students today, the typical exposure to the world beyond American borders is an introductory-level course in comparative government and politics (usually dealing with the major Western European countries) or one in international relations, less often both. An increasing number of colleges, but rarely political science programs, require students to have a course or two "dealing with" a non-Western culture, usually chosen from a long cafeteria list of courses volunteered as suitable by various departments. Political science programs must confront students much more effectively with the fact and the character of the demographic diversity of the world and within individual countries; with the particular problems faced by different peoples in different nations, including the students' own; and with the interconnectedness of the world's political, economic, and social problems. To become competent analysts of the political and social world, students must recognize the ways in which citizens' most deep-seated beliefs and attitudes are rooted in specific cultural stereotypes and myths and how specific cultural biases color their own outlooks as well as those of "others."

Not only the introductory-level but most other American government courses should be taught in comparative fashion: that is, they should be taught with continual explication of the principal differences and similarities in institutions and practice between the American and other major governments, both representative and nonrepresentative.

The character and implications of ethnic and cultural diversity and the international and transnational dimensions of particular problems and policies should be addressed in all relevant courses—"mainstreamed," in the pedagogical vernacular—not treated as a separate and unique problem to be dealt with in a particular course or two or by a particular faculty member.

These recommendations have particular implications for the teaching of American government and politics. Almost all programs have tacitly admitted the minority-blind character of traditional courses by introducing courses on "Race and Politics," "Minority Politics," or "Women in Politics." But the role of women and of ethnic and racial minorities, both historically and in contemporary affairs, must be reassessed and addressed properly not only in such courses but in every course where it is relevant. The educational goal here is the same as that just described with respect to ethnic and cultural pluralism elsewhere in the world: to help students recognize the character, bases, and consequences of their own and others' most fundamental individual and group political perceptions, conceptions, and beliefs.

The introductory-level American government course should emphasize the dimensions and past and present trends of ethnic, racial, and cultural diversity in America.

The implications and role of that diversity should be addressed in every American government course where it is relevant, not only in courses treating it as a problem of a particular age, let alone a never-changing problem.

Significant changes also are evident in the immediate context of political study in America, namely, in the demography of student bodies, the primary clients of political science programs. In more and more schools, Afro-Americans; Cuban, Central American and other Hispanics; Chinese; Vietnamese; and other ethnic and racial minority members constitute a significant proportion of the student body. Student bodies also are more heterogeneous socioeconomically. Cultural and social diversity brings with it diversity of academic backgrounds and orientations to academic study and a changing mix of student interests. Some programs have adjusted to

these changes by adding courses that address the interests and attitudes of particular groups of students. While there is no need to make "knee-jerk" responses to every constituent group's demand for courses relating exclusively to its interest, relevant views must be given proper attention.

EVALUATION

Evaluation of students' overall performance probably is the most neglected element of the major program. It often amounts to little more than a summation of discrete performances in the courses taken. Ideally, students' learning and performance should be measured not only in course examinations and a final round of "comprehensive exams" but at regular intervals against norms or benchmarks based on expectations of where students ought to be at different stages in their undergraduate careers. Unfortunately, we know of no such current practice.

The most common practice now is to rely on students' grade point averages, supplemented in a large but unknown number of programs by some kind of senior-year comprehensive exam. Even where comprehensive exams are the practice, often they are "comprehensive" only in an additive, not an integrative, sense. That is, they test mere recognition of disconnected piecemeal segments of information or literary skill in writing an essay answer to several unconnected questions. Too rarely do they measure students' analytic powers and their grasp of the interconnections between the subject matter of the courses they have taken in cognate disciplines and across their major. Despite objections to their use, standardized tests—such as the Advanced Political Science Test administered by the Educational Testing Service or the PACAT tests, which are tailored more specifically to the particular pattern of a department's program—appear to be becoming a bit more common, probably because they substantially reduce the burden on the faculty of testing.[19]

We believe that, at a minimum, students are owed a valid and reliable overall evaluation of their performance in the major at the end of their program. We therefore make the following recommendation.

Departments should reexamine carefully their procedures for evaluating students' overall performance in their major and take such steps as may be necessary to:

☐ define the goals and standards students are expected to reach—that is, the benchmarks against which they are to be measured—emphasizing not merely the quantity of information retained but the coherence and interconnectedness of their knowledge and their analytic ability in dealing with new problems or situations

☐ devise or acquire examinations and testing instruments appropriate to measuring progress against those benchmarks

☐ evaluate the evaluation process and results regularly and update it frequently.

Evaluation of the effectiveness of the political science program itself is an equally important, even more rarely addressed, problem. Departments and their graduate programs often are compared on the basis of measures such as the productivity of faculty members and their Ph.D. students—indexed, for example, by data from citation indices, publication lists, and so forth. Proposals have been made to compare the average performance of all of a department's graduating majors with that of other institutions' majors measured similarly, much as average group performances on scholastic aptitude and subject-matter achievement tests commonly are used to compare and rank the performance of elementary schools. We think such a procedure is totally unjustified. All the standardized tests have been criticized sufficiently in recent years, by educational and testing experts as well as by hostile critics, raising doubts about their reliability as measures of individual attainments and abilities. All the more reason, then, to doubt their validity for measuring program performance. Even more important, such collective averages are hopelessly contaminated by the wide variation from course to course, department to department, and institution to institution in academically relevant demographic characteristics such as students' race, social class, and general intellectual abilities; institutions' class size and faculty-student ratios; selectivity in admissions; and countless other uncontrolled factors. We do not believe comparisons of aggregated test scores or grade-point averages are valid measures of program performance.

We urge the American Political Science Association, through its Education Division and with whatever member assistance it deems appropriate, to develop and seek support for a study of ways to make reliable and valid evaluations of program performance.

CONCLUSION

It is worth repeating that our recommendations are not proposals to be adopted by departments but suggested guidelines to help them consider how best to improve the education given their students, utilizing their own particular individual and institutional resources, talents, and conceptions. We are convinced that examining, revising, and developing programs for that purpose must become a primary concern of faculty members, departments, and the discipline collectively. We have suggested that such programmatic rethinking calls for examination of the intellectual validity, integrity, and currency of faculty members' grasp of their subject matter, including the analytic tools and skills students need in order to use the knowledge imparted to them. Equally important, evaluating, changing, developing, and conducting programs for the liberal education of political science majors will require us to keep constantly in mind their guiding purpose and goal: to equip majors to use the knowledge and skills they gain not merely in the world of academic political science as students but "outside" and beyond the discipline as adult members of society.

1. The members of the task force that prepared this report are Twiley W. Barker, University of Illinois; Lawrence W. Beer, Lafayette College; Mary Ellen Fischer, Skidmore College; Ronald Kahn, Oberlin College; Kathleen McGinnis, Trinity College; Marian L. Palley, University of Delaware; Randall B. Ripley, Ohio State University; and John W. Wahlke, University of Arizona. Ex officio members were Richard Brody, Stanford University, and Lois Moreland, Spelman College.

   Our perceptions of current political science practice are based mainly on information about political science departments published annually by the American Political

Science Association and on responses to an open-ended solicitation of a nonrandom sample of two hundred departments (out of more than three hundred from which we requested documentary materials about their current major programs.) Student views were obtained from questionnaires completed by varying samples of students at both task-force members' institutions and other institutions. Individual task-force members' discussions with faculty members and students at their own and other institutions provided very useful, even though unsystematic, information and ideas. We benefitted also from discussions at panels of the annual meetings of the American Political Science Association in Atlanta, Georgia, August 31–September 3, 1989, and the Western Political Science Association, in Newport Beach, California, March 22–24, 1990.

The APSA Council formally received and accepted the task force report and passed a resolution urging political science faculty members to consider its recommendations.

We discuss later the four-year study (of political science only) that led to the publication of the American Political Science Association's *Goals for Political Science: Report of the Committee for the Advancement of Teaching* (New York: William Sloane Associates, Inc., 1951). It is extremely unfortunate that comparable time and support was not available for the present study.

Additional references:

☐ American Political Science Association, *Careers and the Study of Political Science: A Guide for Undergraduates* (Washington, DC: American Political Science Association, periodically).

☐ American Political Science Association, *1977–78 Survey of Departments* (Washington, DC: American Political Science Association, 1989).

☐ American Political Science Association, Committee on Instruction, *The Teaching of Government* (New York: Macmillan Co., 1916).

2. Association of American Colleges, National Advisory Committee to the Liberal Arts Major Project, *Report on Study-in-depth*

(Washington, D.C.: Association of American Colleges, 1989), 2.

3. Association of American Colleges, *Integrity in the College Curriculum* (Washington, D.C.: Association of American Colleges, 1985), 15–26.

4. AAC, *Integrity*, 24.

5. AAC, *Report on Study-in-depth*, 2.

6. APSA, *Goals for Political Science.*

7. See the pamphlet *Careers and the Study of Political Science: A Guide for Undergraduates*, 4th ed., ed. Mary H. Curzan (Washington, D.C.: American Political Science Association, 1985). Available from the American Political Science Association, 1527 New Hampshire Avenue, NW, Washington, D.C. 20036.

8. AAC, *Integrity*, 2 and 27.

9. The pattern varied little from one to another of the seven types of institution shown there.

10. From the task force's own data. Despite the limitations of these data, they are consistent with our personal impressions; and where we have parallel data, ours do match closely those of the latest APSA Departmental Services survey.

11. *Roster of U.S. Scientific Personnel and Specialists*, U.S. War Manpower Commission, (1945).

12. APSA, *Goals for Political Science.*

13. American national government; comparative government; international law and relations; political parties; political theory; public administration; public law; state and local government. Fred I. Greenstein and Nelson W. Polsby, eds., *Handbook of Political Science*, vol. 1 (Reading, Mass.: Addison-Wesley Publishing, 1975), ix.

14. Greenstein and Polsby, *Handbook of Political Science*, x–xii.

15. APSA task force survey of two hundred political science departments.

16. One task-force member has described "political science"–or "government," as 5 to 10 percent of the departments are named–as "multidisciplinary with respect to forms of inquiry."

17. The thought is not wholly new. A 1923 report by the APSA emphasized "the need

for political scientists to team up with other social scientists in an attack on common problems." See Committee on Political Research (the "Merriam Committee"), "Progress Report of the Committee on Political Instruction," *American Political Science Review* 17 (May 1923): 276–81.

18. One indication of the concentration on American affairs is that three of the eight subfields in which at least one course is required or recommended for students are American–general American government (97 percent), American public law (64 percent) and various other American government courses (82 percent).

19. PACAT, the Project for Area Concentration Achievement Testing, is surveying curricula and developing examinations in a number of academic disciplines, including Political Science. This information provided by Dr. Anthony Golden (Address: PACAT, Austin Peay State University, Clarksville, TN 37044).

PSYCHOLOGY[1]

The authors of this report teach psychology in an array of institutional settings. Our students bring to their undergraduate classes different cultural heritages and a range of academic preparation. The American Psychological Association urged us to draw on our collective experiences as classroom teachers and as administrators. In framing this report, we listened to the voices of many colleagues. We tried, as William James described the task of exploring another type of experience, to examine "the roots and the fruits" of teaching psychology.

Psychologists have reflected periodically on the objectives of undergraduate education, on what courses best prepare students to attain these objectives, on research designed to understand how students learn, and on innovative pedagogy that enlivens the work of faculty members and students in the classroom, laboratory, and field settings.

In 1951, six psychologists met at Cornell University to "audit" the undergraduate curriculum. In their report, *Improving Undergraduate Instruction in Psychology*, they identified "intellectual development and a liberal education" as primary objectives for undergraduate work. A secondary objective was "a knowledge of psychology, its research findings, its major problems, its theoretical integration and its contributions."[2]

Ten years later, another study group met at the University of Michigan, concerned that teaching had lost its prestige and that research consumed most faculties' energy and creativity. Using survey data collected from 411 departments, they discussed the curriculum, professional and vocational training, the introductory course, methods courses in experimental psychology and statistics, and three model curricula. The authors of that study, *Undergraduate Curricula in Psychology*, characterized psychology as a liberal arts discipline emphasizing breadth rather than narrow specialization.[3]

In *Undergraduate Education in Psychology* (1973), Kulik reported on data gathered from 463 baccalaureate programs, 99 two-year institutions, and 17 site-visit case studies. From analyses of these data he argued that no single curriculum could encompass the diversity of student needs and educational settings: "Pluralism may be a valuable concept in the design of programs in psychology."[4] Moreover, the report questioned whether curricula like those of liberal arts colleges best meet the ideals of liberal education: "Is it conceivable that for some students, occupationally oriented programs may provide a better road?"[5]

In 1982, a special issue of the journal *Teaching of Psychology* was devoted to "undergraduate psychology education in the next decade."[6] The American Psychological Association surveyed psychology departments by telephone.[7] Scheirer and Rogers' report, *The Undergraduate Psychology Curriculum 1984*, mapped the terrain of an increasingly complex field taught in many different academic environments.[8]

The reports issued in the 1950s and 1960s affirmed undergraduate psychology as one of the disciplines in the liberal arts, emphasizing breadth, content, scientific methodology, and intellectual sophistication. Its aim was to teach students to ask questions about behavior and to understand the ingredients of good answers. By the 1970s—against a background of changes in the field

and in the demography of higher education—Kulik was advocating "curricular pluralism" in recognition of the developing conflicts in psychology that will be described in the next section. By the 1980s, however, faculty members still were attempting to resolve the tensions between scientific versus applied concerns and breadth versus depth through distribution requirements: introductory psychology, methods courses, and then a mix-and-match menu based on the expertise of faculty members and the needs of particular student populations at the institution—much the same as in the years preceding earlier reports.

Our report, then, builds on a forty-year tradition of studying undergraduate education in psychology, a tradition shaped by conflicts that have emerged from new developments in the field. The most common definitions of psychology describe it as the science of the behavior of individual organisms. Even William James, who preferred to define psychology as the science of mental life, recognized that mental processes always exist for purposes of doing. Psychology encompasses the roles of groups and the functions of parts of individual organisms. The former often are the context in terms of which individual behavior is to be understood; the latter provide neurophysiological foundations for the concepts that apply to individual behavior. Physiological psychologists (whose work is sometimes indistinguishable from one or another of the biological sciences) and social psychologists (whose work sometimes is indistinguishable from sociologists, cultural anthropologists, or political scientists) are so different in what they do that communication is difficult and conflict probable.

The differing interests of the physiological and social psychologists reflect the branching of the field in the last fifty years. In the 1930s there were still "schools" of psychology—behaviorism, functionalism, Gestalt psychology, and the like—that attempted to embrace the entire subject matter of the field. By the 1940s, these schools had given way to smaller but still "grand" theories that sought to explain such phenomena as learning, perception, and social action. Even these smaller theories were displaced gradually by the current theorizing that tends to focus upon specific types of learning, perception, motivation, psychotherapy, and the like. The potential for misunderstanding and conflict growing out of extreme specialization is obvious.

Another source of stress is that essentially there are two sciences of psychology.[9] One is traditional experimental psychology, modeled after physics. Its procedures involve the manipulation of causal variables. In principle, this science permits both the prediction and the control of behavior. The second science of psychology, psychometric psychology, derives from the development of mental tests and is modeled on astronomy. Its procedures involve assessments of behavior, usually with the aid of tests, for the purpose of predicting, but not controlling, behavior in some other situation. These two sciences have different outlooks. Experimental psychology concentrates on averages; psychometric psychology is concerned with individual differences and variation. They use different statistics. Experimental psychology employs techniques of hypothesis testing; psychometric psychology uses correlational procedures. Again, the potential for conflict is clear.

Differences in temperament and values also invite conflict. Kimble's study of "psychology's two cultures" identifies six dimensions on which psychologists differ:

☐ most important scholarly values (scientific versus humanistic)

☐ lawfulness of behavior (determinism versus indeterminism)

☐ basic source of knowledge (observation versus intuition)

☐ appropriate setting for discovery (laboratory versus field study/case history)

☐ generality of laws (nomothetic

versus idiographic)
☐ appropriate level of analysis (elementism versus holism).
Psychologists associated with institutions and programs devoted to the natural science aspects of the field occupy the positions identified with the first-mentioned terms in the six polarities.[10]

These polarities are associated with the ways that psychologists earn a living. Many traditional research and academic psychologists endorse the scientific values. By contrast, health service providers endorse the humanistic values. Identification by teaching faculty members with either of these two polarities has implications for the shaping of an undergraduate curriculum.

Comments from faculty members on an earlier draft of this report reflect the polarities identified by Kimble. Some psychologists advocate teaching the science of psychology, in depth, through a structured sequence of required content courses and associated laboratory experiences. Others propose a "track" approach to undergraduate training. One track might emphasize general concepts, critical thinking, and a liberal arts approach. A second track suggested by a few psychologists might focus on students' preparation for postbaccalaureate settings or positions (for example, behavioral technicians in community mental health

agencies, personnel officers in corporate settings, and so on). These preprofessional track options would enable students who will work after completing their undergraduate degree in psychology to have an indepth experience focusing their major field courses, field work experiences, and electives on a career specialization.

Comments we received on an earlier draft of this report also point to different views on how best to integrate gender, ethnicity, culture, and class into the study of psychology.[11] Most psychologists would acknowledge that faculty members must challenge campus racism and sexism, but there is less agreement on how to do so. Gender, ethnicity, culture, and class are seen by some faculty members as the central issues that challenge our contemporary curricula; such a challenge also questions traditional research methodologies that are empirical, quantitative, and positivist, and may advocate alternative psychological methods that are contextual, interpretive, and more qualitative. For other faculty members, although these topics and the new knowledge generated by research have legitimacy within the discipline, they should be subtopics best left to treatments determined by an instructor's sensitivities and commitments.

Our report will not reconcile all of

the conflicts that faculty discussions generate. We believe that differences can be explained to students, fostering in them the capacity to make connections between seemingly disparate arguments and knowledge bases. This means that the teacher will see psychology as an evolving subject matter best understood from an array of differing perspectives. The primary goal is not to demand that the student master fixed content, but rather to teach the student how to struggle with ambiguity, how to reflect on this experience, and how to ask more sophisticated questions about behavior and experience.

This report is organized in six sections: orienting assumptions, undergraduate psychology students, common goals, measurement and evaluation of major field outcomes, structure of the major, student learning and self-evaluation.

ORIENTING ASSUMPTIONS

Five assumptions guide our discussion. These assumptions are consistent with the evolving perspective on the curriculum described in earlier psychology reports and our understanding of the major in the context of contemporary American higher education.

☐ Institutions vary in their missions and in the characteristics of their students. In every generation—from the mid-1800s through World War II, Korean, and Vietnam-era veterans—universities and colleges served new student populations.[12] As student heterogeneity increased, uniform curricula and undergraduate programs became increasingly problematic. Balancing curricular coherence with responsiveness to new knowledge, new students, and new epistemologies is always a difficult task.[13]

☐ A liberal arts education in general—and the study of psychology in particular—is a preparation for lifelong learning, thinking, and action; it emphasizes specialized and general knowledge and skills. The skills required to be a successful student do not always match those required to be a good citizen and a happy and productive person. For example, there are differences between education and real life in the type of intelligence that is most useful (abstract intelligence versus social or practical intelligence or aesthetic sensitivity), the knowledge that is prized the most (generalized knowledge versus specific, informal, nonverbal, and implicit real-life knowledge), the definition and solution of problems (problems clearly defined by type and yielding to simple elegant solutions versus recognizing just what are the problems and juggling numerous possible solutions), and the employment of resources (education rewards "pure thought" exercised in independent isolation whereas real life achievements are more often the product of cooperation in behalf of a common, negotiated goal). Our definitions of "liberal education" may need some rethinking.[14]

□ The definition of curricular goals begins with a specific group of faculty members, their departmental and institutional culture, and their specific understanding of the discipline in the context of changing knowledge and changing student profiles.[15] We think there should be no universally prescribed course of study in undergraduate psychology, no hard and fast requirements as suggested for doctoral training in APA accredited programs. Instead, we advocate curricular pluralism. Coherence across curricula should be based on the common goals suggested in the next section of this report.

□ Research has established that faculty members do not teach in only one way and students do not learn in only one way.

□ Students should expect feedback from faculty members. Evaluation and assessment should not be tied solely to the task of assigning grades. Assessment of students and programs is best accomplished using multiple methods. Even more important, students must acquire the skills to evaluate their own progress and their accomplishment of integrated learning.

UNDERGRADUATE PSYCHOLOGY STUDENTS

In 1987, more than forty-two thousand students received baccalaureate degrees in psychology. This was the second consecutive annual increase in the number of degrees, reversing a downward trend from the more than fifty thousand degrees awarded in 1976. As Figure 1 shows, the decline in enrollments was entirely due to the declining number of degrees awarded to men in this period.

Howard and others have analyzed the changing demographics of psychology students, shifts in gender and ethnic composition of graduate and undergraduate student groups, advances in health-care provider specialties, and decline in employment interest in traditional academic/research settings.[16] The authors document that the dramatic increases in the numbers of women in undergraduate and graduate student bodies have not been matched by similar gains in the achievement of tenure and salary parity by women academics.

It is not known why there has been such a significant increase in the numbers of women entering psychology. Nor do we know the consequences for the field of the gender shift in enrollments. For example, has classroom pedagogy become more responsive to potentially different ways of knowing and discourse?[17] As the authors of this and other studies conclude, demographic changes will have a "profound effect on the field both now and in the future."[18]

COMMON GOALS

In spite of the diversity of settings in which the undergraduate degree in psychology is completed, we believe that common goals can be identified. The eight goals offered here as guidelines may lend coherence to the psychology curriculum. We recognize that specific course requirements will be different in different institutions. The works of Halpern and McGovern and Hawks were particularly helpful

in generating these guidelines.[19]
☐ Knowledge base. There are significant facts, theories, and issues in psychology that a student needs to know. The training of faculty members and their interpretations of the field determine what they label "significant." Comparing the past reports, we know that the content of the field changes.[20] Nevertheless, there are common continuing foci such as: biopsychology, learning, cognition, social psychology, developmental psychology, personality, abnormal psychology and adjustment, and principles of psychological tests and measurements. Based in part on analysis of chapter titles and major themes in introductory psychology textbooks published between 1890

FIGURE 1
BACHELOR'S DEGREE RECIPIENTS IN PSYCHOLOGY (1976–1987)

YEAR	TOTAL	WOMEN	(%)	MEN	(%)
1976	50,363	27,376	54	22,987	46
1977	47,794	27,102	57	20,692	43
1978	45,057	26,540	59	18,517	41
1979	43,012	26,363	61	16,649	39
1980	42,513	26,923	63	15,590	37
1981	41,364	26,917	65	14,447	35
1982	41,539	27,783	67	13,756	33
1983	40,825	27,597	68	13,228	32
1984	40,375	27,426	68	12,949	32
1985	40,237	27,422	68	12,815	32
1986	40,937	28,246	69	12,691	31
1987	42,868	29,536	69	13,332	31

SOURCE: National Science Foundation, SRS

and the present, Matarazzo concludes that "there is only one psychology, no specialties, but many applications."[21]

The critical goal is to help students to develop a conceptual framework embracing relevant facts and concepts rather than isolated bits of knowledge, to achieve a base for lifelong learning rather than a static, encyclopedic knowledge of the current state of the field. Because knowledge in our field and parallel disciplines grows so rapidly, we need to recognize the principle that "less is more" in our coverage of content knowledge in individual courses and in the curriculum as a whole.

□ Thinking skills. Advanced work in the discipline requires skills in learning, critical thinking, and reasoning—skills that come in part from working with quantitative information in statistics or experimental methods courses and from critical reading of original texts in all courses. The psychology student also needs to gain familiarity with qualitative methods and to develop a disciplined curiosity about human behavior and experience. Even at the introductory level, students should be able to inquire about behavioral antecedents and consequences and view with amiable skepticism the explanations and conclusions in popular media reports on psychology and other social sciences.

As they advance, psychology students should learn to think critically about themselves, their differences, and their similarities with others; to evaluate their attitudes about people who are different from themselves; and to know how gender, race, ethnicity, culture, and class affect all human perspectives and experiences.

□ Language skills. Research in the pedagogy of composition and its cognitive psychology bases should encourage teaching that gives explicit attention to the development of our students' thinking, reading, and writing skills.[22] The psychology student should be able to comprehend the discourse of the discipline used in textbooks and scientific journal articles and present written arguments in the language of the discipline, using the elements of style and the presentation of scientific information described in the *Publication Manual of the American Psychological Association.*[23]

□ Information gathering and synthesis skills. Psychology majors should be able to gather information from a library, from computerized information and bibliographic systems, and from other sources to present a persuasive argument.

□ Research methods and statistical skills. The skills to utilize experimental methods, statistics, and qualitative methods are essential. These skills should be fostered in separate courses, further developed in laboratory work, and reinforced by the use of critical discussion of research findings and methods in every course. Whatever the mode of instruction, the student should become increasingly independent in posing questions about the study of behavior and experience and in selecting effective methods to answer those questions. Through repeated exposure to the methods of psychology, the student majoring in psychology should develop growing sophistication about research strategies and their limitations, including issues such as the drawing of causal conclusions from experimental versus correlational results.

☐ Interpersonal skills. Interpersonal awareness, sensitivity, and an expanding self-knowledge can be uniquely fostered by the study of psychology. To monitor one's own behavior; to be sensitive to differences and similarities in the way people are treated based on gender, race, ethnicity, culture, and class; to work effectively in groups: these are outcomes that should complement the cognitive achievements of the traditional course of study in psychology.

☐ History of psychology. It is important for psychology majors to have an understanding of the history of the discipline that goes beyond knowledge of major figures and their contributions and includes the sociocultural context in which psychology emerged. Through such knowledge, students may better appreciate the evolution of the methods of psychology, its theoretical conflicts, its sociopolitical uses, and the discipline's place within the broader intellectual traditions of the humanities, sciences, and social sciences.[24]

☐ Ethics and values. The ethical principles of psychology were empirically derived from critical incidents submitted by scientists and practitioners.[25] Since 1948, when the first APA committee met to fashion a code of ethics, the discipline's emphasis always has been on the educational value for psychologists of espousing a set of ethical principles. Undergraduate students should develop an ability to use these principles to understand conflicts, to generate alternative responses, and to act on their judgments. Recognizing the dignity of the person, promoting human welfare, and maintaining academic and scientific integrity are examples of such principles. A particularly important social and ethical responsibility of faculty members is to promote their students' understanding of gender, race, ethnic, cultural, and class issues in psychological theory, research, and practice.

REPORTS
FROM THE
FIELDS

MEASUREMENT
AND EVALUATION
OF MAJOR FIELD OUTCOMES

Outcomes to be evaluated must be consistent with the mission and goals of a particular college or university. At the departmental level, the goals for the major should be viewed within this broader context. Thus, the important outcomes for psychology intersect with the broader goals found in an institution's mission statement or those suggested as a "minimum required curriculum" in AAC's *Integrity in the College Curriculum*—literacy, working with quantitative information, science, historical consciousness, values, and multicultural experiences.[26]

A hallmark of effective assessment in psychology is a multimethod approach.[27] Archival strategies such as transcript analyses; surveys of students, alumni, and employers; portfolios of laboratory reports and class papers; performance on standardized tests such as the GRE; locally developed comprehensive examinations; senior theses and research projects all are potentially rich sources of evaluation information.[28]

Any evaluation of the undergraduate psychology program should be initiated internally and validated by external consultants. Evaluation is an opportunity for periodic reflection and should be a stimulus for

growth and renewal.

Despite the increasing emphasis on assessment as a tool of program and institutional evaluation, students gain most from assessment that takes place in individual courses. Effective use of multiple testing procedures in the classroom accomplishes multiple goals: students gauge their understanding of new and increasingly complex material; faculty members gauge the clarity of their presentation of this material; faculty members and students shape one another's expectations for learning.

STRUCTURE OF THE MAJOR

Most psychology curricula have a beginning, a middle, and an end. The beginning includes an introductory course that exposes students to topics in the discipline. Methods courses in research and statistics and, in some departments, a course in principles of psychometrics and individual differences follow the introductory experience. The methods courses enable students to read and evaluate the research presented in content courses as the knowledge base of the major. Many departments organize these requirements using a distribution model in which students sample several courses offered in cognitive psychology, developmental psychology, social and personality, biopsychology, and so on. Finally, a course in the history and systems of psychology, an advanced general psychology course, or a senior seminar on selected topics in psychology may serve as a capstone for content. The senior research project completed in a campus laboratory or the senior field work/practicum/internship completed in an applied setting may be offered either as a requirement or as an elective. The curricular models in Figures 2, 3, 4, and 5 are traditional and alternative structures for organizing a sequence of learning.

The Generalist Model in Figure 2

most closely approximates the traditional curricular structure. Consistent with our working premise that "less is more," however, and that students' capacity to develop thinking, learning, reasoning, language, and methodological skills is facilitated by an iterative exposure to less content, we recommend reducing the number of survey courses. This requires developing two courses in the traditional knowledge base of offerings, followed by two more specialized courses in the same area and with a laboratory.

The thematic models in Figure 3

FIGURE 2
GENERALIST MODEL:
UNDERGRADUATE PSYCHOLOGY

Introductory Psychology (1)

Methods courses (3)
☐ Statistics
☐ Research methods
☐ Psychometrics and individual differences

Survey courses (2) in knowledge base
EXAMPLES: Social psychology, personality, physiological psychology

Specialized courses (2) with laboratories to follow up survey courses
EXAMPLES (matched to above survey courses): Group dynamics, behavior modification, animal learning

Integrated senior-year project or seminar (1)
EXAMPLES: History and systems, advanced general, special topics, senior research, honors research, field work and seminar

Interpersonal skills and group process laboratory for community service (1)

Elective(s)

FIGURE 3
THEMATIC MODEL:
DEVELOPMENTAL PSYCHOLOGY

Lifespan Developmental Psychology (1)

Methods Courses (3)
☐ Statistics
☐ Research methods
☐ Psychometrics and individual differences

Survey courses in thematic knowledge base (2)
☐ Cognitive development
☐ Social/personality development

Specialized courses (2) with laboratories to follow up survey courses
EXAMPLES: Child psychology, psychology of adolescence, adulthood, psychology of aging

Integrated senior-year project or seminar (1)
EXAMPLES: History and systems, advanced general, special topics, senior research, honors research, field work and seminar

Interpersonal skills and group process laboratory for community service (1)

Electives (s)

(Developmental Psychology), Figure 4 (Biological Psychology), and Figure 5 (Health Psychology) are possible examples of curricula that extend our notion of "less is more" even further. Instead of the traditional introductory course that covers fourteen to sixteen subfields of psychology in a single semester, the student would be introduced to one area (see, for example, Figure 3, Lifespan Developmental) that treats all the topics included in traditional introductory courses in the context of an integrative perspective. Subsequent methods courses could be generalist in nature (for example, Figures 3 and 4) or continue with the theme introduced in the first course by exposing students to more and more complex research and statistical methods on the thematic topic (for example, Figure 5).

Continuing with the Developmen-

FIGURE 4
THEMATIC MODEL:
BIOLOGICAL PSYCHOLOGY

Biological Psychology (1)

Methods Courses (3)
☐ Statistics
☐ Research methods
☐ Psychometrics and individual differences

Survey courses in thematic knowledge base (2)
☐ Brain and behavior
☐ Evolution of behavior

Specialized courses (2) with laboratories to follow up survey courses
EXAMPLES: sensation and perception, learning and cognition, emotion and motivation, health psychology, personality and pathology

Integrated senior-year project or seminar (1)
EXAMPLES: History and systems, advanced general, special topics, senior research, honors research, field work and seminar

Interpersonal skills and group process laboratory for community service (1)

Elective(s)

FIGURE 5
THEMATIC MODEL:
HEALTH PSYCHOLOGY

Health Psychology (1)

Methods Courses (3)
☐ Statistics
☐ Research methods in health and clinical psychology
☐ Psychometric methods and individual differences

Survey courses in thematic in knowledge base (2)
☐ Psychology of personality -OR- social psychology
☐ Biological bases of behavior -OR- learning and adaptive behavior

Specialized courses (2) with laboratories to follow up survey courses
EXAMPLES: Abnormal psychology, child clinical psychology, stress and coping, psychology of prevention, psychology of women, experimental approaches to personality, hormones and behavior, motivation and emotion

Integrated senior-year project or seminar (1)
EXAMPLES: History and systems, advanced general psychology, independent research, honors research, field work and seminar

Interpersonal skills and group process laboratory for community service (1)

Elective(s)

tal Psychology thematic model as an example, the survey courses broaden the students' knowledge by exposing them to two facets of human development in which they must necessarily integrate multiple other subfields of psychology that influence the developmental literature. Specialized courses with laboratories follow these two survey courses based on the same rationale that informed our recommendation for the generalist model.

Critics of the thematic models (which could be designed equally well for social psychology, cognitive psychology, or other areas in the traditional knowledge base) will argue, "This is not 'psychology'; it is too narrow and specialized." We would agree that, while this is not a traditional approach, it can foster both breadth and specialization while encouraging students to integrate their learning in a more coherent manner. In large, research-oriented institutions where distinguished senior faculty members often do not teach undergraduates, the thematic model has the potential for bringing such individuals back to the baccalaureate enterprise. Scholars, graduate students, and undergraduates enrolled in a thematic track may be more likely to work together in and out of the classroom. In sum, we see both the generalist and the thematic models as worthy of consideration be-

cause they reflect what is now happening and what we believe could be designed to facilitate students' integrated learning.

All four models include an integrated senior-year project to be completed in an applied field setting off campus (for example, a mental health agency or corporate personnel office) or on campus (for example, university peer-counseling services) or in a research setting (for example, a neurosurgery laboratory or survey research laboratory). Another example for this senior-year experience could be in the traditional classroom with one or more faculty members teaching the history and systems, advanced general psychology, or special topics courses. A senior-year applied experience enables students to test their accumulated knowledge, skills, and ethical sensitivities. Furthermore, applied experiences integrate for students the goals of liberal learning espoused by most faculty members: that is, to be reflective about all of one's experiences. In contrast, a senior-year classroom experience emphasizes the integration of what has been learned up to that point but focuses more sharply on traditional intellectual outcomes for study in the major.

We recommend an additional component for all undergraduate majors in psychology. An interpersonal skills and group-process laboratory is included in all of our proposed models in order to develop students' abilities to work in groups. Whenever possible, we recommend that this laboratory (or the senior-year applied project) be combined with a community-service component. A volunteer experience should be an integral part of every student's undergraduate education. Such an experience would provide psychology majors an opportunity to apply interpersonal problem solving and decision-making skills, develop their leadership potential, and provide career-related insights. Supervised community service can instill a sense of responsibility that is critical for informed citizenship while addressing a broad range of human needs.

In sum, our assumptions, common goals for the major, and proposed curricular models converge to provide students exposure to many ideas and perspectives, fashioning for them conceptual structures whereby they can "think in psychological terms." We want to emphasize teaching for the transfer of learning. Our students should be able to recognize, and apply appropriately, concepts and skills in a variety of contexts. They should be able to look at relationships, to make connections, to struggle with ambiguity. To accomplish this, our curricular models emphasize students having the experience of practicing (talking,

writing, doing) psychology and listening to psychologists and others talk about the discipline from personal and scholarly perspectives.

As every past report has stressed, the content of courses and the structure of the curriculum are necessary but not sufficient conditions for effective education in a field. Good teaching is essential. Good teaching in psychology is characterized by the active involvement of students (more talking by students and less by teachers). Good teaching, whether in a large auditorium, a smaller classroom, or a laboratory, uses technology directly or indirectly to enhance students' learning and enthusiasm. For example, computers can be used in many ways to enhance students' learning: They can be used as tools to develop statistical and research methods skills; they can be used for demonstrations and for simulations of psychological research; they can be used for student practice and as programmed learning devices; and they can be used to teach problem-solving strategies, further developing the complex thinking abilities that critical reading and writing tasks encourage.

Good teaching presupposes that faculty members continually renew their craft by continually exploring how their students learn most effectively. Joseph summarizes this process well: "How does our field look from the point of view of the learner?... We want to build a cognitive science upon which teaching is based, and we cannot leave it to the specialists alone, good as they may be. We the teachers, as *clinicians of cognitive science* in our classrooms, need to articulate what we do."[29]

STUDENT LEARNING
AND SELF-EVALUATION

The learning process and college's influence on students have been studied by psychologists for many years.[30] We recommend that faculty members use this literature to design individual courses in the same way that they can use the past literature to design their overall curriculum.

Involvement in Learning, the National Institute of Education report, recommends three critical conditions of excellence in the learning process: student involvement, setting clear and high expectations, and regular and periodic assessment and feedback.[31] In specifying learning goals and measurable outcomes, faculty members could consider the eight goals that we proposed in an earlier section, using whatever local modifications seem necessary, and gathering reactions from their students about how the current curriculum enables students to achieve these goals. Grading in individual courses provides discrete markers for stu-

dents about their mastery of knowledge in one content area, but useful evaluation also must include periodic, cumulative evaluation points. Such points can be embedded within required courses or field experiences and designed so that the students know how they are progressing.

As students gradually become independent learners, the department's advising system should enable students and faculty members to work together, to gauge progress, to analyze roadblocks, and to plan for the future beyond the baccalaureate program. Effective departmental advising systems include informational resources (for example: brochures, handouts, videotapes) on career planning, postbaccalaureate employment, and graduate or professional school opportunities and requirements. Ware and Millard and Woods have developed excellent handbooks for these purposes.[32] Departmental chairs and deans can help make advising much more effective by including faculty advising work as bona fide elements of promotion and tenure decisions.

SUMMARY

The world in 1990 is different from the world described by Buxton, McKeachie and Milholland, and Kulik.[33] In the year 2000 and beyond, the knowledge base of psychology may include few of the content areas described above. Hybrid departments are growing out of the combinations of knowledge generated by scientists and humanists in collaborative disciplines. Undergraduates now are studying social ecology, behavioral medicine, health psychology, neuroscience, and cognitive science.

Is there a "canon" in psychology? If there is, it probably is in our evolving methodologies for studying behavior, emotion, and cognition. These methods enabled psychologists and their students to study problems such as racism, educational testing, and computer-assisted learning when the knowledge and social norms in these areas were shifting rapidly.

As one contributor to contemporary undergraduate liberal learning, psychology should sustain its popularity and efficacy. Psychology has the potential to touch the whole lives of students—their intellectual development, their emotional growth, and their behavioral skills. The uniqueness of psychology is in the ability of its faculty members to incorporate what Mann labeled the scientific, healing, and wisdom functions in their teaching of undergraduates.[34] As the Ann Arbor group stated more than thirty years ago:

> We want our students, in encountering the concrete material of

human life, to be skillful in (a) recognizing aspects or properties of it that psychology has helped them to see more clearly, and (b) recognizing processes and relationships they would not have known about except as a consequence of their study of psychology...which, also, commonly involves some emotional involvement on their part.[35]

1. The authors of this report are Laurel Furumoto, Wellesley College; Diane Halpern, California State University–San Bernardino; Gregory Kimble, Duke University; Thomas V. McGovern, Arizona State University West (chair); and Wilbert J. McKeachie, University of Michigan. This report is recommended by the American Psychological Association as a framework for campus discussion of the major in psychology.
2. Claude E. Buxton et al., *Improving Undergraduate Instruction in Psychology* (New York: Macmillan, 1952), 2–3.
3. Wilbert J. McKeachie and John E. Milholland, *Undergraduate Curricula in Psychology* (Fair Lawn, N.J.: Scott, Foresman, 1961).
4. James Kulik, *Undergraduate Education in Psychology* (Washington, D.C.: American Psychological Association, 1973), 203.
5. Kulik, *Undergraduate Education*, 202–203.
6. Special Issue: Undergraduate Psychology Education in the Next Decade, edited by Charles G. Morris. *Teaching of Psychology* 9, 1982.
7. *Results: Phase 1 of Survey of Undergraduate Department Chairs* (Washington, D.C.: American Psychological Association, 1983).
8. C. James Sheirer and Anne M. Rogers, *The Undergraduate Psychology Curriculum 1984*, (Washington, D.C.: American Psychological Association, 1985).
9. Lee J. Cronbach, "The Two Disciplines of Scientific Psychology," *American Psychologist* 12 (1957): 671–84.
10. Gregory A. Kimble, "Psychology's Two

Cultures," *American Psychologist* 39 (1984): 833.

11. Phyllis A. Bronstein and Kathryn Quina, eds., *Teaching a Psychology of People: Resources for Gender and Sociocultural Awareness* (Washington, D.C.: American Psychological Association, 1988).

12. Frederick Rudolph, *Curriculum: A History of the American Undergraduate Course of Study Since 1636* (San Francisco: Jossey-Bass, 1977); Zelda Gamson, *Liberating Education* (San Francisco: Jossey-Bass, 1984).

13. Alexander W. Astin, *Achieving Educational Excellence* (San Francisco: Jossey-Bass, 1985).

14. See Thomas Jeavons, "Connecting the Curriculum and the Community," *Liberal Education* 75 (November/December 1989): 20–25; and Lauren Resnick, "Learning in School and Out," *Educational Researcher* 16 (December 1987): 13–20.

15. Mortimer H. Appley, "The Place of Psychology in the University," *American Psychologist* 45 (1990): 387–90.

16. Ann Howard et al., "The Changing Face of American Psychology: A Report from the Committee on Employment and Human Resources," *American Psychologist* 41 (1986): 1311–27.

17. See Mary F. Belenky et al., *Women's Ways of Knowing: The Development of Self, Voice, and Mind* (New York: Basic Books, 1986); and Blythe Clinchy, "On Critical Thinking and Connected Knowing," *Liberal Education* 75 (May/June 1989): 14–19.

18. Howard, "The Changing Face of American Psychology," 1326.

19. Diane F. Halpern, "Assessing Student Outcomes for Psychology Majors," *Teaching of Psychology* 15 (1988): 181–186; Thomas V. McGovern and Brenda K. Hawks, "The Varieties of Undergraduate Experience," *American Psychologist*, 43 (1988): 108–114.

20. Buxton et al., *Improving Undergraduate Instruction*; Scheirer and Rogers, *Undergraduate Psychology Curriculum 1984.*

21. Joseph D. Matarazzo, "There is Only One Psychology, No Specialties, But Many Applications," *American Psychologist* 42 (1987): 893.

22. Thomas V. McGovern and Deborah L.

Hogshead, "Learning about Writing. Thinking about Teaching," *Teaching of Psychology* 17 (1990): 5–10.

23. *Publication Manual of the American Psychological Association* (Washington, D.C.: American Psychological Association, 1983).

24. Laurel Furumoto, "The New History of Psychology," in *The G. Stanley Hall Lecture Series*, ed. Ira S. Cohen (Washington, D.C.: American Psychological Association, 1989), 5–34.

25. American Psychological Association, "Ethical Principles of Psychologists," *American Psychologist* 45 (1990): 390–395.

26. *Integrity in the College Curriculum* (Washington, D.C.: Association of American Colleges, 1985).

27. Halpern, "Assessing."

28. Thomas V. McGovern and Karen Carr, "Carving out the Niche: A Review of Alumni Surveys on Undergraduate Psychology Majors," *Teaching of Psychology* 16 (1989): 52–57.

29. Joseph Katz, "Does Teaching Help Students Learn?" in *Teaching Undergraduates: Essays from the Lilly Endowment Workshop on Liberal Arts*, ed. Bruce A. Kimball (Buffalo: Prometheus Books, 1988), 183 (emphasis added).

30. Alexander W. Astin, *Four Critical Years* (San Francisco: Jossey-Bass, 1977); Arthur W. Chickering and associates, *The Modern American College* (San Francisco: Jossey-Bass, 1984); Kenneth A. Feldman and Theodore M. Newcomb, *The Impact of College on Students* (San Francisco: Jossey-Bass, 1976).

31. *Involvement in Learning: Realizing the Potential of American Higher Education*. Report of the Study Group on the Condition of Excellence in American Higher Education. (Washington, D.C.: National Institute of Education, 1984).

32. Mark E. Ware and Richard J. Millard, eds., *Handbook on Student Development: Advising, Career Development, and Field Placement* (Hillsdale, N.J.: Erlbaum, 1987).; Paul J. Woods, ed., *Is Psychology for Them? A Guide to Undergraduate Advising* (Washington, D.C.: American Psychological Association, 1988).

33. Buxton, *Improving Undergraduate Instruc-*

tion; McKeachie and Milholland, *Undergraduate Curricula*; Kulik, *Undergraduate Education*.

34. Richard D. Mann, "The Curriculum and Context of Psychology," *Teaching of Psychology* 9 (1982): 9–14.

35. McKeachie, *Undergraduate Curricula*, 88.

CHAPTER TEN

———————————■———————————

RELIGION *

The academic study of religion in America is in some respects as old as the American university itself, and it shares the much older legacy of the European university. But an essentially new conception of this field has developed over roughly the past quarter century, particularly in many undergraduate departments. This report will articulate programmatic designs for concentrated undergraduate studies in religion that emerge from and extend these newer developments.

The 1960s and 1970s were a creative period in the development of the field of religion: a time of pedagogical experimentation, curricular innovation, revisionist scholarship, some confusion, and a great deal of intellectual ferment. This experimental buoyancy has continued to enliven the academic study of religion, making it an especially exciting field in which to teach and study. It also has generated such a diversity of programs that it is difficult to generalize about current practice. Some departments, for instance, have concentrated primarily on religions of

non-European background (Asian, Islamic, African, native American, and so on) while others have centered their attention on Judeo-Christian religions, for which biblical studies are foundational; even within that broad division there are many variations in detail. In every case the multicultural commitment has required studies in more than one tradition.

Whatever traditions are studied, furthermore, the methods of study are appropriate to the modern university and differ markedly from the various venerable practices of textual study, self-interpretation, catechesis, and spiritual reflection that have developed within many of the religious communities themselves. Like other academic disciplines, ours employs many methods, some adapted from kindred disciplines in the humanities and the social sciences, some generated by the exigencies of our particular field of study. Still, after some twenty-five years of development, and despite the diversity of methods and subject matters that certainly will continue to exist across the field, the academic study of religion has matured into a discipline in its own right with modes of discourse that are both discipline-specific and public.

Reaching that degree of maturity as a discipline has been no small achievement, and it is the more remarkable because this discipline has taken form in considerable measure in undergraduate departments. There do exist some graduate programs of high quality that have similar disciplinary goals, but they are still few and far between. The graduate programs from which most undergraduate faculty members in religion are recruited are more specialized and traditional: departments (many of them distinguished) of Protestant or Catholic theology, of Judaica or Buddhism or Islam, of Asian studies or the history of Religions, in which undergraduate faculty members are well trained in their specialties. To integrate these diverse specialties into a coherent program devoted to the newly matured academic study of religion, however, confronts young faculty members with a challenge for which their graduate programs have only marginally prepared them.

This disparity between the undergraduate department of religion and most of the available graduate programs that train its faculty constitutes the most serious problem that

afflicts the field today. Still, for purposes of the present study there is some advantage in the fact that the new wave in the academic study of religion has matured as a discipline primarily in undergraduate teaching. For it has taken shape as a program designed for undergraduates, contextualized by the role it plays among the other liberal arts. Its curricular initiatives, varied as they are, have been directed to the education of liberal arts students over the past twenty-five years, and this report is based specifically on cumulative experience with these initiatives in that context.

In the course of conducting this study, in looking closely at the documents and in discussions with colleagues from many kinds of institutions, this task force became aware of significant and promising curricular ferment in departments that we had classified, perhaps too hastily, as traditional and/or sectarian.

Our consultants also amply confirmed our initial impression of the enormous programmatic diversity in this field. In the details of specific programs the local ethos is of overriding importance. If we or AAC ever were tempted to think that we might prescribe programmatic details for the entire field, our consultations would have crushed any such illusion. Finally, however, the most heartening conclusion we have

drawn from our consultations—
at least in our more optimistic
moments—is that there actually may
be a broad potential consensus brew-
ing concerning basic objectives and
principles of study-in-depth in this
field, a general consensus adaptable
to many of the variations in local
practice.

We conceive what follows to be
chiefly a contribution to the articulation of such an emerging consensus.
Therefore, the determinations of
study-in-depth in religion presented
here are neither simply descriptive
nor entirely prescriptive. They aim
to be something of both. We will say
what we understand study-in-depth
in this field to be, so the report will
sound descriptive. There may never
be a department in North America
whose program conforms entirely to
this description. Still, we shall have
missed the mark if we are only spin-
ning our own fond fancies. To the
extent that we have hit the mark,
what follows will have begun to tag
a wriggling consensus so newly emer-
gent from the womb that it may
never have been seen before in
broad daylight. Yet it will describe,
to the astonishment of practitioners
in this discipline, just the sort of
program they have been implementing, or have been thinking of implementing, in the way of study-in-
depth for students majoring in
religion.

RELIGION AS A MULTICULTURAL STUDY

This report focusses on the student.
What should an undergraduate expect to gain from a concentration in
the study of religion?

Undergraduate studies in religion
are not primarily preprofessional.
They are designed to prepare students for many possible future roles.
Students bound for religious voca-
tions generally make up only a small
minority of religion majors, and
even fewer go on to graduate programs in the academic study of religion. The majority of students
concentrating in religious studies are
liberal arts students who plan no
further formal studies in the field.
They major in religion the way other liberal arts students major in history or literature, to cultivate a
depth dimension in a field of special
interest to them, in their pursuit of
broadly humanistic educational goals
and in their mastery of broadly useful skills.

Typically the department of religion is a university department,
contributing to the education of
students throughout the university.
Its faculty participates in general-
education programs and welcomes
students from every precinct of the
university in most of its courses. Traditionally, in fact, the department of
religion on many campuses has been

regarded as a "service department," its program designed to serve the interests of students in the university at large. The academic study of religion remains outward-looking, but as the discipline has matured we have given more attention to the kinds of discipline-specific studies that are appropriate to the liberal arts student who elects to conduct study-in-depth in religion. So we begin with these more discipline-specific features of our program.

First and foremost, study-in-depth in religion are intrinsically multicultural, directed to more than one religious tradition. This does not mean that a student of religion can expect to acquire no more than a smattering of knowledge of various traditions. To study any one religion in depth, the student should expect to study more than one; to study more than one religion she or he should expect to achieve, over several semesters, a detailed, cumulative knowledge of at least one religion, generally through a series of courses devoted to different periods of its history and to different aspects of its ongoing life.

The study of any one historic tradition (for example, Buddhism, Christianity, Hinduism, Islam, Judaism) or of a native tradition of Africa or the Americas also is a study of the culture or cultures in which it has originated and through which it has developed. It is the study of a culture at the point of its most fundamental values and its deepest value conflicts, to which the student gains primary access by attending to the life of a religious community within that culture and to its literary, musical, iconic, and architectural expressions; cultic practices; social organization; political strategies; and the like. The study of religion, furthermore, is the study not only of a culture but of a society and requires the application of sociological and anthropological methods. That already is a very rich study, and it is common for the student concentrating in the study of religion to pursue it in part through a subconcentration in one religious tradition.

The student cannot study even one religious tradition in depth, however, by attending to this tradition and its attendant culture(s) alone. The student could gain insight into the special features of the tradition in that way, yet not grasp it as a religion. The study-in-depth of religion requires that the student have more than a superficial acquaintance with at least one other tradition in the context of its attendant culture. Knowledge of at least two traditions are required to study religion in depth. It does not matter in principle which two traditions are studied. That will depend largely on local conditions such as the training and resources of the faculty. But religion cannot be studied academically without comparative insight.

The comparative study of religion is not ethnocentric, much less Christocentric, or even theocentric. It is directed to the cultural specificities of each religious tradition under study. It brings no preconceived definition of generic "religion" to its study, but interrogates the tradition itself to discover what is "religious" in it, on its own terms. It proceeds inductively, suiting the methods of study to the specific contours of a common life in its own time and place.

Yet a precise knowledge of a particular religious tradition not only is an end in itself but a source, a rich field of exempla, through which the student pursues an insight into religion as a transcultural phenomenon. No fixed definition of "religion" is presupposed. Any understanding of what is religious that may inform the study at the outset is tentative and heuristic, a way of identifying possibly fruitful questions, but any such understanding is a rough scaffolding subject to dismantling as the subject matter itself gives rise to more refined questions. Still, the ongoing effort to grasp what is, in a humanly significant sense, "religious" in the religions requires that more than one tradition be studied, with

the same attention to the cultural specificity of each. The point is not only to identify what is similar in various tradition but to identify what is different and why it is different. "Religion" as a multicultural phenomenon is the fundamental object of study, but difference is as intrinsic to the phenomenon as similarity, so the understanding of religion is constantly evolving, always provisional, subject to refinement and enrichment.

Of course any understanding of "culture" is as elusive, and as dynamic, as such an understanding of "religion." The multicultural study of religion in depth requires a developing methodological sophistication to keep pace with the student's expanding knowledge of the exempla. Indeed, the relation of religion to culture is itself extremely varied. Religions sometimes have defined themselves against the culture and at other times have been reshaped into primarily cultural religions, with profound internal metamorphosis at each change in cultural role. Some have migrated several times from one culture to another, again with profound inner transformations at each migration, and of course the cultures have undergone changes no less profound. In this sense, an adequate understanding of any one tradition is already multicultural, perhaps making problematic the very notion of a religious tradition. Again, a deeper understanding of these issues requires a study of more than one tradition that is attentive to both similarities and differences in the patterns of variety and change.

Not every discipline in the liberal arts and sciences, at least as presently practiced, is intrinsically multicultural in this way. Fortunately this multicultural scope is not unique to the study of religion, but it is rare, and it is one of the paramount values the study of religion in depth offers the liberal arts student in an increasingly cosmopolitan world.

THE SUBJECT IS RELIGION

Like the study of any discipline in the liberal arts, the study of religion has a great deal in common with kindred disciplines in both method and subject matters. What differentiates the study of religion? As in the case of some other disciplines, but by no means all, study in this field is multicultural; it is alert to symbolic language and gesture; it attends to community-forming narratives and shared moral values but also to private meditations and spiritual journeys, to rites of passage and ways of coping with suffering and death, to ways of celebrating birth and well-being. Nevertheless, what fundamentally differentiates this discipline

from others, even in the way we pursue such matters of common interest, is the fact that we study religion. We focus on religion, not just the better to understand other things, or as a derivative from other aspects of the human scene, but because of its own intrinsic importance. Students of religion learn to ask questions of a distinctive sort, inquiring into the community life and the solitariness of human beings in order to understand their religion.

Many general definitions of religion have been proposed, all of them notoriously inadequate in important respects, and we already have indicated our doubt that there is any reason to assume any generic essence of religion informing all religions. Any definitions in this field are provisional and heuristic, a point of departure for detailed study. Nevertheless, asking any community about its religion is a question that brings to light vitally significant aspects of its life that otherwise would remain in the shadows.

Are there gods? Are there sacred places and times? Are there inviolate decencies and taboos to be observed? Is human mortality a condition to be transcended, or is it the source of a devout courage? Inquiringg about religion plunges the student into the densest and most elusive issues of value, introduces the student into an ancient and enduring conversation—

not always peaceful—about ultimately serious matters, engages the imagination of the student in the most daring imaginative ventures of human experience.

The study of religion is enjoyable. For many students it is a disciplined encounter with an order of questioning that has affinities with their own struggles for personal identity. It is one way of joining the human race.

THE EMPATHETIC STUDY OF THE "OTHER"

The study of religion in depth is both empathetic and critical. If we attend to the empathetic dimension first, we do so because criticism inevitably brings to bear the point of view of the critic. If criticism is uninformed by an empathetic understanding of the criticized, it chiefly serves to confirm the moral or cultural superiority of the critic. For that, a liberal education scarcely is needed.

Empathy does not imply approval or acquiescence, much less conversion to "another" faith or confirmation of "one's own." Securing conviction is not an objective of the academic study of religion. Empathy, on the other hand, entails both aesthetic appreciation for and aesthetic distance from something that remains "other," at least for purposes of study.

The empathetic reading of a text, for instance, entails not only close attention to what is said and precisely how it is said but also requires careful reflection about why it is said, and why it is said in just this way: about its reasons but also about its emotional grounds, about its intended effects on an implied reader, about the institutional objectives served by it, about the mythic assumptions expressed in its metaphors and the hopes and fears betrayed in its rhetorical turns.

The empathetic reading is directed to the intentionality of the text, not to the disposition of the author as such. Where there is a distinctive voice in the text, nevertheless, its special accents are closely attended to, for they are not only expressions of authorial personality but of the social matrix from which they arose, registering the pulses and tensions of a shared life.

Texts, of course, are not the only objects of empathetic study. Indeed, many rich traditions among nonliterate peoples are not textual at all. Ethnographic and anthropological methods are essential in providing access to an empathetic understanding. Rituals, hymns, icons, institutional polities, burial practices, proverbs: all are studied with attention to the shapes and movements of life disclosed in them, the sensibilities, aspirations, and dreads of communities alien to the experience of the student.

They are always alien. The otherness is obvious when the religious expressions come to us from geographically distant cultures, confronting the student with the exciting challenge to comprehend the human meaning of people who understand themselves and their world very differently than the student does. The empathetic understanding grasps the coherence of an alien religious point of view within itself: the student discovers that it makes sense, and the sense it makes enlarges her or his own horizon of human possibility. But that same very substantial educational value, the appreciation of the other, is at stake even when the study is directed to a religious tradition with which the student considers him or herself to be personally acquainted or even identified.

The defamiliarization of the familiar can be disconcerting, but it is the prelude to the arts of empathetic understanding through which the texts challenge the student in a fresh way. The same is true of studies with a more contemporary focus. Of course the student cannot directly study religious movements in every time and place, but to the extent that he or she has mastered some of the empathetic arts, the student will be equipped to inhabit the world alert to

nuances in the words and actions of many "others." Even the student's home town may seem a very different and perhaps more interesting place.

Our sources, the objects of our study, are not passive. They do not make up an inert material that we can form as we choose. Being "other," with their own rich ways of life, they resist our efforts to understand them. They elude neat categorization and defeat reductive "explanations." They talk back. Our best efforts to understand these objects never will be final, but the very effort sharpens our thinking, broadens our human horizons, sensitizes our human sympathies, and confronts us with fundamental human issues. In the academic study of religion, the hermeneutical arts of empathetic understanding are worth cultivating for their own sakes. They also position the student of religion for serious critical inquiry.

CRITICAL MEASURES

The academic study of religion is conducted on the premises of the modern nonsectarian university. A donnish pun, we admit, but not a trivial observation, for the premises on which we conduct our study are located institutionally and intellectually in centers of learning that have their origins in the medieval European university and have been methodologically informed by critical traditions that have developed since the European Enlightenment. Students majoring in this field pursue studies in at least two religious traditions, and they learn from these traditions. They also are initiated into an additional tradition, however, not religious but academic, which dominates the mode in which they study religion. This they learn as well, but in a different way: they learn its methods, as these methods are adapted to this field of study, as critical instruments employed in the very pursuit of the study. Through all their studies in diverse religious traditions, students of religion are studying "religion." Though they pay close attention to the self-interpretations of religious communities, along with other aspects of their belief and practice, they do not privilege these self-interpretations in their own understanding of these communities. To regard them under the academic category of "religious" makes them available for a different sort of investigation, guided by the critical methodologies of the university.

This academic orientation to the subject matter, even entailing its re-signification, is not innocent. "Religion," to be sure, is a construct of academic study. The use of this construct in the study of a tradition does not impose a universal essence under which the exemplum is subsumed. It imposes nothing substantive on the exemplum at all. But its heuristic employment does presume the possible applicability of critical questions and categorizations that have proven useful in other studies in the field. It makes a text or an institutional structure an object of specific modes of investigation, conducted on terms that have evolved in academic study since the Enlightenment. Of course the investigation may generate new questions, superseding or requiring the revision of the ones with which we began. It may even disclose the need for an entirely different method—or a different exemplum.

Criticism of religion is not hostile, but it is independent and suspicious. It does not accept at face value the apologetic self-presentations of religious devotees, or, for that matter, the popular polemics of their opponents. The posture of suspicion is the legacy of post-Enlightenment academic study.

Feminist criticism is especially strong and well-developed in the academic study of religion. The modern rise of feminism in the academy has been virtually coterminous with the emergence and maturation of our discipline, and the numbers of gifted feminist critics attracted to the academic study of religion have achieved an influential critical mass.

The study of religion in depth involves sensitivity to the contributions of women in religious communities and to strategies of male leadership to keep women in subordinate roles in religious institutions and in society generally. Cultic practices, myths and scriptures, images of divinity: all are scrutinized with an eye to issues of gender.

Within the limits of faculty resources and training, students are initiated into the practice of critical methods in the process of studying every subject matter addressed in entry-level and intermediate courses. Some courses concentrate primarily on critical theory and methodology as such, however, so that the critical instruments themselves may be examined and refined. In addition to courses in historic religious traditions, then, there also are courses—some of them required of majors and again within the limits of available resources—in philosophy of religion, psychology of religion, sociology of religion, phenomenology of religion, and hermeneutics. Some of these critical courses are team-taught with faculty members in other appropriate departments.

A LIBERAL ARTS MAJOR

It will be obvious even in our efforts to describe the more discipline-specific features of study-in-depth in

religion just how embedded in the liberal arts curriculum of the American college and university this study is. Still, it is worth mentioning some of the more general goals and skills the student of religion can expect to have in common with other liberal arts majors. High on this list is close reading. Our students should learn to attend closely to the details and nuances of primary sources in a variety of genres, difficult to understand in a variety of ways. Some of the texts our students study, for instance, are densely reasoned treatises, some are poetic and evocative, some are artfully propagandistic. It is challenging to learn to read such different types of texts intelligently, and of course a close reading is inseparable from interpretation and criticism.

To be sure, there are limits placed on close reading when texts have to be read in translation, as they are in most of our courses. For this reason departments generally require or strongly recommend proficiency in at least one foreign language—preferably a language in which original texts can be studied in advanced seminars or thesis tutorials—so that development in the skill of close reading can culminate in the mastery of texts in the language in which they were written.

Writing skills also are mastered in the religion major, since the writing of papers, from brief expository exercises to full essays, is required of students on a regular basis, especially in upper-level and advanced courses, and their work is subjected to criticism. As students progress from entry-level to advanced courses, not only should the writing of papers become the preferred test of comprehension, but discussion should predominate as classroom method. Students learn to be articulate in formulating and defending points of view, raising critical questions, meeting the arguments of peers and instructors.

Close reading, grammatical and coherent writing, articulacy in the give-and-take of discussion, mastery and active use of a foreign language: such language skills are good examples of the kinds of transferable skills cultivated in liberal arts majors. They are hard-won assets, valuable—even marketable—in virtually any career or association our students may eventually pursue. So while a liberal arts major in religion or kindred fields is not narrowly preprofessional, it can be highly relevant to professional and other goals in later life. It is in fact arguable that the cultivation of such broadly transferable skills is more practical for most undergraduates than the pursuit of skills more narrowly applicable to some single profession.

There also are transferable skills

cultivated by the liberal arts major other than the linguistic ones we have mentioned. Students majoring in religion and kindred fields, for instance, learn to do documentary research on specialized topics. They learn how to design a research program, how to find sources in libraries and archives, and how to analyze and present their material coherently. They learn to use computers and other technological aids to study and research. They learn the social skills entailed in cooperative work and productive disagreement. They learn to research and interpret the past from documentary and physical evidence, and they cultivate skills of systematic observation and "thick description" in field work projects devoted to contemporary situations.

Besides such transferable skills, students also pursue broad educational goals consonant with and reinforced by their liberal arts program as a whole. They master a number of critical methodologies applicable to the study of religion and to other fields in which they may be working as well. They gain insight into various dimensions of contemporary civilization, not only through direct study of aspects of the current scene but through the perspective gained by knowledge of other times and other places. They discover the rhetorical and experience-shaping power of symbol systems and the social roots out of which symbol systems grow.

Indeed, students become aware of the extent to which the world they live in is socially constructed, and they become both more and less at home in that world. The world loses something of its familiarity but also something of its intractable givenness and becomes susceptible to invention and discovery, to criticism, wonder, change; and, as it is with the world the students live in, so it is with themselves. They discover the strong ties that bind them in a common origin and a common destiny with other human beings, but they also discover the vulnerability and divisive conflicts of human society. They discover their own power to think.

With respect to all such skills and objectives, the study of religion in depth reinforces studies pursued in the other arts and sciences. It is not so rigidly departmentalized that our students feel they are in alien territory when they venture beyond the curriculum in religion.

TOWARD THE PROGRAMMATIC DESIGN OF THE RELIGION MAJOR

Details of curricular design in religion doubtless will continue to vary from campus to campus. Local insti-

tutional circumstances are bound to be decisive. Usually, too, the religion curriculum must accommodate large numbers of nonmajors, with some courses offered primarily for them and many courses open to qualified nonmajors. In planning a program for majors, however, departments confront the need to design a curriculum that is coherent as a whole, and our suggestions are directed to that effort.

Before offering some proposals about the progression of stages through the major, we will address structural features of the major curriculum as a whole. It seems useful to organize offerings in religion into three general categories: studies in historic traditions, critical approaches to the study of religion, and themes and theories.

☐ Studies in historic traditions: The bulk of a department's courses generally fall into this category, including not only particular religions (Buddhism, Judaism) but also the religions of large geographic areas (native American, African, Asian). Here the student will encounter, in a program extending over several semesters, courses in the history and some of the distinctive features of two or more historic traditions.

☐ Critical approaches to the study of religion: Studies directed to historic traditions already are critical in the sense that appropriate critical methods are employed and tested in interpreting these traditions. But some studies should address the critical approaches themselves, subjecting a body of critical theory (sociology of religion, phenomenology, and so on) to analysis and criticism. Students majoring in religion should take at least two critical or metacritical courses of this sort, perhaps including a required seminar restricted to majors.

☐ Themes and theories: There is a considerable body of literature, some of it by major religious thinkers, that addresses religious themes of overarching significance—theories of ritual, ideas of God, gender issues, social ethics, and personal faith. Students of religion should take some critical soundings in this body of literature, especially in works relevant to their larger interests in this field. Some courses might be organized thematically, for example, around theories of myth and ritual, and some might be devoted to the work of one or more constructive religious thinkers.

We suggest that all three of these elements should be represented in the total structure of a major program. It is not so clear just where each of them should fit in the unfolding of that program from introductory to advanced studies. All three structural elements seem necessary, but their relation to each other is kaleidoscopic, and their integra-

tion into a particular program well may differ from one institution to another.

In addition to finding appropriate places for these three structural elements, it is important that there be a progression through the major program so that students can advance in their knowledge and critical sophistication from one stage to another. A curricular program might be arranged in four progressive stages:

☐ Entry-level studies: Entry-level courses are designed for new or potential majors to introduce them into university studies in this field. The most fundamental entry-level course is the departmental introduction designed to orient students to the curricular program as a whole. It should provide materials that students can use and build on in the more advanced studies offered by the department. This integral relation to a department's program is essential, but it can be achieved in different ways. Some departments, for instance, might focus the introduction on two or more significantly different historic traditions—perhaps one that is text-oriented and another that has developed among nonliterate peoples. A department might even undertake a survey of major world religions.

A different focus might introduce students to some of the critical approaches employed in university studies in religion, with exempla chosen from one or more historic traditions. In that case the design will be determined by theoretical and critical interests, with the exempla chosen to provide appropriate subject matters for the exercise of such interests and skills. Departments with sufficient resources might even offer two alternative departmental introductions—perhaps one of each of these types—and might offer other entry-level courses besides the departmental introduction, that is, one designed to provide an overview of one or another historic tradition in which the department has special teaching strength.

☐ Intermediate studies: The student might take most of his or her courses devoted to major periods in the development of at least two historic traditions or to significant aspects distinctive to them. Critical disciplines should be employed in the interpretation of this material, and students should become self-conscious about their use of these disciplines. At this point, students might take one course focussing on critical approaches and one on themes and theories. Much of the students' course work will be concentrated in this stage.

☐ Advanced studies: Advanced studies should be more specialized, presupposing the materials students have examined at the intermediate level. Seminars restricted to majors and to students who have fulfilled the intermediate-level prerequisites are effective, as are tutorials that permit students to explore more deeply interests that were generated in the intermediate studies.

☐ Capstone studies: These culminating studies for seniors should offer students opportunities to apply and refine insights cultivated in their earlier studies. Since insight and the ability to use methods and concepts critically are more important at this level than cumulative knowledge, the use of comprehensive examinations seems inappropriate. For some students, researching and composing a senior thesis is an ideal capstone study. An alternative might be the preparation of a portfolio of the student's best work, including papers and projects that are revised to represent the best level of thinking that the student has achieved. The composition of an intellectual autobiography also might be appropriate at the end of a senior's year, enabling the student to review and assess his or her own development through the program. Outside faculty members might be invited to the campus to examine some of these materials and to interview graduating seniors, asking them to assess what has gone right and what has gone wrong in their programs.

*The members of the task force on the study of the religion major are: Stephen Crites, Wesleyan University (scribe); Frederick Denny, University of Colorado–Boulder; Carole Myscofski, University of Missouri; June O'Connor, University of California–Riverside; Albert Rabil, Jr., SUNY–College at Old Westbury; and James Wiggins, Syracuse University.

CHAPTER ELEVEN

SOCIOLOGY[1]

Colleges and universities strive to provide an intellectually liberating education for their undergraduate students. Although the nature of a liberal education has generated considerable debate,[2] a truly liberating education requires students to undertake study-in-depth in a given discipline. An earlier AAC report concludes that study-in-depth implies at least the following:

☐ comprehension of a complex structure of knowledge

☐ achievement of critical sophistication through sequential learning experiences (which cannot be reached merely by cumulative exposure to more and more subject matter)

☐ acquisition of abilities and skills required to undertake independent work

☐ development of and disposition to undertake new learning in order to serve themselves and their society as citizens.[3]

In sociology and other social sciences, study-in-depth as part of a liberal education also will include experience with:

☐ a central core of method and theory

☐ a range of topics and variety of analytic tools

☐ a crucial interplay between continuous observation on the one hand and a developing, articulated theoretical base on the other.[4]

The American Sociological Association (ASA) executive office often receives calls from institutions asking for criteria and guidelines with which sociology programs can be evaluated. ASA has never developed a set of guidelines because it recognizes the diversity within the discipline as well as the diversity in the contexts in which sociology is taught. At the same time, the Teaching Services Program promotes effective teaching; provides materials and training; and offers a journal, *Teaching Sociology*, as a way to help departments meet their own goals. The academic climate has changed: as mandated reviews of departments increase, ASA is called upon more frequently to assist in these areas.

ASA and AAC jointly appointed a

task force in sociology in spring 1989 to examine how the sociology major achieves these goals. This report presents an account of the work of the task force, an overview of the current situation in sociology, and thirteen specific recommendations.

The task force recommendations are not prescriptive but specific and significant guidelines. We recognize the diversity in departments: in size, mission, budget, geographic location, student demographics, and other factors. We hope each department will give the report serious attention and determine what parts are pertinent to their own program. This written report is the beginning of a process of reflection and improvement within our discipline. Reviewing the recommendations, even to amend or reject them, will renew the vitality and increase the coherence of sociology programs.

SPECIAL CONDITIONS INFLUENCING THE SOCIOLOGY MAJOR

Three major sets of issues influence the character of most sociology programs. The first is the development of sociology as an academic discipline over the past one hundred years. A second factor is the diversity of specializations found in sociology. The third set of issues arises from the wide diversity of students

enrolled in sociology courses and in sociology as a major.

The development of sociology as an academic discipline

Sociology is a relatively new discipline. Baker and Rau present a synopsis of the growth and ethos of the curriculum:

Sociology was first organized as academic work for students and professors in the 1880s and 1890s. During the first several decades, sociologists struggled against considerable odds to develop a field of study and gain academic respectability. Sociology was driven by the spirit of social amelioration and attempted to make the study of all kinds of social problems academically credible. There was a tendency to add courses to the curriculum around the fringes of economics and the practical concerns of social welfare. While early founders were defensive about organizing the leftovers in the social sciences...they kept busy establishing a curriculum and finding jobs for newly trained sociologists, many of whom were converts from economics or the ministry. The founders enjoyed making pronouncements about the "science of society," but the rhetoric of science did not help create a coherent academic discipline or a well organized curriculum.[5]

Like the other social sciences, sociology's origins lie in philosophy. Its development in the United States as a separate discipline parallels almost exactly the growth of the university and the emergence of the specialized disciplines we know today. By the early twentieth century, the formation of learned societies expressed and expanded all the university-based disciplines and sociology in particular; the American Sociological Society was founded in 1905.[6]

More than any of the other social sciences, sociology was shaped by the momentous changes taking place in Europe and the United States in the nineteenth century. Durkheim, Marx, Weber, and Simmel, sociology's founders, took as their text the industrial-capitalist-urban revolution that was taking place around them. The founders traced the effects of this revolution on traditional values: religion, economic and political institutions, family, and community. Their approaches to these issues combined empirical observation with an understanding of social structure, thereby setting apart sociology as a distinctive discipline.

Sociology appealed to students most, however, for its promise to ameliorate misery and illuminate pressing social concerns. By 1910, when the major was firmly established in the undergraduate curricula of American universities, sociologists were marking the boundaries between their discipline and the other social sciences and philosophy.[7]

The discipline-based department, another hallmark of university development, became the instrument for carrying out this project.[8] Because sociology was a young discipline, separate departments were established more slowly than those in more traditional disciplines such as history. They took hold more firmly in universities than in colleges, where even now sociology sometimes is combined with anthropology or social work.

The dominance of the university, with its accompanying proliferation of disciplines and departments, splintered the nineteenth-century consensus about what constituted a liberal arts education.[9] This was almost as true within the disciplines as they grew ever more numerous and complex; sociology was no exception.

The discipline took shape in the twentieth century with pendulum shifts toward positivism, large-scale social theory, attention to social problems and the dispossessed, and exploration into more social phenomena. Enrollments built to a peak in the 1960s, fell in the next two decades, and are climbing again.

The sociology curriculum has been loosely structured from the beginning. In its American form, sociology has evolved as a cultural entity

with three distinct legacies:
☐ The theoretical legacy, wherein several generations of scholars have written a literature of commentary on the theorists and theories of sociology.
☐ The methodological legacy: Building on the social survey movement of the progressive era, attitude studies, demographic work, and major developments in statistics and computer software, sociologists analyze all kinds of quantifiable social data and pursue qualitative field methods.
☐ The civic legacy of substantive topics: a longstanding interest in distinctly "sociological" topics such as family, crime and deviance, race relations, community and urban culture, gender, death and dying, and complex organizations.

According to Baker and Rau, the undergraduate curriculum has been structured around two professional subcultures—theory and methods—that are loosely grafted to an array of substantive topics.[10]

Diversity of specializations
Sociology is characterized by pluralism in theoretical and methodological approaches, in substantive specializations, and in units of analysis (from small groups through organizations to whole societies). Crosscutting these specialties is the range of pedagogies faculty members use to teach. The resulting diversity limits

consensus on what is important for sociology students to know. Consequently, even among similar institutions, there may be little similarity in the content of the sociology major.

The task force's analysis of catalogues showed consensus on an introductory course, one or more methods and statistics courses, and one or more theory courses. The point at which students are encouraged or required to take these courses, however, varies from sophomore to senior year. Other courses that make up the total credits for the major show no patterns within or across departments. There was no other discernable pattern in requirements for the major in departments of differing missions and sizes.

The substantive courses in the sociology major have led one colleague to describe it as a "7-11 curriculum"—students dash in and out at their convenience, taking what they want when they want.

There are some points of consensus:
☐ Most sociologists agree on the crucial role of different types of social structures—institutions, organizations, even stable communication patterns—in understanding human behavior.
☐ Most sociologists agree on the importance of microlevel processes and interactions that foster the develop-

ment and growth of the "self."

☐ Most sociologists see the value of empirical analysis using a variety of methods.

Diversity of students

Sociology courses provide an important service function in most colleges. Sociology majors often make up a small percentage of the students even in upper-division classes. Student diversity shows itself in these ways:

☐ Students enter the sociology curriculum lacking a conception of the field. Not only is sociology taught sporadically in high schools, the general public lacks an understanding of the discipline. Very few students declare a sociology major upon entering college.

☐ Sociology attracts a diverse group of students: they come from and go into a variety of occupations; come from and go to metropolitan areas, suburban areas, and rural areas; and come from all age groups, both genders, all ethnic groups, and all social classes. This diversity is a strength. Giving voice to different social perspectives is a vital underpinning of the sociology curriculum.

☐ Because of a lack of inherent sequencing in content and few prerequisites, there are nonmajors in all sociology classes, even upper-division courses. Lower-division courses typically include more nonmajors than

majors.

☐ Compared to students in many arts and sciences fields, students in sociology declare the major late in their undergraduate careers. Most other majors are recruited through general-education courses, from other majors, and from among the "undecided." By the time the sociology major is declared (usually late in the sophomore or early in the junior year), the student must rush to take required courses. The "compressed major" complicates the goal of study-in-depth.

RATIONALE FOR STUDY-IN-DEPTH IN SOCIOLOGY

The task force defines study-in-depth within the sociology major as the development of a coherent and mature conception of sociology as a scholarly endeavor. Study-in-depth implies a process of intellectual development whereby students become part of the sociological community of discourse. Social integration fosters cognitive integration.

To move to a rationale for the sociology major as study-in-depth, the task force concentrated on three themes:

☐ acquisition of a sociological perspective

☐ the goals of liberal education

☐ student intellectual development.[11]

The interplay among these themes undergirds our recommendations for how to achieve study-in-depth.

Acquisition of a sociological perspective
Sociologists generally agree that the sociological perspective incorporates three central aspects:
☐ the preeminence of social structures and their influences on micro and macrolevel social processes
☐ the value of empirical analysis
☐ the link, in C. Wright Mills' terms, between private troubles and public issues, or the individual's experience and larger social processes.[12]
The curriculum in the sociology major should offer students multiple experiences for building and testing theory, collecting and evaluating data, and using the sociological perspective in linking their lives to larger social processes. The sociological perspective enables students to become aware of social forces affecting their lives. Such liberation is certainly part of the general meaning of liberal education.

The goals of liberal education
The second part of study-in-depth is liberal, or liberating, education itself. As defined in AAC's *Integrity in the College Curriculum*, a liberal education fosters specific capacities, including logical and analytic reasoning; literacy; numeracy; historical con-

sciousness; understanding of science and scientific inquiry; understanding of values and their relationships to a variety of life situations; appreciation of symbolic expression; international and multicultural competence; experience with study-in-depth; and involvement in a community of learning.[13] Properly structured, a sociology major allows students to achieve reasonable competency in all of these domains.

Sociology further contributes to liberal education by unfettering the mind. Peter Berger describes sociology as a way of seeing, of seeing through things, and going beyond the ordinary, the obvious and what is manifest.[14] He further notes that "...familiarity breeds indifference."[15] There is a need for "debunking" because things are not always as they appear. Selvin and Wilson note that sociology opens "the mind's door to the deceptively familiar world of social arrangements. It prompts us to question the customary. It encourages us to entertain alternatives.... We get a truer view of social reality as sociology reveals the complexity of cause and effect in human affairs—the likelihood of causes other than we had supposed, and effects that may be far different from what we had in mind...."[16]

Students' intellectual development
The third theme is students' intellec-

tual development, one of the central concerns of higher education. The stages of intellectual development differ slightly in various taxonomies.[17] Sociologists should familiarize themselves with different models but focus on their common core: first, a recognition that students at different stages of intellectual development interpret questions and concepts in notably different ways, and second, that stages of intellectual development represent students' increasing capacity to deal with abstraction, organizing principles, and interrelationships. Intellectual development is not automatic, but it can be stimulated by instruction. Therefore, regardless of debates over any one taxonomy, sociologists should consider intellectual development as both a goal and a constraint when organizing and numbering courses and deciding what is taught and how.

In general, the first stage of intellectual development involves remembering facts and description, with students oriented to authoritatively determinable right and wrong answers. This material often is tested with multiple-choice questions. A second stage asks for comparisons of one situation with another: the beginning of analysis. At a more advanced stage, students move from comparisons to identification of variables. By showing how variables relate to each other and offering an interpretation, students begin the process of building theory.

At a fourth stage, students move toward evaluating and synthesizing the various kinds of pertinent theories, comparing one theory to another. For instance, students might contrast the works of Karl Marx and Max Weber on what the two men say about class and power. In sociology, causal analysis draws on different theoretical sources for major explanatory variables. Synthesis and evaluation of theories therefore are essential for students' preparation for independent inquiry.

The task force believes that these three themes ought to converge through study-in-depth in sociology. The major should foster a student's intellectual development, competency in applying the sociological perspective, and ways of seeing fundamental to liberating education.

HOW TO SEQUENCE

Rau and Dale have highlighted three dimensions on which sequencing occurs: skills courses (methods and theory), substantive courses, and critical thinking.[18] The goal is to move students on all three dimensions simultaneously.

To move only on one dimension offers pitfalls. A student may be technically proficient but without substantive grounding; a student may be critically incisive but lack training in the concepts and approaches of the discipline.

The skills dimension is the easiest place to begin sequencing because most departments require at least two skills courses (methods and theory). These courses should be coupled and sequenced. If students can take courses in any sequence, then instructors cannot presume knowledge from prerequisites. Consider the standard methods-statistics-theory sequence. If the sequence were only three courses and if students could take them in any order, there are six different combinations; imagine if the sequence included more courses. This decoupling of courses characterizes many of the catalogues we reviewed.

The task force recommends that skills courses be offered earlier rather than later in the major (that is, late sophomore year to early junior year rather than senior year).

The substantive dimension shows much more variety. In most departments, it is hard to find an underlying logic for the course titles and sequencing of substantive courses.

Some dimensions on which a department might sequence substantive courses are:

☐ requiring increasing sophistication in reading and doing empirical research and theoretical analysis

☐ moving from courses central to sociology to ones that are more specialized and less central, though equally valid and interesting (For example, a course on social stratification might be offered or required early in the major. Courses such as sociology of sport might be senior electives.)

☐ moving from courses aimed at nonmajors to those aimed at majors

☐ moving along a track or concentration of courses in one area—for example, criminology, gerontology, or medical sociology—that progress from introductory materials to more advanced work

☐ moving from microlevel phenomenon to macrolevel units of analysis or vice versa

☐ moving from social institutions (that is, family, education) to social processes (that is, urbanization, change) or vice versa

☐ following a theme or set of themes. At the University of Houston, for example, the department has identified three sociological concerns: the distributive (looking at social inequality), the social psychological, and the organizational. Courses revolve around the application of one theme to several social institutions or application of three themes to one institution.[19] The department groups courses within a theme, and students are expected to take courses within each group in a prescribed order.

For the critical-thinking dimension, the course numbering system should reflect the increasing demands placed on students. Granting the reality that students within a single course are always at different levels of intellectual development, instructors should do as much as they can to stimulate intellectual competence in applying and interrelating the field's concepts, methods, and perspectives. As students progress through the major, they should have more and more experiences with active learning, oral and written communication, application of learning from one context to another, data manipulation and analysis, original research activities, and synthesis of material that has come before.

In sum, departments should plot courses on the three dimensions to reflect accurately their sequencing decisions.

RECOMMENDATIONS FOR SOCIOLOGY PROGRAMS

1. Departments should articulate and publish goals and rationales for their program.

Faculty members in sociology departments should collectively develop, articulate, publish, monitor, and assess goals and rationales for their programs, taking into account the institution's mission and student characteristics.

This task force drafted a set of departmental goals as an example.[20] The goals are phrased in terms of observable behavior. For each goal, the student should be able to do certain things—outcomes that can be demonstrated to faculty members who can assess the quality of the work. The task force strongly encourages departments to think in terms of behavioral outcomes and not stop the process with lofty, immeasurable goals.[21]

2. Departments should assess the needs and interests of their students; departmental goals and practices should reflect and respond to these needs and interests. "Communicating clear expectations for students depends, in part, on understanding discrepancies between expectations instructors establish and those students accept as consistent with their own."[22]

Departments should engage in continual evaluation of their programs with a commitment to a formal review every five years. The important principle is that feedback from students is a central part of the program. Departments could survey undergraduate majors, nonmajors, and graduates; use evaluations of instruction and advising; conduct focus groups; and so forth. They should ask how relevant and understandable the parts of the major are, as well as how major as a whole prepares students for their jobs. Faculty members can use the results from this monitoring to adjust individual courses, parts of the curriculum, advising, and the overall rationale of the major.

3. *Departments should structure the curriculum and pedagogical experiences to increase the intellectual development of students over time. To this end, departments should promote active learning experiences.*

As noted earlier, the content of sociology does not present a compelling, singular, hierarchical sequence of courses. Departments must develop that sequence and its rationale. However, the sequencing should be based on the intellectual sophistication expected of students and reflected in coursework. As a start, the numbering and prerequisite system need to make sense to students, parents, advisors, and colleagues in other disciplines.

Departments should monitor courses and the entire program for the proportions of material at various levels of intellectual functioning, ranging from the lowest level of describing and remembering to the highest level of independent inquiry. Careful examination of syllabi and discussion among faculty members can reveal inconsistencies in numbering, prerequisites, sequencing, and difficulty of material. While it seems obvious that lower-division courses should offer preparation—in content

and skill—for upper-division courses, the task force's examination of course descriptions and syllabi does not show sufficient application of this principle.

4. *Departments should have at least four levels in a sequence of courses in the major.*

Our review of current practices shows a "ferris wheel" model of sequencing. Anyone, freshman to senior, who has the "ticket" (the introductory course prerequisite) can hop on at any point. The few courses required for the major (usually methods, statistics, and theory) require this single prerequisite, and rarely are students expected to take them in any order. As Goldsmid and Wilson note, "Our scanning of college and university catalogues suggests that sociology has far fewer prerequisites for advanced courses than do psychology and economics."[23]

In the four-level sequence, however, the first level consists of an introductory-level course (or courses) designed to give an overall picture of the discipline, including basic questions, concepts, and typical answers to the questions. The task force recognizes the difficulty and importance of teaching this course, and we recommend that departments:

☐ consider teaching introductory sociology as a laboratory course, with some small-group experience (for example, discussion groups) if it is

taught in a large class setting
☐ put their best teachers in the introductory course; those could be senior or junior faculty members. If a few very promising graduate students are used, they should receive teacher training and peer review as a part of their teaching assignments. The same type of support and feedback should be accorded part-time, temporary instructors, who should be used as infrequently as possible.
☐ move toward providing an understanding of society more than an explanation of the intricacies of the discipline of sociology. The courses should be less encyclopedic or fact- and name-oriented and should emphasize powerful ideas in sociology, empirical generalization, and the general sociological perspective. Such emphases come at the expense of coverage. Our best estimate is that 90 percent of students in introductory sociology never take another sociology course. While that number should be lower, departments need to consider the nonmajor as the audience for the introductory course.
☐ model "sociological thinking," preferably through active learning. In every introductory course, students should be asked to read some original writing (even in addition to a textbook), do some writing (even short answers), and critique a piece of sociological work. In short, students should see that sociology is a

creative enterprise.

The second level in the sequence includes required courses in basic sociological skills (statistics, methods, and theory) and substantive courses (for example, sociology of the family or social stratification) designed to provide students with breadth of knowledge without assuming their prior exposure to research training or sociological theory. The task force considers first-level and second-level courses to be lower-division courses.

The third level includes advanced substantive courses that continue to develop breadth and depth. These courses assume that students have a background in social research methods and theory; they require students to apply and develop the analytical skills they have acquired at the second level while they absorb additional substantive information. In short, second-level courses are firm prerequisites for these upper-division courses.

The fourth level includes one or more capstone courses, in which students are encouraged to integrate different parts of their coursework into a coherent and mature conception of sociology as an approach to inquiry and to life. The capstone experience should emphasize students' ability to pull things together rather than pursue a narrow specialty, as might occur in a special topics course. Students may concentrate on certain monographs or write on a specific topic, but their work should bring to bear on the topic at hand all their preparation in the major. As part of the capstone, students should write a senior paper or thesis or complete some other kind of a professional "product" (for example, a videotape or photo display). The capstone should be required of all majors.

5. *Departments should structure the curriculum to recognize explicitly the intellectual connections between sociology and other disciplines.*

One goal of a liberal education is for students to recognize intellectual connections among disciplines. Sociology programs have several alternatives for achieving greater intellectual integration:

☐ Within courses, instructors can integrate material from other disciplines by comparing methodologies, theories, and findings of different disciplinary approaches.

☐ Through careful advising, departments can encourage students to take "connected" courses in other departments. These recommendations should be based on the complementarity of the connected course to sociology. While sociologists might agree that it is valuable for students to take psychology courses, the sociology adviser should know which specific topics, instructors, and pedagogies challenge sociology students.

☐ Taking a minor in another field

enhances students' ability to see connections among courses.

☐ Departments can encourage students to take part in interdisciplinary programs such as women's studies, urban studies, or gerontology, among others.

6. *Departments should design a curriculum that gives students repeated experiences in posing sociological questions and bringing data to bear on them, making full use of computer and communication technologies as available.*

Education in sociology depends on the ability to collect and analyze data as well as construct theoretical analyses. Students' sociological perspective grows from these active learning experiences. Sociology courses, then, must be viewed as laboratory science—requiring appropriate technology, facilities, and small class size. The large lecture format—passive learning—should be phased out.[24] At the very least, passive formats and styles should be modified to include more inquiry through discussion, case studies, critiques, computer-assisted instruction that is not drill and practice, simulations, and so on.

Probably the earliest "test" of a proposition begins with library research and literature review. Here the simple technologies of computerized library searches are appropriate. Part of the major should include instruction in retrieving secondary data and using key abstracting services and reference documents.[25]

Sociology majors should be computer literate. Departments should try to offer basic training in personal computer use and relevant software, including analysis of quantitative and qualitative data, word processing, and menu-driven exercises. If possible, students should have experience on a mainframe system and familiarity with packages such as SPSS or SAS, with coding and file creation and other simple procedures.

Different approaches to data collection and analysis are feasible. Observing behavior in organizations or small groups or working with small-group laboratories or focus groups provides training in the sociological perspective. Using key informants for analyzing sociological patterns, processes, and social constructions can be instructive. Similarly, collecting, organizing, and analyzing historical data can illustrate sociological methods of description and of analyzing change.

7. *Departments should structure activities to promote a productive learning community that includes students and faculty members.*

An important pedagogical tool for students' intellectual development rests on the sociological principle that intellectual integration is fostered in large parts from social-network integration. When students have common experiences, know each other and their professors, and have contact outside the classroom, they can respond to each other's ideas more constructively; they enter a community of discourse. Because of constraints on sequencing the sociology major, it is especially important that departments create conditions that foster a socio-intellectual community for their students.

Sociology traditionally has tried to draw undergraduates into the discipline through departmental clubs, colloquia, and other special events. As more students enroll part-time and commute from jobs and families and as faculty members are pressed in their own work lives, however, these extracurricular activities are more difficult to engineer.

The use of small groups of students to solve problems and work out exercises has become common in sociology courses other than statistics and lab courses.[26] Collaborative research projects also enhance community.

Another approach is to have students take several courses that are clustered around a common theme such as science, technology, and human values. Students can be clustered as a cohort that experiences first-year core courses together.

In addition to the above strategies for socio-intellectual contact, students need to develop an identity as sociologists (or student sociologists). Faculty members should mentor all students, have them work as interns within the department, and encourage them to attend professional meetings and discuss what they have learned.

This professional socialization is hardly indoctrination. Part of the sociological perspective is the drive to critique. The diversity of our field and the lack of consensus about key courses may arise from the self-reflective and self-critical way sociology faculty members think about their discipline. This ability and habit of critique, no doubt, will be passed on to students.

Outside of the classroom, good advising is essential to promoting a community of discourse.[27] The ASA Code of Ethics stresses the importance of helping students with job placement and fostering their involvement in the department and the community of discourse. Departments might develop handbooks about the department and the field, standard packets of career materials, or sample resumes.

As Carol Schneider notes, "We bring students into the academic community...not to make them resident citizens in the academic world but rather to nurture and support them as they develop the capabilities they need to enter and negotiate across many communities of discourse and understanding inside, but especially outside, the academy."[28] Sociology and anthropology provide perspectives to help us stand outside of our own experience and reflect on it. Furthermore, we can anticipate future roles (employee, parent, professional sociologist) as an extension of this "step out" process.

8. Departments should structure activities to help students integrate their educational experiences within the department and across departments.

Most students do not take sociology in high school, and an introductory sociology course in college is their only exposure to the field. This introductory course usually has many purposes and constituencies: general education, prerequisites for other sociology courses, and requirements for other majors.

The task force suggests that these students might best be exposed to descriptions of social institutions and how institutions are organized. Most have had little experience in society's institutions; they have not thought seriously about differences between institutions. Except for voting, they have virtually no experience in political institutions and only meager experience with economic ones. Yet these represent two of the major causal influences on their attitudes and behavior.

Students do have considerable experience in family life, but some only from the perspective of children. Likewise, their experience with education, while substantial, has been in a relatively homogenous environment with their own race and social class. Students should be exposed to other experiences with social institutions.

9. *Departments should structure the curriculum to underscore the centrality of race, class, gender, and culture in society and in sociological analysis.*

Race, class, and gender are "central categories of social experience" that affect us all.[29] Many courses fall victim to the ghettoization of sex and race in particular, with faculty members thinking that offering separate courses on those topics "takes care of it." Introductory sociology textbooks often are written with separate chapters on race and gender and little infusion of that material in other subject areas. In some cases, the experiences of people who are not white, male, and middle class are treated as deviant cases. For example, the black family (or the homosexual family, for that matter) often is relegated to the last chapter in a textbook called "other family forms."

Sociologists should lead the way in showing our colleagues in other disciplines that, in the words of Elizabeth Higginbotham, not only women have gender, and not only blacks (or other minority groups) have race.[30]

In some cases, research has been done on samples that are not fully inclusive. Research on men cannot be generalized to women, nor can findings from one racial or class group be generalized to another. Students can learn the power of race, gender, and class by using these variables as key explanations for variance in social phenomena.

Where scholarship has been inclusive, or work has targeted non-white, non-male, non-middle-class persons, those materials can speak to the experiences of students in the class. Where classes are homogeneous, such readings open students' eyes to new realities.

Faculty members must ask themselves Margaret Andersen's penetrating question: "Does the syllabus teach that all group experience is grounded in race, class, and gender, or is one group generalized while all others are particularized?"[31]

10. *Departments should structure the curriculum to increase students' exposure to comparative and international materials where appropriate.*

The logic behind the preceding recommendation extends to materials that reflect non-American experience. Students learn about differences in cultures by reviewing comparative material. Contrasts with their own experience make them more aware of the world they take for granted. Furthermore, international comparisons call into question theories and concepts developed only in an American context.

11. Departments should structure the curriculum to develop the sociological literacy of students and the application of sociological knowledge to policy issues.

The curriculum should develop students' capacity to read, understand, and respond critically to primary textual materials in the discipline. Starting in the introductory course, students need to be exposed to sociological writings in the popular press as well as in disciplinary journals. They need to be taught and given practice in how to critique published reports, including the newspaper. A theme running through all courses might be how sociology differs from other perspectives on the same general topics. Students need to be taught how to frame questions and determine appropriate strategies for addressing these questions. Students can be given policy issues and asked to highlight the sociological contributions to public discussion of these issues or their policy outcomes.

12. Departments should structure the curriculum to provide opportunities for students to develop higher-order thinking skills and skills in written and oral

communication, at least in upper-division courses.

The task force recommends that every student majoring sociology:

☐ read three or more original monographs and critically comment on them

☐ read at least six professional articles that reflect differing methodologies

☐ write a major paper using sociological concepts

☐ rewrite that paper for at least one other audience: a community group, a letter to the editor or op-ed piece, or a letter to a legislator, for example

☐ participate in a research project that uses primary or secondary data

☐ give an oral report

☐ know how to access library reference materials relevant to sociology

☐ prepare a resumé effectively presenting sociological skills.

13. Departments should assess the major (curriculum, courses, and instruction) on a regular basis using multiple sources of data.

To implement this recommendation, departments routinely should collect data by:

☐ examining their department's goals, missions, needs, facilities, and accessible resources

☐ examining the faculty's goals, needs, resources, and perspectives on instruction

☐ surveying present students—both majors and nonmajors—on needs,

goals, levels of satisfaction with courses and advising, social networks, career goals, and actual plans
☐ surveying graduates on similar issues, as well as on their identification with sociology
☐ monitoring similar data in similar institutions and departments
☐ articulating the findings' implications for departmental programs.
These data would be in place for any administratively mandated program reviews.[32]

Sociologists are well versed in data collection and analysis and should be able to prepare formats for storing such information and putting it into usable reports. Some universities have excellent institutional research offices that can provide data on student demographics. Departments should develop a profile of how sociology majors are, or are not, different from the general student body. For example, in most universities, sociology attracts a greater proportion of racial and ethnic minorities.

If faculty members are interested in pedagogical research, they will find that sociological ideas can be tested using campus settings. Does the research on small-group communication, size, and leadership, for example, help us understand the dynamics of classroom discussion groups? The journal *Teaching Sociology* and other journals are places to submit and read such work.

Reviewing the university-level general-education requirements and the requirements of specific programs (for example, nursing or social work) may reveal paths of student enrollments into sociology courses. For example, nursing students often are required to take a course in sociology along the lines of Marriage and the Family; a statistics course in sociology may be required for several other majors. Knowing this path helps departments know about the students in its courses. In short: know your students.

WHY CHANGE IS DIFFICULT

Time and again, issues of "academic culture" impede the kind of change outlined in this report. Reading the reports of the other task forces, we found many common frustrations.

Educational institutions function in ways similar to other businesses. The organizational arrangements favor the status quo and keep change at bay. This process keeps organizations stable, but it frustrates educational reform. The unstructured curriculum is imbedded in the interests of higher education. However sincere, the recent calls for attention to undergraduate education will be limited in scope unless these changes occur:
☐ Teaching is seen as professional

work, by peers as well as students, and is considered in promotion and tenure decisions.

☐ Teaching ceases to be private activity occurring behind closed doors, out of sight from other colleagues. Teaching is professional behavior that needs to be discussed and subject to peer review.

☐ The department becomes a meaningful decision-making unit that functions with a collective mission. The chair must engage in more academic leadership, and individuals must make some sacrifices.[33]

☐ National learned societies invest in and guide the teaching of their discipline as important work, providing resources and legitimacy for attention to teaching at all kinds of institutions.

These issues are not unique to sociology. Nevertheless, sociologists, along with colleagues in education and other social sciences, should take the lead in offering proposals for organizational change that will enhance the likelihood that these reports will have a beneficial impact on undergraduate education.

American Sociological Association (chair); and Theodore Wagenaar, Miami University (Ohio).

The task force is demographically representative: three men and four women of different age cohorts; one member is black. Task force members came from a range of academic settings. All are active participants in ASA teaching activities and have taught many sociology courses across the curriculum. No one represents a two-year college; AAC's charge was to look at the four-year major. As the project unfolded, however, we became increasingly interested in the links between two-year and four-year programs.

The task force had a dual purpose: to respond to the major issues in the AAC "charge" and to offer help to departments who turn to ASA for guidelines on the major. We held four working meetings from March 1989 through February 1990. Each meeting involved intensive discussion, note-taking, synthesis, and report-writing.

The task force surveyed senior sociology majors about their feelings and beliefs about various aspects of their sociology programs. These data are available from ASA and appear in the unabridged version of this report (see appendix). We have comparative data from other majors. In addition, the task force examined catalogues and program descriptions from eighty-six departments to identify patterns of requirements and sequencing for majors.

The task force held a "town meeting" at the 1989 ASA Annual Meeting to present a preliminary draft report and hear responses. More than one hundred people attended the session, and most of their comments were addressed in the revised document. Members of the ASA Committee on Teaching served as helpful readers of the report. Finally, the ASA Council read and approved the document and voted to send it to all sociology departments.

---

1. The task force that prepared this report included Catherine Berheide, Skidmore College; Kathleen Crittenden, University of Illinois–Chicago; Robert Davis, North Carolina A&T State University; Paul Eberts, Cornell University (scribe); Zelda Gamson, University of Massachusetts–Boston; Carla Howery,

2. Zelda Gamson, "What Should Liberal Education Mean?" in *Liberating Education*, ed. Zelda Gamson et al. (San Francisco: Jossey-Bass, 1984), 1–27.

3. *Integrity in the College Curriculum* (Washington, D.C.: Association of American Colleges, 1985), 27–32.

4. *Ibid.*

5. Paul J. Baker and William Rau, "The Cultural Contradictions of Teaching Sociology" (unpublished paper, 1990), 2–5.

6. Frederick Rudolph, *Curriculum: A History of the American Undergraduate Course of Study Since 1636* (San Francisco: Jossey-Bass, 1977).

7. *Ibid.*

8. Lawrence R. Veysey, *The Emergence of the American University* (Chicago: University of Chicago Press, 1974).

9. Rudolph, *Curriculum.*

10. Baker and Rau, "Cultural Contradictions," 2–6.

11. The term "major" often will be used instead of study-in-depth simply because it is shorter and in common usage. However, the terms are interchangeable only when the major has sequencing, rigor, and increasingly complex intellectual tasks.

12. C. Wright Mills, *The Sociological Imagination* (New York: Oxford University Press, 1959).

13. *Integrity*, 15–26.

14. Peter Berger and H. Kellner, *Sociology Reinterpreted* (Garden City, N.Y.: Doubleday, 1981).

15. *Ibid.*, 39.

16. Hannan Selvin and Everett K. Wilson, *Why Study Sociology?* (Belmont, Calif.: Wadsworth Publishing Co., 1980), 16–17.

17. See Keith Roberts, "Sociology in the General Education Curriculum: A Cognitive Structuralist Perspective," *Teaching Sociology* 14 (October 1986): 207–16.

18. William Rau and Beverly Dale, "Ideas on a New Structure for Sociology's Undergraduate Curriculum" (unpublished paper, 1990), 6.

19. Janet Saltman Chafetz, "Course Sequencing and Semi-Sequencing," *ASA Teaching Newsletter* 6 (October 1982): 2.

20. The sociology major should study, review, and reflect on:

☐ the discipline of sociology and its role in contributing to our understanding of social

reality. The student should be able to describe how sociology differs from and is similar to other social sciences and give examples of these differences, describe how sociology contributes to a liberal arts understanding of social reality, and apply sociological imagination, principles, and concepts to her/his own life.

☐ the role of theory in sociology. The student should be able to define theory and describe its role in building sociological knowledge, compare and contrast basic theoretical orientations, show how theories reflect the context in which they are developed, and describe and apply basic theories or theoretical orientations.

☐ the role of evidence and qualitative and quantitative methods in sociology. The student should be able to identify basic methodological approaches and describe the general role of methods in building sociological knowledge, compare and contrast basic methodological approaches for gathering data, design a research study, and critically assess a published research report

☐ basic concepts in sociology and their fundamental theoretical interrelations. The student should be able to define, give examples, and demonstrate the relevance of culture, social change, socialization, stratification, social structure, institutions, and differentiation by race/ethnicity, gender, age, and class.

☐ how social structures operate. The student should be able to demonstrate how institutions interact in their effects on each other and on individuals, how factors such as population or urbanization affect social structures and individuals, and how culture and social structure vary across time and place.

☐ reciprocal relationships between individuals and society. The student should be able to explain how the self develops sociologically, how societal and structural factors influence individual behavior and the self's development, how social interaction and the self influences society and social structure, and how to distinguish sociological approaches to analyzing the self from psychological, economic, and other approaches.

□ the macro/micro distinction. The student should be able to compare and contrast theories at one level with those at another, summarize research documenting connections between the two, and develop a list of worthy research or analytical issues.

□ at least one area in depth within sociology. The student should be able to summarize basic questions and issues in that area, compare and contrast basic theoretical orientations and middle-range theories, show how sociology illuminates the area, summarize current research in the area, and develop specific policy implications of research and theories.

□ the internal diversity of American society and its place in the international context. The student should be able to describe the significance of variations by race, class, gender, and age and understand appropriately how to generalize or resist generalizations across groups.

Two more generic goals should be pursued in sociology:

□ encouraging students to think critically. The student should be able to move easily from remembering through analysis and application to synthesis and evaluation, recognize underlying assumptions in theoretical orientations or arguments, identify basic premises in particular methodological approaches, show how patterns of thought and knowledge are directly influenced by political-economic social structures, and present opposing viewpoints and alternative hypotheses on various issues.

□ encouraging students to develop values. The student should believe in the utility of the sociological perspective as one of several perspectives on social reality and the importance of reducing the negative effects of social inequality.

21. The task force reviewed the goal statements of the few departments that had them but did not find a set that was measurable. The goals drafted by the task force could serve as the foundation for "outcomes assessment," a trend in higher education.

22. Joan S. Stark, Kathleen M. Shaw, and Malcolm A. Lowther, "Student Goals for College and Courses: A Missing Link in Assessing and Improving Academic Achievement," *ERIC Digest* 6 (1989): 2.

23. Charles A. Goldsmid and Everett K. Wilson, *Passing on Sociology* (Washington, D.C.: American Sociological Association, 1980), 12.

24. Large classes can be well taught, but it is an uphill battle. For guidance, see Reece McGee, ed., *Teaching the Mass Class* (Washington, D.C.: ASA Teaching Resources Center, 1986).

25. An excellent example of such training occurs at the University of Wisconsin-Parkside, where all students must be "library literate" within their own major. Each major has a workbook with questions to complete by using the library to find the answers. The *Student Sociologist's Handbook* (1987) is another useful reference.

26. See William Rau and Barbara Heyl, "Humanizing the College Classroom: Collaborative Learning and Social Organization Among Students," *Teaching Sociology* 18 (April 1990): 141–55.

27. Martha McMillan and Kathleen McKinney, *Strategies for Effective Undergraduate Advising in Sociology* (Washington, D.C.: ASA Teaching Resources Center, 1986); Carla B. Howery, "Effective Advising," *ASA Footnotes* (February 1991), 4.

28. Carol G. Schneider, "Connecting Learning," *Liberal Education* 75 (November/December 1989), 4.

29. Margaret Andersen, "Moving Our Minds: Studying Women of Color and Reconstructing Sociology," *Teaching Sociology* 16 (April 1988): 123–32.

30. Elizabeth Higginbotham, presentation at meeting of Sociologists for Women in Society, Louisville, Ky., February 1990.

31. Andersen, "Moving Our Minds," 131.

32. For guidelines on such reviews, see Charles S. Green III, *Guidelines and Resources for Assessing Your Sociology Program* (Washington, D.C.: ASA Teaching Resources Center, 1986).

33. See Lee A. Bowker and Hans O. Mauksch, *Academic Leadership: The Role of the Chair* (Washington, D.C.: ASA, 1986);

and Michael Brooks, "Building the Commitment to Undergraduate Education: A Structural Response," *Teaching Sociology* 15 (October 1987): 376–83.

CHAPTER TWELVE

WOMEN'S STUDIES[1]

The phone rings at 9:00 P.M. on a Tuesday in January. It's Marguerite, a first-year student in my introductory honors course on women writers, who has been working on her first paper: a discussion of the famous moments of exclusion described by Virginia Woolf in the opening chapter of A Room of One's Own. Wandering around Oxbridge, Woolf is asked to keep off the grass, barred from the library, and made aware that she should not enter the chapel—all because she is a woman, not a "fellow." Marguerite had been in the library and realized too late that she had waited until after dark to leave. Unlike Woolf, she was locked in, not locked out, but for the same reason: she is a woman, not a man. The campus is dangerous to women alone at night. "I couldn't believe I had forgotten the time," she says. "Usually I am so careful." Fortunately, her roommate was home and came in a car to get her.

As Marguerite was waiting, she did a little survey. It turned out that men came and went alone, but no women did. She witnessed several women making calls at the public phone, for what was obviously routine "protection." My student has realized something about Woolf's text that, perhaps, no man could, and she is energized by this new understanding. It was reading Woolf that led to her survey, to her recognition that her experience was shared and was political.

She called because she wants to know whether it's all right if she refers to this evening's discovery in her paper. She knows that you're not supposed to write about "real life" in English papers. Her expressions of relief and gratitude when I give her permission to feel what she is feeling and articulate it as part of her analysis leave me wondering: How will all those other women in the lobby of the library understand their confinement? Which class in this vast university ever will address—or even acknowledge—the fundamental fact that a woman alone cannot go to the library *here without risk after dark?*

Also like Marguerite, however, I am partly exhilarated: Merely by assigning Virginia Woolf, I have precipitated a moment of consciousness-raising which must, I know, be replicated an untold number of times before it will result in a world in which Marguerite can leave the library alone at midnight if she wants—and she, too, will now help replicate that moment.

WOMEN'S EXPERIENCE AND THE FEMINIST CRITIQUE

Marguerite's epiphany is why women's studies exists. The library incident exemplifies how theory and experience work together to transform the student's sense of self and her relation to the world. Women's studies' central responsibility is to facilitate such moments of recognition and to follow them with moments of empowerment. The moments of recognition come when women or men identify the artificial gender constructions imposed by their culture. The moments of empowerment are initiated when, as in Marguerite's case, women replace their internalized acceptance of feminine dependency with a feminist awareness that enables them to critique the conditions of their lives—and work to change them. Many similar examples occur in women's studies classrooms every day, as students reinterpret their own and other women's lives; find multiple layers of meaning in literature, the arts, popular culture, and ordinary conversation; discover a language to describe sexual assaults and differential treatment; recover women-centered views of society, work, and values; and gradually create new strategies for functioning in and changing their worlds.

To foster such personal and intellectual transformation, women's studies both critiques existing theories and methodologies and formulates new paradigms and organizing concepts in all academic fields. It provides students with tools to uncover and analyze the ideological dynamics of their lives and become active participants in processes of social, political, and personal change. What we teach, and the way we teach it, encourages students to imagine alternatives to present systems of inequality and participate in political and social transformation.

WOMEN'S STUDIES AND HIGHER EDUCATION

What we have at present *is* a man-centered university, a breeding ground not of humanism, but of masculine privilege.

Adrienne Rich
On Lies, Secrets, and Silences

The central organizing category of analysis in women's studies is the concept of gender, which we understand as a pervasive social construction reflecting and determining differentials of power and opportunity. From their inception, however, feminist scholarship and pedagogy also have emphasized the diversity of women's experiences and the importance of the differences among women as necessary correctives to the distortions inherent in androcentric views of human behavior, culture, and society.

Women's studies therefore establishes the social construction of gender as a focal point of analysis in a complex matrix with class, race, age, ethnicity, nationality, and sexual identity as fundamental categories of social, cultural, and historical analysis. Women's studies at its best resists seeing "woman" as only white, middle class, heterosexual, and young. The deliberate deconstruction of the term "woman" and the tyranny such a term exercises over "women" is more than a simple recognition of multiple oppressions; our analyses require attention to the entire matrix. Gender, for example, never operates independently of race; it is differently formulated and experienced depending on class or national identity. Lesbian lives, so typically erased or distorted in most accounts, reflect more genuine complexity when analyzed in the context of ethnicity or age.

In the United States, women's studies grew out of the women's movement of the 1960s and 1970s as both faculty members and students clearly saw that women's social and political inequality was reflected in and partly produced by the invisibility of women's experience in the curricula, research priorities, and methodologies in higher education. Women's studies began as compensatory education, but it has become a comprehensive intellectual and social critique which retains its roots in the political women's movement. Of critical importance is our recognition that we, as women's studies faculty members, are working "against the grain" of our privileges—as various as they are, given race, class, ethnicity, and sexual identity—in an effort to extend privileges to all.

Women's studies' location "against the grain" of the institutions in which it operates reflects the marginal position assigned to women generally. The view from the margin, however, has provided women's studies with a theoretical perspective as "other," a perspective essential to our enterprise and one that distinguishes women's studies in important ways from the more established disciplines. Like race-specific ethnic studies programs, women's studies makes central the perspectives, experiences, and cultures of the marginalized. Our position on the boundaries of conventional academic categories has important structural and epistemological consequences. Each profoundly affects the nature and definition of the women's studies major.

Women's studies grew rapidly because it met urgent political and intellectual needs and because its founders took advantage of existing institutional frameworks and structures. These structures are employed by other interdisciplinary units—most particularly African-American and other ethnic studies programs—with which women's studies shares similar intellectual traditions, social definitions, and pedagogy. These other interdisciplinary groups also have unique institutional responsibilities and dilemmas that are the result of our cultural histories.

While women's studies exhibits great structural diversity and flexibility, the field never has had the luxury of designing either programs or curricula without making compromises. The nature and structure of women's studies programs, more than those of most academic fields, are tied directly to resources and to the credibility and legitimacy women's studies has achieved on a given campus.

Like so many other interdisciplinary programs, women's studies is part of what Charles Lemert has identi-

fied as the "shadow structure" integral to nearly every college and university, its "academic other": those programs where few teachers have tenure, where resources typically are thin and rewards rare, but where much, if not most, cutting-edge scholarship is occurring and where faculty members, are most passionately engaged in their research and teaching.[2] As Lemert and others have pointed out, "disciplines" all too often are confused with or even identified with what are, above all, administrative units (departments, divisions, schools, and colleges). Disciplines exert an administrative authority masquerading as an intellectual one and thus render suspect programs and curricula that violate or transcend convention. Curricular proposals, appeals for faculty lines and operating resources, and funding requests for program and faculty development in women's studies often must be accompanied by rearticulations of the rationale for its existence.

The very conditions of structural tension or political and administrative marginality that plague many women's studies programs, however, also are the conditions of women's studies' intellectual strength. By insisting on interdisciplinary flexibility and reflexivity, by refusing conventional categories and labels, and by asserting obligations to a self-conscious critique of the politics of knowledge, we resist absorption into an "acceptable" (and safe) liberal pluralism at the expense of our radical critique. While women's studies calls for a reallocation of material rewards to be applied to programs on the margin as well as at the center, its epistemological power depends on its location in spaces where conventional intellectual boundaries are blurred. In the tensions and contradictions between the need for academic authority and women's studies' refusal of it on patriarchal terms we construct our idea of feminist education in general and of a women's studies major in particular.

Women's studies, then, holds up a deliberately fragmented mirror to the old conceptions of the core curriculum of the liberal arts. It refutes the claim that the liberal arts as traditionally conceived offer the student "wholeness" or "well-roundedness." The emphasis on social construction in feminist scholarship exposes as untenable the primacy of the free and autonomous individual implied since the Enlightenment in the term "liberal." From its position on the margin and by its willingness to identify its own ideologies, women's studies brings to light the ideological nature of all structures of knowledge—most particularly the masculine bias in curricula that once seemed complete and impartial. Per-

haps the most important skill women's studies can pass on to students is the ability to recognize those biases where they seem most invisible.

A feminist analysis also challenges the metaphor of "study-in-depth" as it applies to contemporary structures of knowledge. AAC's *Integrity* report defines the great lessons of the major as: "...the joy of mastery, the thrill of moving forward in a formal body of knowledge and gaining some effective control over it, integrating it, perhaps even making some small contribution to it.... No matter how deeply or widely students dig, no matter how much they know, they cannot know enough, they cannot know everything."[3]

A feminist analysis of this rhetoric reveals not only a disturbing sexual subtext implying an analogy between knowledge and sexual subjugation but, more transparently, an idea of learning as mastery or control. Clearly embedded in this language are unconscious androcentric assumptions of dominance and subordination between the knower and the known, assumptions that too readily bring to mind the traditional relationship of men to women; of the colonizers to the colonized; indeed, of the masters to the slaves. Such phallocentric metaphors for "study-in-depth" raise serious questions about feminist participation in it. Nor are these metaphors the accidental usages of one report; they replicate the dominant discourses of Western empiricism that women's studies (along with other postmodern interpretive systems) critiques.

Such language indicates a misdirection for any intellectual project. Interdisciplinary study is becoming the prototype of organizing academic inquiry as we move into the twenty-first century. More appropriate metaphors for the idea of the major, therefore, are those now operative in women's studies: matrix, connection, dialogue, network. Women's studies does not seek to give students control over knowledge; rather, it helps students understand their place in social and cultural matrices and negotiate their environment, learning from—as well as resolving contradictions through—dialogue. In place of metaphors of mastery, feminism offers metaphors of intimacy and intersubjectivity; rather than relationships of dominance, we prefer those of reciprocity; for conceptions of knowledge as acquisition, we substitute ideas of exchange and community.

We certainly do not want to be locked out of the library; neither do we want to be locked in. We locate our description of the women's studies major between our discomfort with some of the assumptions of "study-in-depth" and our belief that a women's studies curriculum helps articulate the nature of the undergraduate experience.

WOMEN'S STUDIES AS A MAJOR

Those of us who stand outside the circle of this society's definition of acceptable women; those of us who have been forged in the crucibles of difference—those of us who are poor, who are lesbians, who are Black, who are older—know that *survival is not an academic skill*. It is learning how...to define and seek a world in which we can all flourish. It is learning how to take our differences and make them strengths.

Audre Lorde
Sister Outsider

Since its inception, women's studies has aimed to provide curricula for students who want to concentrate or major in that area. A parallel and equally important goal, however, has been to influence the entire educational environment to move away from exclusionary androcentric perspectives and practices in courses and activities. The latter focus means that women's studies unravels the very idea of a "major" as a self-contained program with clearly defined boundaries and a stable identity. One of women's studies goals is providing a sequence of coherently interrelated courses; a concomitant goal is dispersing itself among and acting upon other fields.

Women's studies degrees, majors, minors, and programs are built from a variety of curricular building blocks. The infrastructure of most courses is a series of separate courses on women and gender grounded in and usually offered through traditional disciplines or departments. These cross-listed courses serve both the concentration and dispersion of feminist scholarship. Virtually all women's studies programs supplement cross-listed courses with "interdisciplinary" or "transdisciplinary" courses sponsored by the women's studies program itself.

Even long lists of courses about women, however, are not sufficient to ensure gender balance in the curriculum as a whole. Since 1980, therefore, some 150 "mainstreaming" or "transforming of the curriculum" projects have been infusing feminist scholarship into a wide range of courses not necessarily focused on women or gender. Essential to the success of these curricular transformation projects is the expertise of women's studies faculty members.

Women's studies, then, has an unusually intense dialogue with other departments. At the root of the intellectual and political vitality of women's studies is this philosophical openness to dialogue: a dialogue that already has transformed the knowledge base of most of the humanities and social sciences, many of the natural sciences, and, of course, women's studies itself. As the UCLA Women's Studies Program describes it, "Women's perspectives challenge notions of causality and periodization in history [and] the content of the Western canon in literature and art; they bring the concept of cultural diversity and alternative values into economy; they challenge markers of class in sociology and concepts of universal power and authority in anthropology; they reveal the role of psychology and medicine in medicalizing women's bodies through disease categories; and they call into question the given, the 'divinely ordained,' and thus the authority on which male political institutions rest."[4] The commitment to self-reflection through dialogue is most evident in the redefinitions initiated by women of color, whose critique of women's studies has significantly changed the analysis, paradigms, and terms of feminist discourse.

The first women's studies program in the United States was formally approved in 1970 at San Diego State University. By 1977, when the National Women's Studies Association was founded, there were 276 women's studies programs nationwide. Today there are 520 programs, of which 235 include undergraduate majors and 404 include minors in women's studies. Women's studies programs and departments now exist across the full range of postsecondary educational institutions in this country. A recent survey by the American Council on Education reveals that 68 percent of all universities, 48.9 percent of all four-year colleges, and 26.5 percent of two-year colleges offer women's studies courses.[5]

More students take women's studies courses, however, than major in women's studies. Of the fifty-six institutional respondents to a recent NWSA survey of women's studies majors, 57 percent of the respondents enroll five hundred to twenty-six hundred students each year. However, 57 percent of the responding women's studies programs that have majors have fewer than ten majors and only 30 percent have twenty or more majors.[6] Double majors are the norm, not the exception.

Although there is great variety in women's studies programs and majors, we can identify shared principles and a range of topics that are found in most programs. Along with the central concept of gender as a social construction, most women's studies educators assume the authority of female experience in feminist theory. Consequently, women's studies emphasizes race, ethnicity, nationality, class, age, and sexual identity, as well as sex and gender, as categories of analysis. Gender always

is experienced from within this complex matrix.

While we emphasize the authority of women's experience, we also critique the myths of objectivity and value-free analysis and emphasize the ideological nature of all experience and all theories, acts of interpretation, and cultural representations. Beyond the need simply for methodological connections among disciplines, exploring these topics requires—and teaches—dialectical ways of thinking that emphasize making connections of all kinds and holding together things that seem contradictory: an epistemology of breadth and tension rather than depth and clarity.

The subject matter of women's studies is all of women's experience as it has been constructed and described for women and by women in a gendered world. More than simply a body of information, however, women's studies also is an approach, a critical framework through which to view all knowledge.

The following composite emerged in separate surveys on the women's studies major.[7] A typical women's studies major takes thirty-five semester hours divided among an introductory course; a series of electives equally distributed between the humanities and the social sciences and equally divided between courses offered by the women's studies program and courses cross-listed by the departments; and a final capstone experience in the form of a senior seminar, field study/internship, or independent study. Increasingly, women's studies programs are adding a feminist theory requirement (38 percent) to their major. They also are adding a requirement for a course on race, ethnicity, or non-Western culture. Ninety-five percent of the programs in one survey offer courses representing cultural diversity; one-third of all programs surveyed now require some kind of course or courses on race, ethnicity, or cross-cultural perspectives for their majors.[8] The addition of the feminist theory course and the emphasis on cultural diversity speak to the maturity of the discipline and its willingness to question the nature, structure, and politics of its own field. Women's studies instruction also typically emphasizes debates within feminism: the contentious history of the women's movement; the varieties of feminist theories; debates over biological difference and the relation between nature and nurture; the debates over the relation between feminism and other powerful contemporary explanatory systems such as Marxism, psychoanalysis, and postmodernism.

Introductory courses

Women's studies is one of the very few subjects that is virtually never addressed in high school. Most students come to their first women's studies course knowing nothing about the field or possessed of many misconceptions about it. Sixty-six percent of women's studies programs offer an introductory course and 84 percent of those who offer one require their majors to take it.[9]

To replicate in the academic setting the powerful transformative effects of the consciousness-raising techniques of the early women's movement, most introductory courses include class discussion, journals, and the sharing of personal experiences in an analytical context. The introductory course typically is organized thematically to introduce students to some of the key feminist issues such as identity formation, cultural representations, work, family, sexuality, violence, class stratification, and racial and cultural diversity. Studying such topics requires an interdisciplinary approach that teaches students to connect their inquiry across several disciplines. This interdisciplinary approach frequently introduces students to feminist critiques of some of the traditional disciplines. Fundamental concepts of feminist theory and methodology usually are woven into the reading, lectures, and assignments. Because of the broad scope of the introductory course, it sometimes is team-taught or is taught by a faculty member immersed in interdisiciplinary research and teaching; it also frequently employs guest lecturers.

Middle: electives

All women's studies major curricula include a middle section in which students choose electives from an approved list. Common requirements in the women's studies major include:

☐ a requirement that some courses be in arts/humanities and some in social sciences (66 percent)

☐ a requirement for at least one course on women of color, race, and gender, or global perspectives (33 percent)

☐ a requirement for at least one course on feminist theories and/or methodologies (38 percent)

☐ a required practicum or internship course applying feminist knowledge to institutions in the community or on campus (38 percent).

Only 26 percent of the programs offer all of their required courses for the major exclusively in courses with a women's studies prefix. A far larger proportion, 72 percent, offer their required courses through a combination of courses sponsored both by the women's studies program and by other departments.

Some disciplines are more widely represented in women's studies electives than others. Four in particu-

lar—literature, history, sociology, and psychology—are nearly universally represented and sometimes offer several women's studies courses within a single college or university. In one survey, all forty-five programs listed some courses in the social sciences, with the total ranging from three to forty-two and an average of thirteen.[10] All but one listed courses in arts and humanities, with a range of two to thirty-seven and an average, again, of thirteen. Not surprisingly, only sixteen programs cross-listed natural sciences courses, with an abbreviated range of one to three and an average of one. Professional schools, like the natural sciences, also have lagged behind in transforming their curricula to include gender and feminist scholarship. Thus, what is available to women's studies students is heavily dependent on the cooperation, goodwill, and expertise of other academic units.

This dependence on other academic units is a nagging problem; it breeds frustration for women's studies programs because curricular planning and quality review are very difficult. Women's studies has difficulty, for example, establishing criteria and legitimate authority about which courses offered by other departments will be acceptable electives for the women's studies major. Because many still see feminism only as ideology and not as methodology, attempts on the part of women's studies to control academic and intellectual quality too often are perceived as unacceptable "advocacy" or as "merely" political control.

Problems with the availability and content of the electives that are the heart of the women's studies major have led many programs to press for increased faculty hiring, faculty development, or both. Some programs, especially in larger institutions, enjoy administrative support for joint appointments shared by women's studies and a department, for endowed chairs, or for new faculty members appointed full time to tenure-track lines in women's studies. Tenure especially signals fundamental recognition of the legitimacy and authority of women's studies as an academic specialization and a long-term commitment of university resources.

Capstone courses

This is the part of the women's studies major on which there is least consensus and greatest flux. According to NWSA's survey, 57 percent of the programs queried required a senior seminar for the major, while 38 percent required field study, an internship, or independent study. There currently is no consensus in women's studies about the purposes and functions of a required senior course. Sometimes, however, the senior seminar is the only course in which ad-

vanced women's studies students are not outnumbered dramatically by students who are taking their first women's studies course; these women's studies students feel a need to spend time in academic environments with their peers. The first seminars were modeled after the prevailing academic standard: individual research projects in a seminar context. Various programs have experimented with changing the nature of the individual project, permitting action projects or group projects, or encouraging nontraditional projects. Other programs have replaced the research seminar with a reading-and-discussion course on theory.

THE FEMINIST CLASSROOM AND STUDENT LEARNING

Learning a new way of seeing the world is not like learning algebra or when the Nineteenth Amendment was passed. Rather, learning feminism is a process—an ongoing journey that is, for me, filled with both joy and pain.

> Abby Markowitz
> 1989 Women's Studies
> graduate of Towson
> State University

Women's studies always has questioned not only what we teach but also how we teach. From the earliest women's studies courses twenty years ago to NWSA's current three-year

FIPSE project on student learning, "The Courage to Question," empowering students as active learners has been an unbroken thread of continuity. This commitment affects curricular decisions, influences how individual courses are structured, and determines the nature of faculty development priorities and rewards. It also frequently puts women's studies in tension with a university system that too often devalues teaching, advising, and faculty investment in student programming.

In many ways the university hierarchy that propels tenure, promotion, grants, and public recognition imitates conventional, stereotypical divisions of male and female labor. Research is "men's work." It is public; it is national rather than local; it typically is connected to money; it usually necessitates leaving the "home" of the university to present research findings; and it relies on the mind, the intellect, and rationality. Teaching and advising, however, really are only women's work: something done at "home"; something done locally and privately; and something drawing on the heart, feelings, and emotions. Teaching becomes like raising children; advising and counseling students like volunteer work with the PTA or at the hospital; working with students on programming and student services like housework. Just as women's

studies validates the worth of women's lives by virtue of the subjects it investigates and the questions it poses, it seeks to validate the worth of women's lives in the way it structures the experience for the major and the roles faculty members play in that interactive process.

Nowhere is that clearer than in the feminist classroom, where theory and practice are tested with each class. Once again, the task of women's studies is to connect rather than rank research, teaching, counseling, and action. Women's studies values a link between heart and head, action and idea, feeling and intellect. They are not in opposition but rather in dialogue: informing, correcting, and enlarging knowledge in the process.

To accomplish that complex integrative process, women's studies has sought to be self-reflective about how knowledge is conveyed and acquired. Feminist pedagogy is discussed at least as much as feminist scholarship in an effort to highlight the connections. Feminist pedagogy aims to be participatory, experiential, and empowering. It typically fosters dialogue, a safe arena in which to express disagreements, and an engagement with difference. "It starts," as one faculty member explains it, "from the radical act of taking women seriously and validating them."[11] There is much more attention to group work, self-defined papers and projects, discussion, spatial arrangements in the classroom, methods of presentation, varieties in course assignments, journals, and invitations to tie theory to one's personal experience.

By decentralizing authority, faculty members encourage students to assume more active responsibility for what they learn and how. Students are taught how to produce knowledge as well as how to reproduce it. Decentralizing authority also dramatizes for students that women's studies faculty members are learners in the classroom as well as sources of authority and expertise. One faculty member says, "In teaching my first women's studies course many years ago, I found myself changing as I talked; I discovered the extent to which I had been in complicity with the system, male-trained into the system; I deconstructed myself and reconstructed myself through dialogue in that class."[12] Another explains, "The discomfort that comes from the withdrawal of white privilege in the multiethnic classroom is the most powerful lesson I've learned in women's studies."[13]

One program describes the ideal classroom setting faculty members seek for their women's studies students as one "in which knowledge is understood to be partial and contingent but not equally valid, and where analysis of competing perspec-

tives is encouraged."[14] That same program also views the classroom as needing to be one "in which students are encouraged to clarify their beliefs and values and to look at evidence, ideas, beliefs, and concepts that may be inconvenient for them to know."[15] While the women's studies classroom aims for a safe, hospitable learning environment, then, it often finds itself in tension because of its commitment to competing perspectives and to inconvenient pieces of knowledge. The classroom becomes for many a source of discomfort and disturbance as well as nurturing and affirmation.

Women's studies students typically undergo a profound transformation as they claim more knowledge. They pass through an identifiable series of moments of recognition, just as Marguerite did when she found herself "locked in" the library. Such insights are followed by moments of empowerment in which patriarchal frameworks and perceptions are modified, redefined, or rejected altogether and replaced by a newly emerging view of the self and society. The difficulty and complexity of this process—and the degree to which it influences our curriculum and pedagogy—cannot be overemphasized.

Breaking what feminist writer Tillie Olsen calls the "habits of a lifetime" is no trivial matter. It is accompanied by the full range of human resistance, by continual attraction and repulsion—denial and recognition—as the release of anger or the self-indulgence of viewing oneself as a victim or a victimizer are gradually replaced by an ability to live, work, and think within conditions of tension and contradiction necessary to a productive life in a world with unequal arrangements of power.

Because such moments are inextricably a part of being a women's studies major, the task of the faculty in facilitating students' movement to a new integration of knowledge and experience is especially complex and demanding. It involves, for faculty members as for students, the imperative to connect felt experience with analytic theory in order to understand both. This attention to the learning process causes women's studies classes to have unusually high ratings in an AAC comparative study of students by majors.[16]

Students repeatedly talk about their classroom experiences in women's studies as being vital to their perception of themselves as learners. In one survey, students overwhelmingly saw women's studies "as an intellectual discipline providing them with information they had not received elsewhere...and a new, critical way of thinking that nevertheless also validated them as perceivers and knowers."[17] One student comments,

"I felt like more pieces of me got to be there," while another says, "It felt like coming home...and I felt affirmed somehow, that all this stuff I was carrying around in my head was indeed real, that it was there." For others, the profound effect is captured by one student's comment: "It changed my life." Overall, they agree with the student who argued that women's studies classes "were more rigorous than those found in more traditional disciplines, precisely because they demanded more self-exploration and questioning of received information."

The enterprise of women's studies, like the best of education, is a multifaceted one. More than establishing a sequence of courses, outlining a subject area, or positing fresh critical frameworks, women's studies also is about personal and intellectual growth, both for the faculty and for the students. It is attentive to and creative about the classroom climates and methods that enhance learning. It empowers male and female students as active learners and as social change agents.

As students learn to validate their own inner voices, they also learn to respect the inner voices of others, whose skin color, sexual identity, or political views may differ from their own. By providing students with analytical frameworks in which to view knowledge and the courage to trust their own personal experiences, women's studies helps the Marguerites of the world, trapped in the institutional structures of knowledge, to find a safe way to get home. Our hope is that in the process she and others eventually will work to make all places safe: places where, male or female, lesbian or heterosexual, white or black, old or young, affluent or poor, we all can move freely.

RECOMMENDATIONS

☐ *Free women's studies programs from institutional constraints that weaken curricular offerings.*

Too often, programs lack resources to offer a full and balanced range of elective courses. The most substantial remedy can be achieved by hiring faculty members with expertise in women's studies. In addition to dispersing such faculty members among various departments, women's studies as an academic unit itself must secure full tenure lines or joint appointments so that core courses can be guaranteed. Inconsistent, unpredictable staffing has hampered women's studies programs, many of which must rely on visiting professors, part-time faculty members, and the good will of other departments.

☐ *Increase the overall budget in women's studies programs.*

Reallocating university resources

will reduce the problem of curricular constraints by providing funding to "borrow" faculty members from other departments, offering faculty development or research grants, sponsoring lecture series and institutes, and allocating funds for travel to conferences.

☐ *Identify specific locations in the curriculum where issues of race and ethnicity will be addressed.*

These central issues will not be addressed until at least one specific place—preferably more—in the curriculum focuses on the intersection of race and gender. Ideally, at least one required course in the major should be devoted exclusively to these issues; it should be taken relatively early in the student's course of study. In addition, the analysis of race and class as well as gender should be pervasive in all women's studies courses.

☐ *Recruit faculty members of color for women's studies programs.*

Women's studies programs need multiracial faculties and student bodies, not just a multicultural curriculum. One of the most valuable ways to attract students of color is to employ faculty members of color, especially in lead positions such as program director.

☐ *Enhance interactions between women's studies programs and ethnic studies programs or other programs where race is a prominent area of study.*

Such formal and informal interactions would ensure a greater emphasis on the crucial intersections of gender with race and ethnicity in our academic project. Programs might, for instance, cosponsor projects and events, create cross-listed courses, and hire jointly when possible.

☐ *Remove administrative obstacles that lock both students and faculty members too narrowly within one academic unit.*

Inventive ways should be initiated to enlarge course offerings and stimulate dialogue across disciplines. Currently, students in one unit often are prevented from taking courses in another, or faculty members tenured in one unit are prevented from offering a course that could be cross-listed with a unit from a different school, division, or college within the university.

☐ *Minimize unnecessary course overlap, especially among electives.*

Women's studies programs regularly should review discipline-based courses in the major to reduce unnecessary overlap and ensure academic integrity. Such reviews ought not be perceived, as they are occasionally by colleagues outside the program, as some sort of ideological "police action." Women's studies needs and deserves authority over the content of its discipline, and programs should devise formal ways to take responsibility for it.

☐ *Seek a balance in course offerings*

among humanities, social sciences, natural sciences, and, in larger universities, professional fields.*

Substantial recent scholarship about women and gender is available in all of these areas. Women's studies programs should be vigilant lest they become overbalanced in either humanities or social sciences and neglect important work in the natural sciences.

☐ *Institute formal and informal interaction with teacher education programs for the benefit of both women's studies majors and students preparing to become teachers.*

☐ *Be proactive about publicizing women's studies programs.*

Because of women's studies' emerging but less visible status in the overall curriculum, programs need to be more aggressive about describing their offerings. Students also can be advised directly about curriculum options. Regular, one-on-one student advising is especially important for the women's studies student.

☐ *Provide an organization, or at least a series of activities, for women's studies majors.*

This non-classroom interaction is extremely valuable as students address intellectual and personal challenges to dismantle the inherent power of distortions and exclusions in knowledge due to racism, classism, sexism, heterosexism, and ethnocentrism. These activities should be student-led and student-run whenever possible. On some campuses—especially commuter campuses—and for some students—especially those with heavy responsibilities for families and jobs as well as courses—programs should be attentive to and creative about the design and timing of such support activities.

☐ *Design a required senior course or project specifically to help students anticipate the next set of life choices following their women's studies undergraduate major.*

This course ideally should be reserved for women's studies majors or at least have a majority of women's studies majors in it. If the institution or the number of majors is large enough, programs should seek to guarantee several upper-level courses in which women's studies majors are in the majority.

☐ *Offer students majoring in women's studies an option to do "applied women's studies."*

Internships, field research, and senior seminars designed for projects that apply theory to practice are ways that the curriculum can provide this experience.

☐ *Structure a variety of ways through which faculty members can improve as feminist teachers.*

Some possible structures might include training sessions for graduate students who teach women's studies courses, peer classroom visits, mid-semester faculty development symposia on teaching, or resource packets that describe innovative course assignments.

---

1. This report was written by Johnnella Butler, University of Washington; Sandra Coyner, Kansas State University; Margaret Homans, Yale University; Marlene Longenecker, Ohio State University; and Caryn McTighe Musil, National Women's Studies Association. Early drafts were discussed at the NWSA National Conference in June 1989 at Towson, Maryland; at NWSA's National Conference for Women's Studies Program Directors in October 1989 in Washington, D.C.; at the NWSA National Conference in June 1990 in Akron, Ohio; and widely circulated to faculty members, administrators, and students throughout 1989–1990.

The authors are grateful for the many helpful suggestions made during the long but stimulating process of producing this report. We also would like to acknowledge the research and clerical support given by the National Women's Studies Association staff, especially by Melinda Berriman, whose careful eye and unending patience through many drafts was invaluable. The Coordinating Council of NWSA considers the task force report to be an official report of NWSA about the women's studies major.

2. Charles C. Lemert, "Depth as a Metaphor for the Major—A Postmodernist Challenge," unpublished remarks delivered at the Association of American Colleges' 76th Annual Meeting in San Francisco, California, January 11, 1990.

3. *Integrity in the College Curriculum* (Washington, D.C.: Association of American Colleges, 1985), 24.

4. Dixie L. King, report submitted to NWSA as part of a FIPSE project, "The Courage to Question: Women's Studies and Student Learning," 8.

5. Mariam K. Chamberlain, editor, *Women in Academe: Progress and Prospects* (New York: Russell Sage Foundation, 1988), 137.

6. A survey of women's studies programs with majors was conducted by the National Women's Studies Association in the summer and fall of 1989. Compilations and analyses were prepared by Leigh Harris, Debra Humphreys, Astrida Levensteins, and Caryn McTighe Musil. Forthcoming in *NWSAction*, Vol. IV, No. 4.

7. The composite draws upon the NWSA survey mentioned above and on a survey of program and course descriptions from college catalogues, "A Survey of the Women's Studies Major," by Marcia Westkott and Gay Victoria of the Women's Studies Program, (University of Colorado, February 5, 1990). Forthcoming in *NWSA Journal*, Vol. III, No. 3.

8. Westkott and Victoria, 5–6. A more extensive analysis of the status of racial diversity in women's studies curricula is being done by Patricia Bell Scott of the University of Connecticut and Beverly Guy-Sheftall of Spelman College. Their data from two hundred women's studies programs will be interpreted in a future issue of *Sage: A Scholarly Journal on Black Women*.

9. Westkott and Victoria, 5.

10. Westkott and Victoria, 9.

11. King, 15.

12. *Ibid.*, 9.

13. *Ibid.*

14. Report submitted by the Women's Studies Program of the University of Colorado as part of the NWSA-FIPSE project, "The Courage to Question: Women's Studies and Student Learning," 2.

15. Westkott and Victoria, 2.

16. As part of AAC's examination of "Liberal Learning and Arts and Sciences Majors," members of the participating task forces were asked to distribute student questionnaires in classes. In a compilation of the results, women's studies was rated the highest of the eleven majors on ten of the fourteen questions and was in the top four rankings in the remaining four categories. Checking the column "usually true," students gave women's studies the highest marks for connecting different kinds of knowledge (89.2 percent); connecting course materials and assignments to personally significant questions (86.5 percent); identifying and exploring problems in the field in relation to significant questions for society (97.3 percent); exploring values and ethics important to the major (81.1 percent); and helping students develop an overview of the field's intellectual history (83.1 percent). Although the number of students in the sample was modest, the results echo similar commentaries from students about the value of women's studies courses in their lives and in integrating knowledge. (Washington, D.C.: Unpublished study by AAC, 1990).

17. Barbara Scott Winkler, " 'It Gave Me Courage': What Students Say About Women's Studies," *NWSA Perspectives* 5 (Fall 1987): 29. All subsequent quotations in the paragraph are taken from pages 29–31.

UNABRIDGED REPORTS

The task force reports in this volume are (with one exception) abbreviated. Responding thoughtfully and carefully to the charge presented to them by the project's National Advisory Committee, the twelve learned societies' task forces generally produced documents considerably longer than AAC could publish together in a single volume. Those documents were abridged and edited in consultation with the task forces to produce the versions the reader finds in this volume.

The unabridged versions of these reports should be of interest, however, to those concerned with the shape and character of the undergraduate major and especially to those working in any of the fields represented here. Accordingly, AAC's Project on Liberal Learning, Study-in-depth, and the Arts and Sciences Major has provided support for the publication and distribution of the reports in their unabridged forms in whatever medium each learned society chooses.

The longer versions of these reports are available from these sources:

Biology
"The State of the Biology Major," in *BioScience*, October 1990: American Institute of Biological Sciences, 730 11th Street, NW, Washington, DC 20001.

Economics
"The Economics Major in Liberal Arts Education," in *The Journal of Economic Education*, Summer 1991: Joint Council on Economic Education, 432 Park Avenue South, New York, NY 10016.

History
"Liberal Learning and the History Major," in *Perspectives*, May/June 1990: American Historical Association, 400 A Street, SE, Washington, DC 20003.

Interdisciplinary Studies
"Liberal Education, Study-in-depth, and Interdisciplinary Studies," in *Issues in Integrative Studies*, Winter 1990: Society for Values in Higher Education, Box B-2814, Georgetown University, Washington, DC 20057.

Mathematics
"Challenges for College Mathematics: An Agenda for the Next Decade," in *Focus*, November/December 1990: Mathematical Association of America, 1529 18th Street, NW, Washington, DC 20036.

Philosophy
"The Philosophy Major and its Place in Liberal Education," in *Proceedings and Addresses of the American Philosophical Association*, 1991 (tentatively): American Philosophical Association, University of Delaware, Newark, DE 19716.

Physics
"The Undergraduate Physics Major," in *American Journal of Physics*, Winter 1990 or Spring 1991: American Association of Physics Teachers, 5112 Berwyn Road, College Park, MD 20740.

Political Science
"The Political Science Major in the Liberal Arts Curriculum," in *PS: Political Science and Politics*, March 1991: American Political Science Association, 1527 New Hampshire Avenue, NW, Washington, DC 20036.

Psychology
"Liberal Education, Study-in-depth, and the Psychology Major," in *American Psychologist*, sometime in 1991 (tentatively): American Psychological Association, 1200 17th Street, NW, Washington, DC 20036.

Religion
"Report of the Task Force on Study-in-depth in Religion": inquire of American Academy of Religion, James Wiggins, Department of Religion, 501 Hall of Languages, Syracuse University, Syracuse, NY 13244.

Sociology
"Study-in-depth in Sociology": inquire of Carla Howery, American Sociological Association, 1722 N Street, NW, Washington, DC 20036.

Women's Studies
"The Women's Studies Major," in *NWSA Journal*, Winter 1990 or Spring 1991: National Women's Studies Association, University of Maryland, College Park, MD 20742-1325.